Martin Ferguson Smith, OBE, is professor emeritus of Classics at Durham University. He has an international reputation for his editions and translations of the Epicurean writers Lucretius (first century BC) and Diogenes of Oinoanda (second century AD). Diogenes, whose ruined home city is in the mountains of southwest Turkey, set out his philosophy in the form of the longest known Greek inscription. It is addressed to the people of Oinoanda and to so-called foreigners who are actually fellow citizens in a world which is one country for humanity. To the discovery and interpretation of Diogenes' extraordinary work Martin has devoted nearly sixty years of his life, during which he has been much influenced by Epicurean philosophy.

Martin the Epicurean, as well as describing the author's long engagement with Diogenes and his spectacular fieldwork in Turkey, contains chapters on his unusual adventures in communist Albania and Romania and on his modern work, which includes his acclaimed books *Dearest Jean: Rose Macaulay's Letters to a Cousin* (2011), *Madeleine Symons: Social and Penal Reformer* (2017), *In and Out of Bloomsbury: Essays on Twentieth-Century Writers and Artists* (2021), and *The Artist Helen Coombe 1864-1937: The Tragedy of Roger Fry's Wife* (2023).

The book also describes the thirty years he has spent living on the remote island of Foula in Shetland without a shop, television, or smart phone, in fulfilment of a childhood ambition.

MARTIN THE EPICUREAN

MARTIN FERGUSON SMITH

Published in 2026 by SilverWood Books

SilverWood Books Ltd
14 Small Street, Bristol, BS1 1DE, United Kingdom
www.silverwoodbooks.co.uk

Back cover photograph of the author by Lucinda Smith
All other photographs from the author's collection,
unless otherwise indicated in the list of illustrations

This work depicts actual events in the life of the author as truthfully as recollection permits. Some dialogue has been retold in a way that accurately evokes the meaning and feeling of what was said. The story, the experiences, and the words are the author's alone.

ISBN 978-1-80042-324-4 (paperback)
Also available as an ebook

British Library Cataloguing in Publication Data
A CIP catalogue record for this book is available from the British Library

Page design and typesetting by SilverWood Books

Contents

Illustrations

Preface

A few years ago I received two separate requests from published authors for permission to write my biography. Having established that each one was serious, I felt somewhat flattered that others should think my life and work of sufficient interest to warrant investigation and public exposure. At the same time I could not bear the thought of another person attempting the story of my life. In my own writing, I have always attached great importance to factual accuracy. Biography often turns out to contain a large measure of fiction. The same may be true of autobiography as well, but to a lesser extent, provided the author is neither an amnesiac nor dishonest. Anyhow, in most of my adult life I have preferred to be in the driving seat rather than a passenger.

Another motivation is that for me personally it is a useful, if not always edifying, exercise, as I near death, to review my life from beginning to end. It is just a pity that one does not have the opportunity to go back and do things better. I have made many mistakes and often failed to take full advantage of the opportunities open to me, but it is surprising how many happenings, which seemed at the time to be disappointments and setbacks, turned out to be blessings in disguise, necessitating or even inspiring changes of direction which turned out to be advantageous. Sometimes the spurs were the unfavourable assessments of teachers and others. One such example was the remark the headmaster of Shrewsbury School, J.M. Peterson, penned at the end of my final-year school-report in December 1957: "I fear his work is nearing its ceiling now". The previous year he had written "I hesitate at the moment to say that he will make a scholar", contradicting a young assistant master, D.L. Dundas, who, unlike Peterson, had actually taught me and found "the qualities necessary for a 1st class scholar". I did not forget Peterson's low opinion of me and was determined to prove him wrong. My sister, Carol, was similarly inspired to success in the nursing profession by the dismissive assessment of a hospital matron, issued just as she started her training.

The writing of this book, the third of my eighties, has been something of a gamble with mortality. I began it in March 2025, two days after coming home from Shetland's Gilbert Bain Hospital (GBH!) in a weak state and with a poor prognosis. The title, echoing that of Walter Pater's novel, *Marius the Epicurean* (1885), refers to my adult-lifelong interest in Epicurean philosophy, especially as expounded by Lucretius and Diogenes of Oinoanda, and my imperfect attempt to live my life by its teachings – least imperfect in the last three decades of it, when I have lived in contented isolation on Britain's remotest inhabited island, without a shop, television, or smart phone.

Isle of Foula, Shetland
September 2025

Acknowledgements

First and foremost, I am indebted to my daughter, Lucinda Ferguson Smith for huge help. For their encouragement I thank my niece, Anna Hill; my nephews, Keith and Christopher Arrowsmith; my granddaughter, Ciara, and her partner, Ian Birtwistle. I also thank: Jane Abram, Maria Bacconi, Victoria Chance, Rita Chiarini, Caroline Dawnay, Alain de Botton, Rose and Jay Deutsch, Christine Else, Barbara Fraser, Barbara Gould and Alan Hirschfeld, Nancy Green, Linda Elisabeth LaPinta, Sally Lovecy, Nicholas Milner, Wendy Jones Nakanishi, Jan Piggott, Alison Rendall, Robin Simon, Dawn Thomas, and Marianne Thormählen. I thank also my publisher, Helen Hart of SilverWood Books. I am grateful not least to the islanders of Foula in Shetland for their generous tolerance of me and my eccentricities for over thirty years.

Abbreviations

BIAA	British Institute of Archaeology at Ankara
CND	Campaign for Nuclear Disarmament
Fr. / fr.	Fragment of Diogenes of Oinoanda's inscription in Martin's edition of 1993
GMB	Graduates' Memorial Building, TCD
NF	New Fragment of Diogenes of Oinoanda. Numeration of Martin and, since 2007, of Jürgen Hammerstaedt as well
TCD	Trinity College, Dublin
UCNW	University College of North Wales (Coleg Prifysgol Gogledd Cymru), Bangor

See also "Key to Selected First Names" (Chapter 15)

Notes

"Diogenes" is always "Diogenes of Oinoanda". In titles of publications "Oinoanda" is sometimes spelled "Oenoanda".

Quotations of Diogenes are taken from Martin's translation: *Urbi et Orbi: The Epicurean Inscription and Prescription of Diogenes of Oinoanda*, Doxai series: Testi e studi di filosofia antica, tab edizioni: Rome, 2026. Paperback and Open Access.

Quotations of Lucretius are taken from Martin's translation: *Lucretius, On the Nature of Things*, Hackett: Indianapolis/Cambridge [MA], 2001. Paperback.

1

Ancestry, Parentage, Upbringing, First Schools (1940–1948)

I was born in Birmingham, but, since I only lived there for about two years as a young child, I have little feeling of being a Brummie. When I rather sheepishly told Dafydd Wigley, former MP and leader of Plaid Cymru, the Welsh Nationalist Party, where I was from, he sympathetically responded with the information that he was born in Derby. But England's second city was perhaps an appropriate location for my birth, being roughly midway between Scotland and Cornwall, the parts of Britain from which many of my ancestors had come. Moreover, it was a city in which some of those ancestors, mostly on my mother's side, had settled in the mid-nineteenth century.

My mother, Barbara Catharine Tangye, was a granddaughter of George Tangye, one of five brothers who moved from the Redruth area of Cornwall to Birmingham, where in 1857 they established an engineering business that prospered, much helped by a spectacular early success in January 1858, when Tangye hydraulic jacks managed to get Isambard Kingdom Brunel's great iron ship into the water at Millwall, after all other attempts had failed. The firm boasted: "We launched the *Great Eastern*, and the *Great Eastern* launched us". A few years later, a new Tangye factory, the Cornwall Works, was built in Smethwick, Birmingham. The Tangyes were Quakers, very enlightened employers, and philanthropists – major funders of, for example, the Birmingham Art Gallery. During the Second World War the firm won contracts for important work in several areas, including the top-secret Operation Pluto to pump fuel across the English Channel to supply the Allied forces in France. The development team was headed by Barbara's younger brother Christopher ("Chris") Tangye, a brilliant engineer and inventor. The firm continued to produce high-quality machinery until well after the Second World War, but went into decline thereafter.

Barbara was born in Edgbaston, Birmingham, on 16 June 1904. Although she was probably never aware of it, and, even if she had been, would have been unimpressed, this was the original Bloomsday, the date on which the events of James Joyce's *Ulysses* are imagined as taking place. She was generally well read in English literature, but I am sure she never read Joyce or any other Moderns. In contrast, I was introduced to them as a teenager by an unusual teacher, and my interest in *Ulysses* naturally grew when I went on to spend five years as a student in Dublin, where the novel is set and I had the good fortune to be taught by W.B. Stanford, author of *The Ulysses Theme: A Study in the Adaptability of a Traditional Hero*. Barbara was educated at The Mount School, a Quaker boarding school for girls in York. She excelled at art and music as well as history and English. After leaving school, she spent time in Paris, improving her French and extending her knowledge of art and music. She used to say that the French were the most civilised nation on earth.

My father, Henry Ferguson Smith, was descended on his father's side from the Smiths of Craigend and Jordanhill on (respectively) the north and west sides of Glasgow, and his mother, Anne ("Nannie") Georgiana, was a Macaulay, a daughter of the Revd Samuel Herrick Macaulay, who was a son of the Revd Aulay Macaulay (1758–1819), a nephew of the slave-trade abolitionist Zachary Macaulay, and a first cousin of Thomas Babington Macaulay (Lord Macaulay). The writer Rose Macaulay was Nannie's niece. Henry's father, Charles ("Charlie") Stewart Smith, had served as an officer in the Royal Navy until 1889. Fluent in Swahili, he had been employed in the interception of Arab dhows carrying off African slaves – a long-established but sometimes overlooked part of the slave-trade. He personally rescued many victims. I have the curved dagger called a *jambiya*, still in its scabbard, which he seized from one of the traffickers. After 1889 he remained in East Africa for four years, serving as British Consul in Zanzibar, before being appointed Consul in Bilbao. His next appointment, in 1900, was a promotion, as Consul-General in Odessa, chief port on the Black Sea and the fourth-largest city of Imperial Russia, with a population of 450,000, about a third of whom were Jews. It was an important post, carrying responsibility for a dozen or so consular districts in southern Russia and around the Black Sea, and he witnessed some momentous events, including the mutiny of sailors aboard the Russian warship *Potemkin*, the rioting and massacre that followed, and several pogroms. He held it until 1913, when he was transferred to Barcelona. Henry, the youngest of nine children, was born in Odessa on 21 January 1902. He retained vivid memories of his early childhood there and of the long journeys to and from England, usually by train via Warsaw, Berlin, and the Hook of Holland. He and his elder siblings had their schooling in England. He was at Malvern Link (Preparatory) School and Shrewsbury School. He joined the Bombay Company in India in 1924 after serving an apprenticeship in Manchester with Glazebrooke, Steele & Company, a firm closely linked to the one in India in the cotton and textile trade. He continued to serve the Bombay Company until 1948 and was managing director of its Calcutta (Kolkata) branch from 1941.

At Shrewsbury Henry was a slightly senior contemporary of the mountaineer Andrew ("Sandy") Comyn Irvine, and both of them were in School House. A few months after Henry started work in India, he wrote a letter to Irvine, who was a member of the 1924 Everest Expedition:

> THE BOMBAY COMPANY LP.
> CALCUTTA
> May 13th /24.
>
> Dear Irvine,
> By the time you receive this you will have returned, I hope safely, from your great expedition. It is somewhat superfluous to hope that you were successful since most of the world is waiting to hear your news. I must however congratulate you for having been chosen for such a show so early.
>
> I am now living here in rather a pleasant chummery and working in a merchant firm. I wonder if you would come to stay with us for a day or two when you come back to civilisation? I think we will be able to amuse you and I am sure you will be able to amuse us – if you are prepared to talk!
>
> Come along if you possibly can.
> Yrs sincerely
> H.F. Smith.

Sandy was still alive when Henry wrote to him, but he never received the letter, which was addressed to A.C. Irvine Esq at Mount Everest Expedition,

Darjeeling, and forwarded to him from Pharijong, Tibet, on 18 May. Sandy and George Mallory's attempt on the summit was made on 8–9 June, and it is still not known if it was successful.

Henry's letter was returned to him by Sandy's elder brother, Hugh:

28 Gt Ormond St
W.C.1.

29-7-24

Dear Mr Smith
Here's a letter I had returned unopened to me from Tibet. I am sorry he never got it. But it was a stout show wasn't it?

Yours

Hugh Irvine

Although I have never been a rock-climber, the story of the attempts on Everest has always fascinated me, as has that of the first definite conquest of the mountain in 1953. Some years later I got to know a member of the successful team, another Old Salopian, quite well. This was its deputy leader, (Sir) Charles Evans, who was Principal of the University College of North Wales for most of my twenty-five years as a member of its teaching staff. Sadly, by that time he had been crippled by multiple sclerosis. His leadership of the institution, now Bangor University, was controversial, and his mountaineering exploits are his greatest claim to fame. Another member of the 1953 Everest expedition whom I later met was the Welsh historian and travel writer Jan Morris, who spent her last years near Criccieth and was a friend of my cousins Sir Jeremy and Lady Cecilia ("Tiggy") Chance and their daughter Victoria Chance. Until 1972 Jan was James Morris, who, working for *The Times*, was the only journalist in the Everest team and managed to get the news of its success, conveyed in a pre-arranged code, to the paper just in time for publication on the day of Queen Elizabeth II's coronation on 2 June. At the time I was introduced to Jan, she was living in a civil partnership with her former wife, Elizabeth, mother of their five children.

Barbara hardly knew Henry when they married, and she was never in love with him. They met in autumn 1929, when he was home on six-month leave from his employment with the Bombay Company in India. He was nearly twenty-eight and in a hurry to find a wife before he returned to India. He was staying with his parents in the village of Clent, Worcestershire, and Barbara's family lived a mile or two away in Broome House. On the first occasion he called to visit, she and her younger sister, Lou, hid in the shrubbery alongside the drive until they had seen him depart. But he persisted, and, after much wavering and contrary to Lou's advice ("I wouldn't marry a man like that"), Barbara, then aged twenty-five, agreed, and the engagement was announced at the end of February 1930, just before he sailed back to India. The reasons for her hesitation were, in addition to her very slight acquaintance with her fiancé, his different background and interests and the need to live in India, but what swayed her was what she perceived to be a marked similarity of his looks to those of her adored uncle Ted Hodgkin, who had died in 1921, when she was seventeen. She had many doubts about her decision during the next nine months, including on the long lonely voyage out to Bombay (Mumbai) for the wedding at All Saints Church, Malabar Hill, on 5 December 1930 (Plate 1). But the thought of the disgrace and the need to return all those expensive wedding presents ...

The couple's Indian home, owned by the Bombay Company, was 21 Belvedere Road in Alipore, an affluent area of south Calcutta which contains the Zoological Garden. The house no longer stands. She continued to paint, and paint well, in the early years of her marriage, and I have a collection of her delightful "Indian" watercolours, but, probably due to a combination of diffidence and Henry's lack of encouragement, she soon gave up drawing and painting.

Although her home in the 1930s was in India, her children were born in England – Colin Ferguson Smith in Edgbaston on 12 October 1932, (Alison) Caroline ("Carol") Ferguson Smith, again in Edgbaston, on 13 July 1935. Colin and Carol spent most of their early years in India, and Colin especially retained vivid and happy memories of the freedom and excitements they enjoyed not only in Calcutta but also on holidays at Kalimpong and Darjeeling in the Himalayan foothills of West Bengal.

The family returned to England in March 1939. Henry was on leave for several months. Their base was Cross Bank, his widowed mother's house in Clent, and Colin and Carol remained there while their parents enjoyed a summer holiday on the Continent. During it, Barbara conceived their third child who, until he was born, was expected to be a girl, which is said to be why Anemone, his favourite early toy, a gift from Alice, the Cross Bank cook, was pink.

1) Bombay (Mumbai): Henry and Barbara on their wedding day, 5 December 1930

War broke out on 3 September 1939. Henry returned to Calcutta in November. Colin was sent to boarding school, while Barbara and Carol stayed in a rented flat in Birmingham – 21 Westfield Hall on the north (and less fashionable) side of Hagley Road. It was there that I was born, just in time for lunch, on 26 April 1940, weighing seven pounds and eight ounces. Unlike my brother and sister, I was breast fed, which may partly explain why I had a closer relationship with my mother than they did. When I was well into my forties,

I learned from Colin that I was our mother's favourite child, and it became increasingly clear to me that his resentment about this was the main cause of his sometimes-scratchy relationship with me. Another (and, to some extent, associated) difficulty was his homosexuality, which I had long suspected before he confirmed it to me. Although unpleasant experiences at Shrewsbury School mean that I dislike the idea of sexual intimacy between males, never once did I express or imply any criticism of Colin's sexual preference, but his life with his homosexual friends and partners was something he did not share with me or any other member of the family. Indicative of this is that, after his death in 2021, it emerged that he had been in a civil partnership with a male friend since 2014 – information he never divulged to me or Carol or the nephew and niece whom he chose as his executors. Despite the problems, he and I maintained regular contact, and the affectionate feelings we had when we were children were by no means entirely lost. After education at Leighton Park School, Reading, and Gonville and Caius College, Cambridge, where he read Law, he spent a few years working for Tangyes before pursuing a successful career as a stockbroker. All his life he was much interested in music and history, including family history, and very knowledgeable. In some ways he was closer to our sister, Carol, than I was. They were closer in age, and both spent most of their adult lives in Birmingham. Carol's admirable qualities included strong loyalty to family, but she had different tastes and interests.

Because of the risk from bombing, hurried arrangements were made for me to be baptised in the Church of England, to allay the fear of my paternal grandmother that I might otherwise languish in limbo for all eternity. The ceremony was performed privately on 24 June 1940 by the Revd Montague Stanhope Newland, vicar of St Thomas's Church, Stourbridge, on the dining-room table at 21 Westfield Hall. So hastily was the arrangement made that not even one godparent was procured.

The plan had been for Barbara to take all three children out to India soon after my birth, but this was now judged to be too risky, and, when Henry first returned to England in October 1944, after being away for five years, I was aged four and a half. The next time I saw him, late in 1946, I was six and a half. So to me he was a remote figure. I do not think that I minded that, but his absence from my early childhood probably affected my psychological development or lack of it. I did not much like let alone love him in the early years of our acquaintance, and I am sure he did not love me. He was very inclined to pick on me, and I suspect that he was jealous of my close relationship with Barbara, who did love me, but did not love him. On occasions when I was harshly treated, Carol, always fair-minded and never afraid to speak her mind, sometimes intervened if she was on the scene. Although my relationship with him improved with time, and he was a generous man who was supportive of my career, we never progressed beyond a handshake. On the last occasion I saw him, just before he died in a nursing home on 17 May 1992, I spent an afternoon reading to him, at his request, pieces of poetry and prose which he knew as a child. After that we said our goodbyes, and I had a train to catch. As I made to open the door of his room, he beckoned to me and spoke his last words to me. For a moment I wondered if he was going to express regret for the problems between us in the past and assure me of his love, but the whispered message was that a nurse had shown him a better way of managing his urine bottle.

In 1941 Barbara moved from Birmingham to Colwall, a village on the Herefordshire side of the Malvern Hills (Plate 2). An arrangement was made to share with its owner and occupier, Beatrice Ballard, her house called Maybole, Walwyn Road, situated on the approach to Colwall from Great Malvern, on the left side. The house, built about 1925 with some features suggestive of a castle, is reached up quite a long drive past trees and bamboo canes. From one of the bamboo clumps a sizeable grass snake slithered across the drive when I was skipping ahead of the rest of the party, causing me to shriek in terror. The creature was harmless, but I did not know that at the time, and I have never been comfortable with snakes. Beatrice had been recently widowed: her husband, Fred, seventeen years her senior, died on 13 September 1940, after giving long public service in the locality. He had been a member of Herefordshire County Council from 1901 to 1937, and its Chairman from 1926 to 1937. A plaque on Jubilee Drive, high up on the Herefordshire side of the Malvern Hills, records his achievements, including the conservation work he carried out in the area for over sixty years. I do not know how Barbara came to share Maybole with Beatrice, but my best guess is that the two were recommended to one another by Barbara's aunt Isabel Wilson of Perrycroft, a fine Arts and Crafts house, designed by Charles F.A. Voysey and situated high above Colwall on Jubilee Drive. "Aunt Bee", as she was known in the family, became in 1919 the second wife of John William Wilson, MP, Barbara's "Uncle Jack", for whom the house, completed in 1895, was built. A wealthy Birmingham industrialist, he died in 1932. Beatrice and Isabel will have known one another well in any

2) Malvern: Barbara with Martin, 1941

case, and may have been drawn closer together by their Scottish ancestry, their maiden names being Macara and Ballantyne respectively.

I remember Perrycroft from early-childhood visits, but I was much too young to appreciate its Arts and Crafts architecture and decoration. The only feature that fascinated a boy of seven or eight was the wondrous apparatus that caused the entrance-gate to swing open when an approaching car put its weight on a metal platform, and then close after the vehicle had moved on. Apparently there is now no trace of the device, and the present owners of Perrycroft have no knowledge of it. It was almost certainly made and installed by Tangyes of Smethwick, the Tangyes and the Wilsons being closely related. Barbara's mother, Anna Deborah Wilson, who married Allan Tangye, was a younger sister of Jack Wilson. In any case, the "wondrous apparatus" is a part of the property's history.

I have only a sketchy recollection of what Beatrice looked like – slim, grey-haired, wearing a hairnet. Although the arrival of the Smith family may have been a welcome distraction and comfort, Barbara did her best to ensure that we were not a burden to her. Colin and Carol were sent to boarding schools in Colwall – Carol to St Nicholas', across the main road from the end of the Maybole drive, and Colin to The Downs on Brock Road, preceding me there by seven years. One important service Beatrice performed for Barbara was to teach her to cook. Since both her parents' home and the house in Calcutta had been fully staffed with servants, she had had very little experience of work in a kitchen. She used to say that she had not even learned to boil an egg. Well, she must have managed a bit of cooking in the Westfield Hall flat, but it was thanks to Beatrice that she became an excellent cook of traditional British food, making economical and clever use of what was available when rationing was in force and certain items could be in short supply or unavailable. Rationing of foodstuffs began in January 1940, and the number of rationed items soon increased. Among the first items to be rationed was butter, and it was soon followed by margarine. I disliked both, and other members of the family were pleased to use my rations. Beatrice taught Barbara not only cooking, but also how to make delicious chutneys and jams, how to bottle fruit, and how to preserve runner beans in salt. The end of the war, so far from bringing rationing to an end, actually brought an extension of it: most notably, bread, unrationed throughout the war, was rationed between 1946 and 1948. Shortages of certain other foodstuffs persisted, and rationing of some of them continued until July 1954. Barbara's culinary repertoire included excellent desserts and puddings. What it did not include were dishes cooked in olive oil (an item she kept only in the medicine cabinet) or ones that contained garlic. There was consternation when a visiting aunt volunteered to make a spaghetti dish which required both, and many mutterings about the number of saucepans that needed to be used and washed up.

Between the ages of three and five (1943–1945), I attended St Nicholas' School as a day-pupil. My earliest-surviving report, written in the early spring of 1945, when I was not quite five, notes a growing self-confidence and independence, "a great interest in all the class activities", and progress in writing, arithmetic, art, and rhythmic response. As for dancing, "Martin is a charming little member of the class, taking a keen interest and trying hard". Barbara used to say that all her children were more attractive at an early stage than later, and the curly blonde hair I had in my earliest years attracted more admiring attention to me than I ever received later in life. It was much envied by Carol, whose hair was straight.

By the end of the war, as well as developing a carbuncle of prodigious size on my chin, I had contracted most of the available infectious diseases – chicken pox, measles, mumps, and scarlet fever. The last necessitated hospitalisation in Hereford. Carol, who preceded me there by a day or two, was disappointed that she was driven in a taxi, whereas I was conveyed in a proper ambulance. I remember only two other things about the hospitalisation, which was in 1944 or early 1945. One is that a fellow-patient called Ruth, aged about ten, made a big fuss of me, which I much enjoyed. The other is that, at the hour of discharge, Anemone, from whom I had been inseparable since birth, was spared incineration, contrary to the hospital quarantine regulations.

When the war came to an end, on 2 September 1945, Barbara and the children left Colwall and moved back to Birmingham – this time to 78 Westfield Road, a detached house in Edgbaston at the junction with Nursery Road, close to Harborne and the Chad Valley Toy Company. The house was to be the family home until the spring of 1948, except in the winter months of 1945–1946, when Barbara was with Henry in Calcutta. During this period I was cared for by Joyce and Humphrey Drake, a childless couple who lived at Red House in the village of Drayton, just outside Norwich. "Aunt" Joyce was not a relative, but a lifelong friend of Barbara. I can still remember the painful separation and handover at Liverpool Street Station in London. Colin and Carol were at boarding schools and came to Drayton in the holidays. Letters survive in which Joyce describes to Barbara the activities and attitudes of the children, including at Christmas. Although I undoubtedly missed my mother, I was well looked after and attended a small school in Drayton kept by the two Misses Plowright. They taught, as well as reading, writing, and arithmetic, the importance of good manners, and it caused Barbara and my elder siblings some amusement, when we were reunited, to see how before each meal I placed my hands neatly on the table with the fingers of both hands interlaced. My stay with the Drakes was so much enjoyed by them, especially by Joyce, that after my departure they adopted a boy of similar age, in the hope and expectation that he would bring them the same fulfilment and happiness that I had. Sadly, it did not work out like that at all, instead bringing them a great deal of difficulty, worry, and misery.

On Barbara's return from India, she and I returned to 78 Westfield Road, with Colin and Carol joining us in the school holidays (Plate 3). Colin had now moved on from The Downs to Leighton Park, and Carol started at The Mount School, York, in 1946. Both schools were Quaker. Barbara told me, when I was an adult, that the two years back in Birmingham were the happiest of her life. The war was over, Henry was in India, I was at home attending a day-school, and she was free to do the things she wanted to do, and see the people she wanted to see. She attended Quaker meetings in Bull Street, taking me with her for Sunday school. There were frequent visits to the Botanical Gardens, a short distance from Westfield Road. I remember playing games in big Edgbaston gardens. I remember too the mounds of delicious tomato sandwiches made for me by Clarisse, the Hungarian wife of our cousin Sir Basil Tangye. I remember the bitter cold and deep snow in 1946–1947, and the cosiness of sitting by a small gas-fire toasting pikelets after school. I remember viewing the severe flooding that came with the snow-melt, specifically the scenes at Bewdley on the River Severn.

My school was Fairdays, run by a Mrs Grice, at the top end of Harborne. The teaching was good, and I progressed happily and well. I made my own way there and back, on foot and by bus. To catch a bus, I walked along Nursery Road to a pub called The Green Man. But a problem developed: I was frequently ambushed by an unpleasant raggedly-dressed girl several years older than me. She was verbally aggressive and abusive, and on at least one occasion she took hold of me and shook me. Barbara expressed concern, but did not take any action like involving the police or even escorting me to the bus stop. What she proposed was that on the journeys to and from school I use a bus stop nearer the city centre, so as to avoid Nursery Road. I took her advice, only to find that one of the grand houses I had to pass had a big dog which bounded down the drive barking fiercely every time a pedestrian passed. So I found myself trapped, as if between Scylla and Charybdis.

I loved the bus rides and wanted to be a bus driver or conductor when I grew up. I spent much time on the stairs at home, pretending they were those of a double decker, and for my birthday I was given a conductor's cap and ticket-dispensing machine. Games were often played on my own – rarely with Colin or Carol, who were significantly older and often absent, sometimes with Harborne friends, notably Peter and Malcolm Lee, descendants of lawyers and destined to become lawyers themselves, sometimes with my cousins Nigel and Miranda Clark, children of Barbara's elder sister, Cecilia, and her husband Rudolf Kynoch Clark, Birmingham's Official Receiver. To Nigel and Miranda, who lived at Kinver in Staffordshire and later near Kidderminster, I became closer than to my siblings, and we often stayed in one another's houses. My affection for them has been a lifelong one, and I was much grieved when Miranda (Overend) died of cancer in 2010. Another early playmate was canine – a Scottish terrier called Chippy, for whom I shed tears when, soon after we moved into the countryside in 1948, she was put down after repeatedly killing chickens.

3) Martin, ca. 1946

During my time in Drayton, I reportedly enjoyed helping Humphrey Drake in the kitchen garden, and Barbara, who was a keen and knowledgeable gardener all her life, gave me a small patch of the Westfield Road garden, in which I grew flowers, radishes, mustard and cress, and lettuces. It was a small start, but one on which I was to build in my schooldays, whenever I had the opportunity, and in adulthood. A less wholesome early interest I had was in cigarettes. I loved the smell of tobacco and was fascinated by the packaging, which in those days carried no health warnings and indeed sometimes claimed to be good for one or at least not harmful: an example is Craven A, with its endearing black cat and the slogan "will not affect your throat". Barbara did not smoke, so, being unable to steal cigarettes from her, I bought a packet of ten in Harborne, fibbing to the shopkeeper that they were for Mummy. But all I did was hoard them and eventually unroll them. I do not think that I

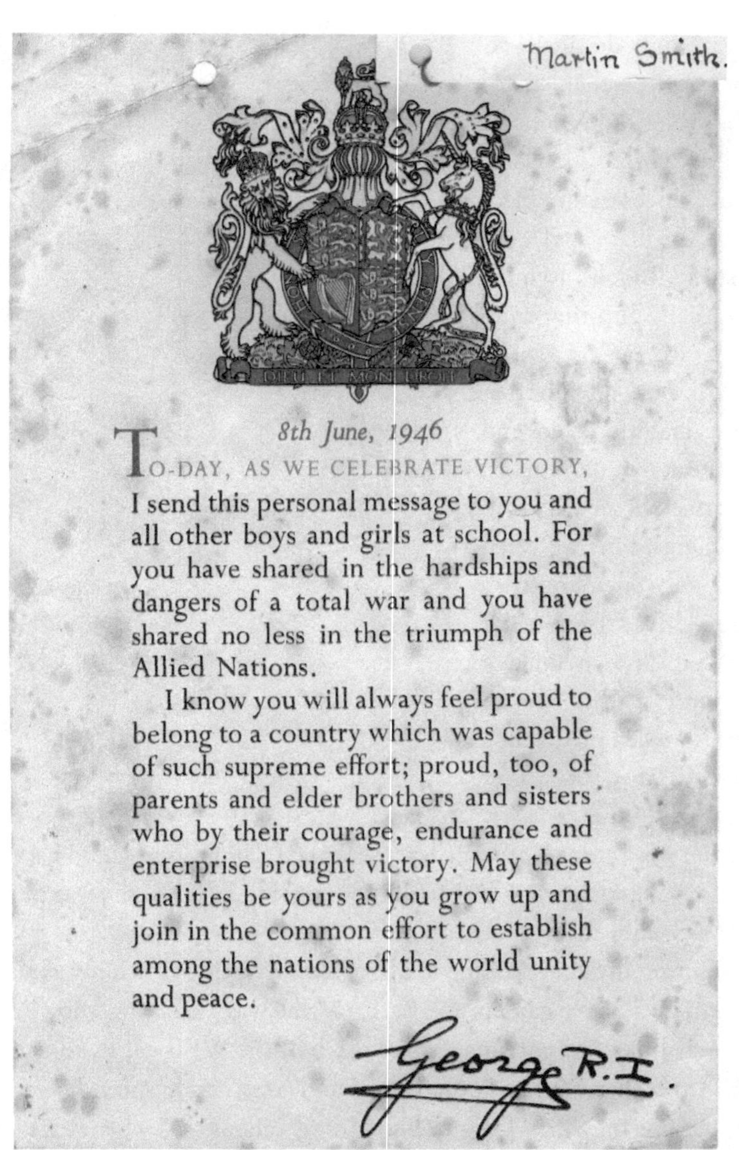

8th June, 1946

TO-DAY, AS WE CELEBRATE VICTORY, I send this personal message to you and all other boys and girls at school. For you have shared in the hardships and dangers of a total war and you have shared no less in the triumph of the Allied Nations.

I know you will always feel proud to belong to a country which was capable of such supreme effort; proud, too, of parents and elder brothers and sisters who by their courage, endurance and enterprise brought victory. May these qualities be yours as you grow up and join in the common effort to establish among the nations of the world unity and peace.

George R.I.

4) King George VI's message to schoolchildren, 8 June 1946, Martin's copy

actually smoked a cigarette before my first year at public school, when I was thirteen. I remember doing so on a Sunday afternoon walk, and then doing it regularly in the boarding house. Another boy, who preferred a pipe, and I volunteered to stoke the coke boiler which fired the central heating. Once we had descended the steps into the boiler-room, our smoking could not be detected. We were known to the other boys as Pipes Thomas and Smoker Smith. I resumed smoking early in my time at university in Ireland, preferring Turkish-style cigarettes. On one occasion I bought from a Dublin tobacconist a box of 100 of these. The price was very low, and when I peeled off a small label, I discovered why. Underneath, I read "Product of the kingdom of Egypt", which meant that the contents were at least six years old, Egypt having ceased to be a monarchy in 1952. After university, my consumption of tobacco was confined to the occasional after-dinner cigar and to cigarettes smoked while mowing grass on a midgy day.

My early childhood reading included: Beatrix Potter; Alison Utley; *Worzel Gummidge*; "BB", *Down the Bright Stream*; Arthur Ransome; adventure stories, including *The Wonder Book of Daring Deeds*; J.W. Fortescue, *The Story of a Red Deer*; and Kenneth Graham, *The Wind in the Willows*. It was probably soon after I started at Fairdays that I received my copy of King George VI's "personal message", on the occasion of the nation's victory celebration on 8 June 1946, "to you and all other boys and girls at school" (Plate 4).

Barbara had two employees at Westfield Road. Both were characters. One was May Owen, the cleaner. Her standards of hygiene at work left something to be desired, and one dreads to think what her own house was like, for it was full of cats, twenty or thirty of them. She had a novel perception of feline pleasure: approaching a cat from behind, she would surprise it by lifting up its back legs before dropping them with the words: "Look how (s)he loves it!" Over the years I have done the same to hundreds of cats, always using the same words, sparing only those creatures known to be decrepit or arthritic, and most of them have actually seemed to enjoy the experience. I have even claimed that the exercise is rejuvenating for them. The other characterful employee was the gardener, Old Joe, a pensioner whose wife had abused him all through their loveless marriage. The garden of no. 78 was a blissful refuge for him: he loved the work, and he loved the tool-shed in which he enjoyed the tea, biscuits, and lunches Barbara provided. She tried to persuade him to leave his tormentor, but he replied: "I have made my bed, and I must lie on it".

2

Herefordshire: The Downs School, Colwall (1948–1953)

All good things come to an end, and the happy time at Westfield Road ended all too soon. Henry had been on leave late in 1946 and early 1947, and in April 1948 he returned from India for good, having resigned from the Bombay Company. This was one blow for me. Another followed later in the month, just after my eighth birthday, when I was sent to The Downs, Colwall, the Quaker preparatory boarding school attended by Colin during the war and previously by Barbara's two younger brothers. It felt as though my world had fallen apart.

I was taken to The Downs by Henry. Barbara did not come as well because it would have made things worse for both of us. On the same day my cousin Nigel was starting at another school in Colwall, The Elms, and the two families met up for a picnic lunch on the Malvern Hills before he and I were delivered. I vividly remember what a member of staff said as she took charge of me: "The other new boys have gone off with Dick Barton". Her words were supposed to make me feel more at home, but had the opposite effect. I had no idea what she meant, apparently being one of the few children in the country who had never heard an episode of the BBC radio thriller series *Dick Barton, Special Agent.* The popularity of the series ensured the instant popularity of Downs new boy Richard Barton, who, by the way, turned out to be agreeable company and had little in common with his fictional namesake. After this baffling start, I was a victim, a day or two later, of an unpleasant practice called "new-nip flicks", when some older boys used their fingers to flick the ears of new boys. I do not expect that I mentioned this and other miseries in the letters home which one was required to write every Sunday morning.

I never found the atmosphere at the school entirely congenial. Each day began with a cold shower before breakfast, even on freezing-cold days in winter, and there was an under-matron watching to ensure that each boy turned round twice in the shower before exiting. After breakfast, junior boys queued first for a spoonful of cod liver oil and malt, then for the toilet, outside which the same under-matron would wait to make an inspection before it was flushed, to ensure that no boy required a spoonful of syrup of figs as well. I disliked this, both the regimentation and the invasion of privacy. I disliked also the way boys in the dormitory were required to relieve themselves in a communal chamber pot, the unofficial aim of filling which to overflowing was often achieved. But what I hated most were the PT (Physical Training) sessions in the gymnasium and, in summer, the nude activities in the outdoor swimming pool as well. I had not learned to swim, and some of the exercises in the gym, especially forward and backward rolls, seemed to me dangerous, and still seem so. Why risk damage to one's neck or back at any age?

In Spring Term 1949, I enjoyed a blessed respite from PT. At the end of the autumn term the school doctor, named Meikle, had cleverly diagnosed an inguinal hernia, and after Christmas I had an operation in Birmingham to repair it. After a brief convalescence at the Selly Oak home of my aunt Lou Cadbury and her husband, John, during which I remember having a delicious breakfast of scrambled eggs on toast brought to me in bed, I was returned to The Downs with instructions, fortunately not in writing, that I was not to do any PT for a few days, maybe a week. I was grateful to be missing any PT, and, when the convalescence-time was up, I pretended not to know about it, and continued to read in the library rather than funk forward rolls in the gym. It was not until near the end of term that I was found out. The headmaster commented on the matter in my report as being "due to a misunderstanding on his part, I hope".

A more serious medical problem, which arose near the beginning of the summer holiday in 1950, was rheumatic fever, which necessitated several weeks of bed-rest and might have caused heart damage. Another problem was my eyesight. Both Barbara and Colin were short-sighted, and it seems strange that no check was made to see whether I was too. My vision was so defective that I could read very little on a blackboard, and when a short comic film was shown as a Saturday-evening treat, I could not see what was on the screen, despite sitting at the front, and had to ask other boys what they had been laughing at. The handicap, which could so easily have been remedied, undoubtedly retarded my progress, and my teachers were as negligent as my parents in failing to detect it. I refer mainly to damage done in the classroom, but my short-sightedness also drained my confidence in other areas: but for it, I might have been less cowardly in the gym and swimming pool. Eye problems of one sort or another have recurred throughout my life, interfering with the preparation for my degree examinations, precipitating my early retirement from university teaching, forcing me to resign as director of an excavation, and culminating in the loss of the sight in one eye. These occurrences have been obstacles, but I consider myself very fortunate that they have not been worse.

From early in my time at The Downs, I formed an ambition to get away from other people and live by myself in some remote place, probably with just a cat for company. The ambition became more precisely focused when I found in the school library H.V. Morton's book *In Search of Scotland* and was captivated by his account of the Scottish Highlands and Islands. I pored over maps of the area and identified several small Hebridean islands as desirable places to live. At this stage I knew very little about my Scottish ancestry, so my interest in Scotland was not influenced by that. In 1952 I started learning Gaelic with the help of *Maclaren's Gaelic Self-Taught* and Neil Macalpine's *A Pronouncing Gaelic-English Dictionary.* In September of that year, when I first set foot in Scotland on a family holiday, my father told our Gaelic-speaking waitress that I was a learner and invited me to say something to her in Gaelic. She was serving our evening meal in a hotel by Loch Lomond at the end of our long day's drive from the English Midlands, and, without a moment's hesitation, I made the appropriate comment "*Tha mi sgìth*" ("I am tired"), and was commended for my good pronunciation. I felt rather pleased with myself. Forty-three years later, my ambition to live by myself on a remote Scottish island would be fulfilled, but there would be no Gaelic and no cat.

By no means everything about The Downs was bad. It was set in lovely countryside. Neighbouring Brock Wood was full of bluebells and wild garlic in spring, and the Malvern Hills were near. Each boy was allowed to cultivate a small patch of garden. There was a working miniature steam railway for those interested, which I was not particularly. There were well-equipped areas for hobbies, including pottery, printing, metalwork, and woodwork: a teak boot-remover which I made in 1953 survives intact after more than seventy years of daily use. Other good things included art, drama, music, and the school magazine, *The Badger.* Art was the province of Maurice Feild, an artist of note as well as a fine teacher. He went on to become a tutor at the Slade School of Fine Art in London. While at The Downs, he painted W.H. Auden, who was a colleague on the staff in 1932–1935 and 1937. Auden produced good work during this period, some of it first published in *The Badger*, and was a stimulating if unorthodox teacher: on one occasion the headmaster, showing prospective parents around the school, took them to Auden's classroom and was disconcerted to find teacher and pupils playing cards. Lilian Tyler was in charge of music and singing. One of her assistants, of a somewhat rotund physique, was nicknamed "Barrel". On one occasion, when she was walking past the main school building, a group of boys, observing her from a high-up window, gave a spirited rendering of "Roll out the barrel". The culprits refused to identify themselves to the headmaster, so the whole school lost a half-holiday.

Sports were taken seriously – rugby in winter, cricket in summer. It was for alleged misbehaviour on the sports field that I received an inexplicable punishment. In an interval of training on a winter's afternoon, the supervising French master, a Monsieur Aubert, took offence when I uttered the words "*Je jette une boule de neige*" ("I throw a snowball") and sent me to the headmaster, W. Frazer Hoyland, who beat my bare backside with gusto. Whatever the exact context of my remark was, it is hard to see that it was vulgar, and one might think Mr Aubergine would have been quite gratified to hear a comment in correct French. I have often wished I had asked the headmaster to explain, and also to justify his administration of corporal punishment in a Quaker school. Was it for his enjoyment?

From the age of nine, I had poems printed in *The Badger*, starting with "The Nile" and "A Storm at Sea". The former suggests that my interest in geography was already developing. In 1951 news that I had won a prize in the subject reached Henry's brother Bill and his wife, Isadore, in America, whereupon I was sent a book by their friend William Beebe describing his underwater explorations off Bermuda in 1934. The charming manuscript dedication on the title page of *Half Mile Down* reads:

> To / Martin Ferguson Smith / hoping that we explorers / may get together soon. / Will Beebe / Christmas 1951.

Other poems include the humorous "It Isn't Worth Learning Lessons", "Winter", and "The Bridge at Bewdley". I am also the anonymous author of one of the witty "Sayings of the Wise" (Spring 1952): "A Deponent Verb is Passive in Form and Active in Free Time".

More important than geography for my career was Ancient Greek, which

I began learning in October 1951, when I was eleven and a half. The subject had only just been introduced, as an alternative to singing, and was poorly taught by a master who had a smattering of languages and had recently added Greek to his repertoire, but it was a beginning. I already knew some Latin. In 1951 I passed the Eleven-Plus examination, qualifying me for admission to a Grammar School, but soon afterwards Henry put me down for the public school he had attended – Shrewsbury School, to enter which I needed to pass the Common Examination for Entrance to Public Schools. That was to happen in June 1953.

A momentous event was the death of King George VI, at the age of 56, on 6 February 1952. He had been on the throne since the abdication of his elder brother, Edward VIII, in 1936, and there was genuine sorrow across the country when he succumbed to the lung cancer caused by his heavy smoking, because of the courageous and selfless way he and his wife, Elizabeth, had conducted themselves during the war, continuing to occupy Buckingham Palace, despite the threat and reality of bombing, and visiting communities that had suffered damage and destruction. The news reached us during an English lesson, which was abandoned, leaving us to talk among ourselves and with the teacher.

Another fatal event occurred during my last term, in summer 1953. One day Colin came to Colwall on his bicycle and took me out to lunch at the Horse and Jockey, an inn at the lower (Ledbury) end of the village. After he had drunk a brandy and smoked a cigarette, we began the walk back to the school. We had progressed perhaps 250 yards when a lorry came thundering down the hill towards us, travelling much too fast as it approached a corner. We did not see what happened. We heard a sound like that of rolling dustbins, but had no inkling that the lorry had mounted the bit of pavement we had traversed a minute or two earlier and killed three pedestrians. The incident had a lifelong effect on me. If Colin had been a bit slower finishing his brandy, he and I might have been mown down. Never again have I felt comfortable walking along a pavement with traffic speeding past, especially if it is coming from behind.

While I was at The Downs, all three of the grandparents I had known died. The first to go was my maternal grandfather, Allan Tangye. He was a benign figure, but a retiring man, and I did not get to know him well. Nevertheless I may have inherited some of his likes and dislikes along with his inconvenient propensity to heavy nosebleeds which Barbara also experienced. Like him, I am not naturally sociable, tending to agree with Mr Woodhouse in Jane Austen's *Emma* that "the sooner every party breaks up the better", and I am inclined to agree with my grandfather in preferring funerals to weddings: the former enhance gratitude for still being alive, the latter induce sad thoughts about the unhappiness that awaits so many couples. My paternal grandmother was not retiring, but fairly formidable, and her death in 1950 moved me much less than that of Barbara's mother, Deborah Tangye, two years later. I loved her, as I loved Barbara, very much, and I treasure my memories of her as well as her affectionate letters full of "thee" and "thy" in the traditional Quaker manner.

I had few regrets at leaving The Downs, but did keep in touch with it for many years, until the Old Downian Society more or less faded out and the Newsletter ceased publication. Two senior contemporaries crossed paths with me – both, as it happens Knights of the Realm. One was the late Nicholas Maxted Fenn, distinguished diplomat and, later, chief executive of the Marie Curie cancer charity. I had bumped into his parents in 1991, when I was exploring the grounds of Broome House, Clent, which at that time was a residential home for the elderly. The other was John Hamilton Scott, Lord Lieutenant for Shetland when I went to live there. For my leaving present from The Downs I chose Lowell Thomas Jr., *Out of This World: Across the Himalayas to Tibet*. It is signed by W.V. Berkley, the headmaster – and a good one – in my final year. I have good memories also of Margaret Sant, who taught the youngest boys; Donald Boyd, an Old Downian who devoted his whole life to the service of the school; E.J. Brown, who taught geography and wrote a history of the school, *The First Five* (1988); and "Harpic", as a long-serving lady cleaner was affectionately known. The master in charge of PT, Ken ("Snappy") Ricketts, was the bane of my life, but was actually, I later discovered, an amiable man.

Compared with The Downs, home life was, if not entirely harmonious, much more congenial, and holidays were eagerly awaited by me as by most of the boys. The number of days to go was chalked up on blackboards, and celebrated in chants:

Five more days to the end of term,
Do da, do da;
Five more days to the end of term,
Do da, do da day.

This time next week, where shall I be?
Not in this academee.

3

Shropshire: Silligrove (1948–1992)

It is time to describe home and home-life after the move out of Birmingham. Henry was a businessman through and through, and, when conditions in India precipitated his retirement from the Bombay Company in April 1948, he was in something of a quandary. No offer from the company's London office had been forthcoming, he was only 46, and with some hesitation he took up farming. At least one rural property had been inspected and rejected when he was home on leave in 1947, and in the absence of a more attractive alternative, he and Barbara decided to take on Silligrove, a black-and-white half-timbered house, of notable cruck-beam construction (Plate 5), dating from around 1400 and incorporating some material from an even older house. Silli- may well be derived from Old English *saelig*, "blessed". Its earliest known occupant, Sir John de Sylygrove, was vicar of Kinlet early in the fifteenth century. It came into Tangye ownership sometime in the late nineteenth century, serving as the home of Albert Charles Tangye, Barbara's Uncle "Plaster", until his death in 1941 and as a shooting lodge and recreational place for other members of the family.

Although less than thirty miles west of Birmingham, the location in the scattered parish of Kinlet is very rural and quite remote, on the very edge of the Wyre Forest, just inside Shropshire from Worcestershire, between the River Severn and the Clee Hills. The area is described by A.E. Housman:

> As through the wild green hills of Wyre,
> The train ran, changing sky and shire,
> And far behind, a fading crest,
> Low in the forsaken west

Sank the high-reared head of Clee.
A Shropshire Lad 37.1–5

"Housman's train", crossing county boundaries no fewer than eight times on its quite short run from Woofferton Junction to Bewdley, and on to Kidderminster, afforded great convenience as well as lovely scenery. Wyre Forest Station, neatly maintained by its stationmaster, Mr Griffith, who wheezed because of the gas he had inhaled in the First World War, was frequently used by me and other family members until its regrettable closure in 1962.

Silligrove was draughty and quite primitive, although from the beginning we had running water, thanks to the pipeline which conveys Birmingham's supply from the Elan Valley reservoirs in mid-Wales. The massive pipes were buried under the meadow just in front of the house. For a while, the water for Silligrove was untreated and excellent, but the awful day came when the Water Board insisted on chlorination and substituted inferior water pumped up from the River Severn. When that happened, Barbara and Henry refused to use tap-water to make tea and instead got a farm-worker to fill plastic containers from a spring in the woods. This supply was remarkably rich in vegetable and animal life, but they thrived on it.

5) Silligrove, ca. 1975

For many years there was no mains electricity. For lighting, we relied first on "Aladdin" paraffin lamps and candles. Then a small petrol generator was installed in an outbuilding. Its output was sufficient for the lights, but not for much if anything more. There was competition not to be the last one to bed, so as to avoid having to cross the farmyard with a torch and turn off the generator. The small engine was replaced by a larger one, made by Tangyes, but we still had no refrigerator, freezer, or washing machine. Mains electricity did not arrive until the early 1960s. Cooking was done on an Aga range, fuelled by anthracite, and a coke-burning boiler provided hot water. The dining room, which included a sitting area, was heated by a large open log-fire (Plate 6). When we arrived, the fireplace was so large that one could stand up inside it. Building works to reduce its size revealed that a crucial beam was near to failure. They also brought to light brickwork from the pre-1400 house. An unusual feature of Silligrove was that the first-floor rooms were served by two staircases, without any connecting door or passage at that level. This proved convenient when Barbara and Henry's marriage hit the rocks in the 1960s: her bedroom and bathroom were up one staircase, his up the other.

6) Carol, Barbara, and Martin at Silligrove, 1952

For me, Silligrove was an exciting playground, especially its gardens, orchard, barns and other outbuildings, and nearby woods, stream, and pool. In the spring The Dingle, where the stream and pool were, was a stupendous sight with its display of many tens of thousands of wild daffodils. The big problem for Henry and Barbara was that most of Silligrove's land had been let to a neighbouring farmer, Mr Guest, and it took a long time to get it back. So we had very few animals at first. What these lacked in numbers, they compensated for in character. They included Bessie, a Large White sow, who was a wonderful mother to countless piglets, and The Black Cow, of somewhat ungainly appearance, who soon revealed herself to be expert at jumping over fences and even gates. She did not supply milk. That was obtained each morning from Meaton, Mr Guest's farm about a quarter of a mile away, and I often carried the can to collect it from the milk parlour. After the novelty wore off, I found it rather a chore. We kept chickens, and that was about it at the beginning. There were tabby cats, most of which lived in the outbuildings and were untamed. They included one called Pumphrey, who was a prolific and excellent mother of great longevity. When I was about twelve, I had a grey and white domesticated cat called Tiddy-Widdy, until she failed to return from one of her nocturnal hunting expeditions, perhaps a victim of Devereux, a gamekeeper who was a near neighbour. After Chippy turned chicken-killer and did not reform, there was no dog until 1952, when on the aforementioned Scottish holiday Henry bought Carol a Cairn Terrier in Bunessan on the Isle of Mull. Molly's mother was a working dog, expert at rounding up cattle, but the daughter never did a stroke of work, except perhaps when hunting grey squirrels, which sent her into a frenzy of excitement. In the 1950s the UK government, in the hope of reducing the damage done by grey squirrels (including bark-stripping and taking birds' eggs and fledglings) revived a scheme which offered a bounty for each grey squirrel tail handed in. A common way of hunting them was to poke the dreys with extending aluminium poles and to shoot the occupants when they ran out. Later, at the end of a summer vacation from university, I used the poles for a quite different purpose – to knock the upper branches of tall perry-pear trees after spreading tarpaulins on the ground to catch the fruit. It was a bumper crop, and I sold the bulging and dripping sacks to Bulmers of Hereford for about £80 – an enormous sum of money in those days.

Affectionate and loyal to the family, Molly was less good with strangers, including postmen. Approaching people with wagging tail, apparently inviting them to stroke her, she would suddenly lose her nerve and give them a snap. Her successor, Pete, of the same breed, drowned in a part-frozen pond after mistaking thin snow-covered ice for firm ground. I did not witness the incident, but recovered Pete's body the next day to the relief of Barbara and Henry, so that the beloved animal could be buried down in the Side Dingle, where other pets had been buried and where their own ashes were to be scattered.

Henry bought a 4WD Land Rover in 1948/1949, soon after the famous vehicle first became available; also a Ferguson TE20 ("Little Grey Fergie") tractor, which had been manufactured since 1946. When he unwisely allowed me to drive the tractor at the age of eight or nine, I promptly steered it into a pear tree, without harming myself, the tractor, or the tree. There was a different outcome when he, working on the land of another farmer, about a mile from Silligrove, somehow managed to run himself over with the Ferguson. He was trapped and lucky not to be killed. His cries for help were heard and he was rushed to hospital.

In the early years we had annual visits from a German girl roughly the same age as Carol. Margot came from Hamburg under a scheme that encouraged reconciliation after the war. She kept in touch with our family for many years, and each Christmas she would send Barbara and Henry a German sausage. They appreciated the kind thought, but did not find the sausage to their taste. The giving came to an end when Barbara put the usual cylindrical package unopened in the larder and wrote to thank Margot for the sausage, describing it "as delicious as always". She was much embarrassed when Margot replied that what she had actually sent was a telescopic umbrella.

A weekly visitor to us was John Henry Tangye, Barbara's Uncle Harry. A retired director of Tangyes Ltd and a former part-owner of Silligrove, he was a pioneer of motoring. When he became a founder member of the Automobile Association in 1905, he had already been driving for seven years. His first car was a French Panhard. He claimed to be the first person to have driven a motor car in Cornwall and related how he had been stoned there and chased across Bodmin Moor by irate men on horseback. When we began our occupation of Silligrove, he was already over eighty, but insisted on driving himself out from Birmingham every Saturday morning, accompanied by his housekeeper, Florence Broome, with a yapping Sealyham under each arm. He would stop on the way for a gin and tonic at the Button Oak inn in the Wyre Forest. Gin was his favourite tipple, and there was always a bottle in his bathroom. On arrival at Silligrove, he would drink more gin and tonic and join us for lunch, his lunch being breast of chicken which he brought with him and shared with the cat. After lunch he retired to the drawing room and the veranda in front of it and had a snooze, sometimes after calling to the owls in the old yew-tree in the garden. He played the piano well and could be entertaining company. I remember him explaining to Barbara why he had remained unmarried: "I never had the pluck". His attitude to other road-users was arrogant: "Halt signs are only for inexperienced drivers". But his driving career came to a sticky end in 1951, when he was 87. Driving his car down a hill in Hagley, he lost control of it, hit a lady pedestrian pushing a bicycle, carried her through a three-foot hedge, and deposited her with a broken leg in a field. He had probably depressed the accelerator instead of the foot-brake. He was acquitted of dangerous driving, but never drove again. After that, he continued coming to Silligrove until his death at the age of 98, but was driven by a chauffeur. Florence remained in his employment, despite her heavy drinking. When one of Barbara's brothers took the matter up with her, her defence was: "I drink a lot to prevent him from drinking more".

In July 1951 there was a burglary at Silligrove. Carol and I were away at our boarding schools, but Barbara, Henry, and Colin were in the house, and they had planned to make an early start to drive to London and enjoy a picnic lunch on the way. In readiness, all the requirements for the trip were assembled the previous evening and placed on a chest in the hall. During the night three youths, who had absconded from a Borstal institution near Redditch, broke into the house and cannot have believed their luck when they found the items all ready for the taking, including a delicious meal for three. After disabling the telephone, they took from the hall and living kitchen nearly £50 in cash, a gold watch, a silver cigarette-box, silver cutlery, whisky, cider, and of course the ready-packed picnic basket. After trying but failing to start the Rover car, they made off into the forest with their loot. When Henry discovered the robbery, he went to the Devereuxs' house up the road to ask to use their telephone. He had to make quite a din to rouse the couple from their sleep. Mrs Devereux stirred first and, still only semi-awake, said to her husband: "Devereux, there's a cart-horse in the garden". The youths were arrested in the neighbourhood a day or two later, and most of the items were recovered. In retrospect, the whole episode was acknowledged to have been rather comic.

I am sorry to say that I had been guilty of stealing cider earlier, when I was eight or nine. It was a hot summer's day, I was thirsty, nobody else was around, and the sight of a bottle of Bulmers Woodpecker cider in the cool pantry was irresistibly tempting. I poured myself a glass, and would have got away with my crime, had I not omitted to replace the stopper. Later, as the family sat down for a meal, Henry asked first Colin, then Carol, if they had been helping themselves. They denied it. When he asked me, I denied it too. Although I had already been smacked by him for another offence and feared his wrath again, telling a lie was not very smart. I had probably gone as white as a sheet or as red as a beetroot, and who else could have been the culprit? After a second denial, I burst into tears and left the room. The situation became extra-upsetting when Barbara followed me up to my bedroom and told me *she* believed me. That was very sweet of her, but made me cry again.

Very different from the Woodpecker drink was the cider or scrumpy which Colin and friends made on one occasion. They gathered up Silligrove apples, took them to a cider-press, and allowed the juice to ferment and mature. It was strong stuff, and unpalatable to me, probably then only about twelve years old. Those who drank a quantity of it were reported to think it innocuous at first, then to find it quite lethal. A farm worker who was given some failed to make it back to his cottage a mile away, but collapsed in a ditch. On one occasion a container of it leaked in the boot of Colin's car and corroded a tool-set. No wonder it corroded human stomachs as well!

Annual summer visitors were two elderly ladies, Christina Hendricks and Miss Linforth, who lived together in a deprived area of Birmingham. They would spend two weeks in a bungalow on Sturt, an area of scrub and woodland that belonged to Barbara's brother Chris. It was our responsibility and privilege to look after them and bring them water as well as provisions. They were not able to walk far, but loved breathing fresh country air and seeing all the green things not present in their slum near Five Ways. To witness their pleasure and appreciation was deeply moving.

The closest house to the bungalow was occupied by a Mr Morris and his family. He kept working horses, and one day Henry and I called on him to request two buckets of horse manure for the mushroom bed I was establishing in a disused duck-pen. He very readily granted the request and filled the buckets in a stable. Unknown to us, he had been summoned to hospital the next day for an operation. But he never made it there. Early in the morning he went out with his gun, and at a short distance from his house shot himself dead. The news made everyone who knew him very sad. What made it even worse for me is that I had been with him just hours earlier.

Despite most of the Silligrove land being unavailable at the beginning, help in looking after it was required, partly but not only because of Henry's inexperience in farming. Ben Trow, a gentle and kind man in his early sixties, who lived just across the road in Silligrove Cottage, had been a gamekeeper, but was now employed mainly as a gardener, good with flowers and vegetables. Suspicious of machines and wedded to the old ways of working, he liked to cut grass with a scythe rather than with a motor mower. He enjoyed discussing gardening with Barbara, who treated him with proper respect, but was wary of Henry, who did not share her passion for gardening, and who had a habit, no doubt developed during his time in India, of loudly shouting from the farmhouse door or farmyard the name of anyone he wanted to speak to and expecting him or her to come running straight away, even if engaged in a piece of work at the time. Although Ben never complained, one could tell from his face that he found such behaviour disrespectful and annoying, and at his age he found it difficult to come running. I too frequently heard my name called. Another ingrained habit of Henry's was to whistle almost non-stop when he was outside, mostly tunes from the 1920s. It was so ingrained that he was not always aware that he was doing it. It had one advantage: it revealed he was somewhere in the vicinity, and where.

Henry never felt comfortable leaving Silligrove to take a holiday, maintaining that the two most enjoyable things about a holiday are planning it and returning home after it. Understandably, he became more reluctant to travel far after he developed Ménière's Disease, with periodic bouts of vertigo and tinnitus, in the 1950s. Another consideration was that he was soon to have more land to look after. In 1952, when the lease of most of the Silligrove land to Mr Guest was still in force, he bought Winwoods, a farm of just over 150 acres, reached along a track from Sturt, about two miles from Silligrove by road. I attended the auction with him in Kidderminster. There was little interest in the property, which he acquired for £5,250. Included was the solid but unmodernised farmhouse, and a young farmworker, Henry Knott, and his wife, Gwen, soon occupied this. I was the first to do any work on the land: there were piles of manure, left by the previous owner in one field, and I was paid threepence a pile to spread them. Not long afterwards, Henry also acquired Rotten Row, a farm of 93 acres. It was a little more distant than Winwoods, but bordered it on one side. The price was £3,750. When the Silligrove land was at last free of its tenant and came into Barbara and Henry's ownership, the total acreage, including that of wooded areas, was about 400.

The main crop grown was barley, but the chief occupation was rearing sheep and beef cattle.

Sometimes I accompanied Henry to market, usually in Bridgnorth or Kidderminster. I did not like seeing our animals being sold, often for slaughter, but enjoyed the buying. The patter of the auctioneers could be entertaining. I recall one of them euphemistically describing a pen of particularly scraggy beasts as "good improvers". In the course of my university teaching career, I was often tempted to describe some of my pupils similarly.

More land meant more farm workers. Henry Knott was always on the scene, strong and willing and a good all-rounder. He could not always say how many sheep there were in a field, but he would know immediately if one were missing. Others were usually employed part-time or at particularly busy times. They included Tom Hinton, who had been brought up to handle horses, but had retrained for general agricultural work and especially forestry, for which he was employed increasingly by Chris in his plantations on Sturt. Tom, who did not pronounce his aitches, liked to enliven his conversation with metaphors and maxims, but not always accurately: "You see, Mr Smith, what we've got to do is kill a bird with two stones". On one occasion, when Barbara, Henry, and I were holidaying in southwest Ireland, and it had been arranged that Tom would be by the telephone at Silligrove at a certain time, Henry rang and, just before a weak line died, heard Tom report the alarming news: "It's raining 'ard and 'Enry's mowing", meaning Henry Knott of course. Fred Perkins, a foxy-looking bachelor who lived alone, was good at almost everything and brilliant at laying a hedge. Masefield (I never heard his first name) had a special way with animals, including cattle. I can still hear him say, with reference to a pregnant cow: "Aye, she be bagging up pretty well now, she be". I once used the same words as a compliment to the heavily pregnant daughter of a friend, and she pretended to be amused. Strong and tall, Masefield found himself in Cleobury Mortimer Magistrates Court after a drink-fuelled argument in The Eagle and Serpent in Kinlet escalated into a brawl in the car park. Masefield easily got the better of his opponent, but unwisely threw him over the fence into the village policeman's garden. Henry arranged and paid for his defence. While waiting in court for the case to be called, he witnessed the trial of a learner driver who had been prosecuted for failing to display L-plates. When asked why he did not display them, the accused replied: "because it was a sunny day". The magistrates scratched their heads in puzzlement. When it was Masefield's turn, he was asked how many bottles of beer he could consume before getting drunk. His reasonable reply was: "It depends what size". It seemed inevitable that he would be found guilty, until his defence lawyer demanded sight of the by-law under which he was being prosecuted. All the police had in Court was a copy, and, after one of their number had bicycled to the police station in a vain search for an original, the case was dismissed.

The drink with which most of the men refreshed themselves at work, including when laying hedges and haymaking, was cold tea with milk and sugar brought from home in lemonade bottles. I never sampled it, but imagine it was an acquired taste. Anyhow, it worked well for them and was probably more healthy than some of the drinks which many folk take to work nowadays.

Barbara was always busy. A young local woman, Vera Lane, gave her good help in the house, but she did much housework herself, including the laundry, all done by hand and needing to be ironed. Henry's brother Reginald, a priest in the Anglican Community of the Resurrection, once infuriated her by calling her a Martha. The gardens occupied much time: she loved being in them, but often wore herself out, and there were frustrations when her white magnolia was ruined by a late frost, or deer got in overnight and did much damage: they were particularly partial to her early roses and young beetroot. In summer there was soft fruit – strawberries, raspberries, red and black currants, and gooseberries – to be picked. There were cherries, damsons, plums, apples, and pears too, and in the autumn walnuts. Not least important, there were blackberries in the hedgerows. We all helped with fruit-picking if we were at home, but Barbara made all the jam and did all the bottling. Often she acted as hostess: relatives and friends loved visiting Silligrove, often for tea, for which she made the scones, flapjacks, and cakes. There was a particularly large gathering on Boxing Day. It was a day I disliked because there was always a pheasant shoot, and killing creatures for fun has never appealed to me. At times I was a beater, because it was expected of me, but, as I grew older and, I should like to think, more mature, I declined to participate. Anyhow, it was a hectic day for Barbara, with perhaps sixteen seated at the long table in the dining room and several others on chairs in front of the fire. On other occasions the parties could be much fun. I count myself fortunate to have been brought up in a family and society that entertained itself not with television, but with radio, books, conversation, and all sorts of games – not only board games and card games, but also charades, sardines, and Up Jenkins, for the last of which the dining room table was ideal.

Barbara's activities were by no means confined to the care of Silligrove. She continued to be an active member of the Society of Friends (Quakers), although she did not get to a meeting house for Sunday worship as often as she wished. This was partly because the nearest one was in Bewdley, about seven miles away, and she did not drive, and partly because the historic Norman church at Kinlet had no organist unless she agreed to play. This she did for many years. In the holidays I used to enjoy pumping the organ for her. On one occasion the organ gave up the ghost during a hymn, whereupon she walked up the nave to a harmonium and continued on that. Congregations tended to be small except at Christmas and Easter. It did not help attendance that the church is next to Kinlet Hall, quite a way from the village. One who never failed to turn up, despite having to walk with a pronounced stoop at least two miles there and two miles back, was an elderly lady called Mrs Kinnish, the widow of a drunkard husband. After I had learned to drive, I was glad to give her lifts. Conversation was virtually impossible because she was stone-deaf, and this could be a problem in the church: she liked to join in the hymns, despite having one of the most unmusical voices I have ever heard, and if she had not grasped that certain verses were to be omitted, she would sing them after the rest of the congregation had finished. Barbara was generous to charitable causes with her time and money. Henry sometimes criticised her for being too generous, but, after she died just over a year before him, followed her practices.

From the beginning, she was a member of Kinlet Women's Institute, through which she made valuable contacts and friendships and learned as well as offered much. She became its president. For some reason, but I think unjustifiably, the WI was often a butt of humour in the 1950s. I remember the hilarity which greeted the reformed witch's last words in a London pantomime starring Arthur Askey: "I'll join the Women's Institute".

Visits to London in the 1950s were always exciting, partly because of the bright lights and the Tube. Henry booked rooms at the huge Regent Palace Hotel near Piccadilly Circus. I considered it the last word in luxury and comfort, despite the lack of private bathrooms. Of the shows we saw, the most memorable for me was one at the Victoria Palace by the Crazy Gang, with Bud Flanagan, Chesney Allen, et al. The group, formed in the early 1930s, was a favourite of the Royal Family and had helped national morale during the war with its comic sketches. On at least one of the London visits I was taken to the British Museum, where I took particular interest in the Rosetta Stone and bought a booklet about it. Found in Egypt and inscribed with a decree of 196 BC in three scripts, including Egyptian hieroglyphics and Greek, it enabled the hieroglyphics to be deciphered. I found this fascinating. It was my first introduction to epigraphy, a subject that was to become important to me from 1968.

It was at about the same time that I became increasingly interested in local history. One manifestation of this interest was to scour the cultivated fields at Silligrove in search of slipware pottery made in earlier centuries. Only fragments were to be found, but they were numerous and sometimes quite sizeable. When a ceramic item in use was broken and thrown out, its pieces often ended up in the fields after being carted out along with compost and manure. They were often thick, the glaze was predominantly brown and yellow, and the decoration varied from the very simple to the quite elaborate. It was great fun for me, but my collection was never examined by an expert, and I fear that it does not survive.

Much fun was had in games on the Silligrove lawn – croquet, bowls, and French cricket. I can still remember exactly where each croquet post and hoop was placed. The games were the more challenging, and sometimes frustrating, because the lawn was not entirely flat, so that allowance had to be made for slopes and bumps. If visitors were playing, they were immediately at a disadvantage compared with the home team. Barbara rarely played and was extraordinarily good-tempered when errant balls sped into her herbaceous border and had to be located and retrieved.

4

Shrewsbury School (1953–1958)

My five years at The Downs School were followed by five at Shrewsbury School. Founded in 1552, it counted among its early pupils two Elizabethan poets who were also statesmen – Fulke Greville and Philip Sidney. The latter was also a soldier, and the famous story is told that lying wounded at Zutphen he declined the offer of water, because another soldier had greater need. An anonymous Salopian (I suspect Mike Dibb) who went on, like me, to university in Dublin, composed a witty stanza which went something like this:

> "Thy necessity is yet greater than mine",
> Said he as he declined the water.
> But would he have said the same
> If it had been a glass of porter?

Sidney's bronze statue stands just inside the main entrance-gates to the school (the Moss Gates), close to Rigg's Hall, to which I belonged. The school's most spectacular success was to come in the nineteenth century under three exceptional headmasters – Samuel Butler, Benjamin Hall Kennedy, and the Revd Henry Whitehead Moss. Under these outstanding scholars, teachers, and administrators, the results achieved by their pupils, especially in Classics, were astounding. During Moss's headship, the school moved in 1882–1883 from its cramped quarters near the centre of Shrewsbury to a spacious new site across the river at Kingsland. His daughter, Rosalind, born at the school in 1890, became a distinguished Egyptologist and worked for many years in collaboration with Ethel Burney. The two lived together in Oxford, and in the 1970s bought an apartment on the Anglesey (Ynys Môn) shore of the

Menai Strait (Afon Menai). There my wife, young daughter, and I used to visit them, usually on Sunday mornings. They were most delightful and interesting company, and for me the link to Shrewsbury School in the Victorian Age was extraordinary. Rosalind died in 1990, aged 99, Ethel in 1984, aged 93. The school continued its strong Classical tradition in the twentieth century, and the teaching methods of the Head of Classics, D. Stacy Colman, in my time were not vastly different from those that were so successful in the nineteenth century. They included reading prodigious quantities of Greek and Latin in the original, learning by heart long passages of Greek and Latin authors, especially poetry, translating ancient texts orally in class, and undertaking verse and prose composition in both languages. Stacy concentrated most of his attention on those pupils reckoned to have the best chance of winning scholarships or exhibitions to Oxford or Cambridge. I was not one of them. After I became a Foundation Scholar of Trinity College, Dublin, he kindly congratulated me, and he did the same when I obtained the Chair of Classics at Bangor. In 1980 he came to Bangor, at my invitation, to give a talk on "The Classics at Shrewsbury School". Rosalind and Ethel had recently moved to Epsom, but returned specially for the lecture. It was extremely surprising and deeply embarrassing when he declined to meet them before or after it. Many years later I learned from another pupil of his, Nicholas Barber, that he had fairly recently had a frontal lobotomy that was intended to deal with severe depression, but had brought about big personality changes. I have vivid memories of specific incidents in his classes. A boy, reading Horace aloud, was savaged for pronouncing the first vowel in *frigidus* short. During the prolonged outburst, Stacy shrieked "not a fridge, a freedge!". Of course one never forgot. Another explosion followed his discovery of a boy eating chocolate in class. His annoyance, already considerable, was increased when it emerged that the chocolate was not a time-honoured brand, but a new one with which he was unfamiliar:

> "Now, if it had been *Cadbury's*, it would not have been quite so bad, but *Tiffin, Tiffin* – this is intolerable".

Of my other Classics masters I have the best memories of William B. Cook, B.M.S. (inevitably nicknamed "Bums") Hoban, and Laurence R. Edbrooke. All three were delightful men and good teachers. The first two were to go on to prestigious headships elsewhere. An elderly retired teacher, who was brought back to fill a gap, caused a sensation by appearing at the first class of the day, held before breakfast, with all his fly-buttons undone. It was rumoured, probably falsely, that the same man had a wooden leg and once got it stuck on the accelerator, with the result that he drove from Shrewsbury to Oswestry in half the usual time.

I was thirteen when I entered the school in September 1953. As when I went to The Downs, I was extremely nervous. Again, Barbara did not join in the delivery of me to the school. I was taken by Henry and Carol, the latter having just left The Mount. There was a tea party hosted by the Rigg's housemaster, Richard H.J. Brooke ("Brookie") and his wife. After that I was taken the short distance to The Poplars, a so-called waiting house, accommodating pupils for whom there was not yet room in the main building. There were about six of us, and we were in the charge of a mathematics master called Arnold Hagger. John Ravenscroft, better known as John Peel, who entered Rigg's one term before me and also started in Hagger's house, has written about his time at Shrewsbury School (John Peel and Sheila Ravenscroft, *Margrave of the Marshes*). His experiences, perceptions, and recollections are often similar to mine, but by no means always so. One of his recollections is that he punched me after I had been put up by several of his friends to pouring a bottle of Quink ink over him. He is mistaken. Pouring ink over somebody, unless perhaps accidentally, is something I would never have done, nor at that age would I have burst into tears after being punched. Peel has confused me with someone else, possibly another Smith. Another thing about which I disagree with him is his assessment of Brooke. He hero-worshipped him because he, and seemingly he alone, sympathised with his career ambitions and gave him encouragement. That is to Brooke's credit, and there were other good things about him, including his lively teaching and his campaign to make Rigg's more cultured. I gratefully acknowledge the encouragement he gave me at times. But I could never wholly admire one who was not just very right-wing (he regarded *The Observer* and *Manchester Guardian* newspapers as dangerously subversive), but also racist: "What I always say is flog the wogs". He spent the last years of his life in Holy Orders. As for Peel, I certainly owe it to him that I am (as some think) surprisingly well informed about skiffle and the beginnings of rock 'n' roll. But whether he much influenced my cultural development and taste is doubtful. He complains that "there was depressingly little interest in either Lonnie [Donegan] or Elvis [Presley] in Riggs" (p. 49). Rummaging through assorted items from my time at Shrewsbury, I see that on 16 December

1956 he and I had parts in the Rigg's Hall Dramatic Society's production of A.P. Herbert's farce *Two Gentlemen of Soho*. I was Hubert, the Duchess of Canterbury's dancing partner, while he was Sneak, a private detective. I may have slightly envied him because, after abandoning my early ambition to be a bus driver, I thought it would be a fine thing to be a detective. What influenced me far more than hearing any of Peel's gramophone records was seeing a performance of *The Gondoliers* by the D'Oyly Carte Opera Company at Stratford-upon-Avon. Instantly, I became an ardent Gilbert and Sullivan fan. Several of us in Rigg's sang snatches from the operas in the evenings, and I composed parodies for performance at house entertainments.

An advantage of starting in the Poplars was that for one term I was spared much contact with the senior boys, whom I had been warned, both by the headmaster of The Downs and by Henry, to be wary of, if, for example, one of them invited me to join him for a walk. The warning was scary, and also mysterious because it was not fully explained what might happen if one accepted the invitation. Certainly I had no idea that I might be buggered in a toilet at Shrewsbury Cemetery, as John Peel says he was. Luckily I was not considered to be as attractive as he evidently was, but one could not but be aware that some of the younger boys were being targeted and abused by some of their seniors. One perpetrator of abuse went on to become a distinguished professor of Law. I found it all utterly disgusting, and lived in fear that I might be targeted too. No doubt there would have been much less homosexual activity if some contact with girls had been allowed or arranged. Two Riggites senior to me made their own arrangements by meeting up with girls in the town. I could not understand why one of them wanted to borrow for their excursions the jar of vaseline I had for my chapped lips. He went on to take Holy Orders.

Another unpleasant thing was the douling system. "Doul" is connected with the Greek word for slave, *doulos*. You were a doul for your first two years, at the service of monitors (house prefects). If a monitor wanted some task performed – his shoes cleaned, for example – he would go into the passage in the study-area and call "doul" in a loud voice, whereupon all the douls within earshot were required to race to him. One enjoyable task I was given, probably in 1954, was to go to the café in the School Shop to be a waiter. It was enjoyable because, as well as being rewarded with a portion of chips, I had the thrill of asking Billy Wright, captain of the Wolverhampton Wanderers and England football teams, whether he would like some more chips. He replied: "No, thank you". He had come up by coach with the Wolverhampton Wanderers Colts to watch them play the School. I boasted about my conversation with him at the time, and I have been boasting about it ever since.

Monitors were empowered to give beatings for all kinds of offences, including failure to observe the rules, rightly ridiculed by John Peel, about who was allowed to talk or walk in particular places or sit on a radiator. These rules and many others were examined by the monitors in a so-called Colours Test – a test that might have had some utility if it had been confined to the colours of the different houses, instead of covering all sorts of infantile absurdities. When I became a monitor, I refused to use the douling system, unless I needed to delegate a task that involved official business, such as taking an urgent message to another house. I also refused to give any beatings.

Housemasters too sometimes administered punishment, including corporal punishment. Anthony Chenevix-Trench, of School House, beat boys so frequently that he was described as a flagellomaniac. Some masters were known to be homosexual. Whether any of them in my time ever subjected pupils to sexual abuse I cannot say. But a paedophile act brought about the instant dismissal of a young Classics master in 1956. He had asked a small boy (not a Salopian) to sit on his chest. He went on to have a distinguished academic career and was elected a Fellow of the British Academy. When I was a young university teacher in Bangor and he came to give a talk to the local Classical Association, one of the Bangor professors introduced him to me, prompting me to say that he had taught me at Shrewsbury. Unsurprisingly, the professor had not been aware of that. I am sure that the visitor was relieved that I did not say more.

At the beginning of my first term I was placed in a form that required Greek to a much higher level than I had achieved at The Downs, so I was demoted to Lower IVb, in which I was, according to the form master, "easily at the top". I was first in Latin among other subjects. It cannot have helped my Greek that no Greek classes were offered in the new form. But the next year, when I was in Vb, the picture changed: I was first in Greek as well as Latin, and reports of my work in Classical Remove confirmed the good progress, one teacher reporting that I had overtaken almost all the pupils who previously were reckoned to be ahead of me. One very important reason for the change is that during the summer holiday in 1955, Barbara and Henry arranged for me to receive private tuition in Greek from a retired Classics schoolmaster in Stourbridge. This involved taking the train three times a week from Wyre

Forest Station and changing in Kidderminster for Stourbridge Junction. It took a bit of a bite out of my holiday, but I have always been grateful for the push it gave me. In addition to performing well in class, I won the T.O.K. Cross Classical Essay Prize, 1956, for a piece on the Greek theatre.

The summer holiday in 1956 was quite a busy one. Instead of going home at the beginning of it, scores of us marched to Shrewsbury Railway Station on our way to a week of CCF (Combined Cadet Force) training at Castlemartin in Pembrokeshire. It was no fun, and not only because the weather was poor. We slept in tents on lumpy palliasses – a word which caused us some amusement. National Service existed all through the 1950s, and the aim of the CCF was to prepare boys for it and turn out young men who were well enough trained to be short-tracked for commissions. There were two examinations to pass – Certificates A and B. I was successful in them, as most candidates were, and I was classed as a "first class shot", but, as a practising Quaker (I had joined Barbara in the Society of Friends when I was about sixteen), I asked permission to be spared further military training. My request, submitted through the housemaster, was refused, but a sort of compromise was reached: I was transferred to Signals, which meant that on field days, instead of crawling along ditches with a rifle, I walked about with a radio on my back or, better still, operated a radio carried by someone else. The radios were so large and heavy that Signals trainees had to work in pairs. It was quite fun until the novelty wore off.

Later, in early August, I made my first visit abroad, flying from Elmdon Airport, Birmingham, to Paris Le Bourget on my way to stay with the d'Amarzit family near Chalon-sur-Saône, south of Dijon. It was quite an adventure for me. I was on my own, I had never flown before, and, although my knowledge of French was adequate, I had had virtually no practice at speaking it. I was met at the city-centre air terminal by the French husband of a cousin of mine. He drove me about in his small Citroën, took me to a café, and dropped me off at the Gare du Nord in good time for my train. I had not relieved myself since Birmingham, and the need was urgent. Leaving my suitcase in the compartment, I hurried off in search of a loo. Opening a door marked "*Lavabo*", I was dismayed to see only the (admittedly advertised) wash-basin. It had to be sufficient for the purpose, but had me puzzled: do the French not have facilities like those at home? I spent the journey to Chalon looking out of the window until it got dark and silently rehearsing "*je suis enchanté de faire votre connaissance, Madame*" and other useful phrases. The reception by Madame Monique d'Amarzit was very friendly. Neither she nor the elderly parents with whom she and her two sons shared a château spoke any English, which was good for my learning of French. Jean-Guy and Éric, to whom I gave English lessons in the mornings, were aged seventeen and twelve respectively, and Éric was the quicker learner. Their mother was a war-widow. Her husband had been interned and tortured by the Gestapo and conducted himself heroically. Unsurprisingly, the family hated *les Boches.* When I was shown to my room and its en suite bathroom, I was puzzled, for the second time since arriving in France, by the incompleteness of the facilities. The bathroom contained something that looked rather like a toilet but was different from any toilet I had ever seen. Like Crocodile Dundee when he first saw a bidet, I could only guess what it was for. Fortunately, exploration revealed a real WC separate from the bathroom. Monique's boys and I did a lot of bicycling and played a lot of tennis. The Suez crisis was developing, and I picked up the latest international news, as well as the British County Cricket scores, faintly on my hosts' crackly wireless. The news provided useful material for conversation with the family.

At the end of August my aunt Jean Smith introduced me to Gilbert Murray, renowned as a Greek scholar and for the work he did to establish the League of Nations. For a sixteen year old studying Classics, it was a remarkable privilege to meet the great man. It came about because just after the First World War Jean had been Murray's private secretary. That was only for just over two years, but she remained a friend of his and his wife, Lady Mary, until their deaths many years later. We went to Yatscombe, their house at Boars Hill, near Oxford, to have tea. On arrival, we learned that she was in bed, gravely ill. She died on 2 September. I had an awful fear that Murray might test my knowledge of Greek irregular verbs, but he did not do anything like that and soon put me at my ease. Later, my work in Turkey brought me into contact with Oliver Gurney, his next-door neighbour at Bayworth Corner. Gurney was an expert on the Hittites and for many years editor of *Anatolian Studies*.

The sport I had enjoyed most at The Downs, and was best at, was cricket. My poor eyesight for several years was an obstacle when batting, but I was successful as a quick bowler. I was also an ardent fan of county- and test-cricket. The county I supported was Worcestershire, and I went as often as possible to the delightful New Road ground just across the River Severn from Worcester Cathedral. Often I bicycled the twenty miles or so from Silligrove.

My number-one hero in the early days was opening batsman Don Kenyon, whom I first watched playing against the Australian touring side in 1953 and scoring a century. At Shrewsbury I continued to play and enjoy cricket. I also took up tennis. But my forte was cross-country running, which suited my temperament as well as my body. As house captain of running, I was commended by Brookie for my excellent training of younger boys, one of whom was Michael Palin. On Palin's eightieth birthday, I wrote to congratulate him and reminded him of the training I had given him. Most of the cross-country running was and is modelled on a hunt, and the Royal Shrewsbury School Hunt (RSSH) is said to be the oldest cross-country running club in the world. The competing runners are "hounds". The captain is the "huntsman", assisted by the senior whip and junior whip. The other places in the school first VIII go by the somewhat unfortunate name of Gentlemen-of-the-Runs – Gents for short. I was made a Gent in December 1957 (Plate 7). Most of the runs (one of them named The Bog Run!) were non-competitive for most of their distance, which varied considerably but could be in excess of ten miles. There were usually three or four "all-ups", when runners at the front slowed down or stopped to allow those at the back to catch up. From the last all-up there was a race to the finish, and the winner was said to "kill".

7) Royal Shrewsbury School Hunt VIII, 1957-1958. Martin standing, second from L

The most remarkable of Shrewsbury School's teachers in my time was Frank McEachran ("Kek"). I had the good fortune to be in his English class when I was in the Upper Sixth. It is a dismal thought that his methods would be regarded as completely unacceptable in schools today, despite the extraordinarily beneficial influence he had on his pupils. He encouraged boys to stand up on chairs and declaim more or less any passages of poetry or prose they chose. It did not matter what the language was, so long as the piece had sound-quality, like a patriotic Hungarian tramcar inscription, or this:

> Unda her brella mid piddle med puddle she ninnygoes nannygoes nancing by
>
> (James Joyce, *Finnegans Wake*)

Or this:

> Where the breadfruit fall
> And the penguin call
> And the sound is the sound of the sea
> Under the bam
> Under the boo
> Under the bamboo tree.
>
> (T.S. Eliot, *Sweeney Agonistes*)

Such pieces are what he called "spells", and *Spells* and *More Spells* are the titles of two anthologies he published. The range of the passages he selected is wide in date, language, style, and content. Homer and other classical authors are there, as are (among many others) Dante, Shakespeare, Milton, Goethe, Coleridge, and Keats, but so are modern writers, including Auden, e.e. cummings, Louis MacNeice, and Ezra Pound. Before his appointment at Shrewsbury in 1935, Kek had taught briefly at Gresham's School, Holt, where Auden was one of his pupils and came under his influence. The noise that emanated from his Shrewsbury classroom was disturbing to those in neighbouring rooms who were trying to get on with "serious" work, but he inspired in many pupils a life-long love of literature. Among my contemporaries who have or had an abiding admiration for him are Christopher Booker, Paul Foot, Richard Ingrams, and Willie Rushton, all of whom were founders and/or editors of *Private Eye*, which originated in *The Wallopian*, a satirical counterblast to the Shrewsbury School magazine, *The Salopian*. I was younger, as well as less talented, and did not cross paths with them, except literally because Rigg's was very close to Ingrams and Rushton's boarding house, Churchill's, and School House, to which Foot belonged.

One text which Kek insisted we read in "my" year was Samuel Beckett's tragicomedy *Waiting For Godot,* first performed in Great Britain in 1955 and first published in English in 1956, so something very new, and it is doubtful if anyone apart from Kek introduced British schoolchildren to it so early. It is an indication of the impression it made on me that I chose Estragon, the name of one of the two protagonists, as a pen-name for my last contributions to *The Salopian* in 1958. I also used it at least once as a disguise at Trinity College, Dublin, Beckett's *alma mater*.

One of Kek's spells was the Italian Fascist hymn, "Giovinezza" ("Youth"). At a bibulous party after a lecture he had given in Bangor on 17 January 1978, I sang it to Arnaldo Momigliano, the distinguished ancient historian. Since he had been driven out of Italy by the Fascists in 1939, it was a risky thing for me to do, but he was amused and intrigued and wanted to know how I had learned it. He said that he had not heard it sung since he was driven into exile.

My contributions to *The Salopian* (not all of which are signed "Estragon") are quite a mixture. They include pieces on "House Food", "Epitaph on One Who Died on Steeplechases", "Homines Sapientes", "Gallup Poll", two short poems entitled "The Promise of Spring" and "Magic Flower", and a nine-stanza poem, "The Boat Race", roughly in the style of Coleridge's *The Rime of the Ancient Mariner*, relating how a boat, forecast to win a Shrewsbury School bumping race, performs brilliantly until it reaches Kingsland Bridge:

> But on the road, in "Windsors" clothed,
>   Were "Teddies" from the town;
> They took a rock (a biggish block)
>   And let it drop straight down.
>
> They aimed it straight, it sealed their fate,
>   It broke the boat in twain;
> They all were drowned without a sound
>   And ne'er appeared again.
>
> And so, my friends, the story ends

And further words do fail;
Sabrina stores those gallant oars,
The "Teddies" are in jail.

Teddy Boys were one concern of conventional society in the 1950s. Another was the threat posed by a paramilitary organisation mentioned in the *Salopian Traditional* "Nursery Rhyme":

Major Fowler, Major Fowler,
How does your C.C.F. go?
The I.R.A. came one day,
And took the bolts away.

This too was my doing. In "Self Portrait" Estragon identifies himself as "an angry young man", a member of another 1950s' movement, spearheaded by, among others, John Osborne, author of the play *Look Back in Anger* (1956), and Kingsley Amis, whose first novel was *Lucky Jim* (1955). In January 1958, when I was seventeen, I submitted to the Quaker newspaper *The Friend* an article entitled "A Time to be Angry", in which I railed against the possession of weapons of mass destruction:

> Who will deny that this is a dark world, a world overshadowed by the threat of the hydrogen bomb? Is it not time to be angry – angry with those who by their lack of foresight have landed us in this chasm of darkness, and those who by their inaction are making no determined effort to bring us up to the light again?

Because I had stupidly forgotten to sign the article, the editors of *The Friend* had to do some prolonged detective work to discover the author, and publication was delayed until 18 August 1958. The article does not mention the Campaign for Nuclear Disarmament – understandably because CND did not hold its first public meeting until 17 February 1958, at least a month after I had submitted the piece. After its publication, I received a small fan-mail and also an invitation from Peggy Duff, CND's first organising secretary, to organise a Midlands youth section. I declined because I was soon no longer to be a Midlander.

In my last months at Shrewsbury, I became more and more restive about the rules and restrictions, some of which I ignored. Every now and then the school declared a Whole Holiday, which boys were expected to spend exploring the Shropshire countryside. A small group of us took a train down to Church Stretton and installed ourselves in the Long Mynd Hotel, where we played snooker and clock golf, enjoyed a sumptuous lunch, and drank beer and spirits. More daringly, on another occasion we took a train to Wolverhampton, where we patronised a good restaurant before going to the cinema.

My relations with my housemaster, already strained, snapped in spectacular fashion late one summer's evening. As a monitor, I was exempt from the rule that one must be in one's own dormitory by a certain hour, and I was visiting another dormitory when I heard approaching footsteps. Brookie walked with a limp, and sometimes, for amusement, the monitors imitated the distinctive sound of his footsteps and his heavy breathing. Rashly assuming that this was the present scenario, I stood behind the door with a raised slipper. The door opened, and I heard the heavy breathing, but was horrified to see that it emanated from Brookie, who, before storming off, told me to come and see him in the morning. Badly shaken, I immediately went to see the Head of House, Christopher Hewetson, and related what had occurred. I was much cheered when, instead of criticising me, he laid all the blame on the housemaster, saying that he was fed up with him snooping around the dormitories, instead of trusting the monitors to do their job. The upshot was that, instead of Brookie dealing with me alone, he had a visit from all the monitors. I do not think I had to say a word. Christopher spoke robustly (I remember him saying something about making mountains out of molehills), and, faced with a near-mutiny of the monitors, Brookie gave ground and made a subdued almost apologetic response.

5

Dublin, Trinity College (1958–1963)

During my life, I have made many unwise decisions, but also some good ones, and my choice of university, uninfluenced by either schoolteachers or parents, was definitely a very good one. The "done thing" was to go to Oxford or Cambridge, but, probably because it was the done thing, I was not keen on doing it and preferred to try for somewhere very different. Interestingly, my daughter, Lucinda, made the same sort of decision about thirty years later. My chosen destination was Trinity College, Dublin, the sole constituent college of the University of Dublin, founded by Queen Elizabeth I in 1592. I had never set foot in Ireland, and the idea of studying there, right in the heart of the capital city, greatly appealed to me. Other Salopians who made the same decision at the same time included Michael Beloe, Mike Dibb, Peter Hunt, and Timothy Stephens.

Before starting the Honours course in Classics in October 1958, I went on an August camping holiday in France with two Shrewsbury contemporaries. The holiday was not a success, although my companions were congenial enough. One of them provided a car, a Morris Minor, the driving of which I shared with him. In retrospect it seems a bit rash that two very young and inexperienced drivers had gone motoring on the Continent, but I do not recall any parental misgivings or warnings, and we came through unscathed.

We travelled to France via the Silver City air ferry from Lydd to Le Touquet. My recollection is that there were just two other vehicles on the aircraft. During the first night, in a campsite, there was heavy rain, some of which got into our tent, and I discovered that my borrowed Lilo air mattress had a slow puncture. The rain continued the following day, and we resolved to get down to the Mediterranean coast as quickly as possible. Arrived there, we marvelled at Nice and Cannes, and enjoyed the heat until, ignorant of the need for skin protection, we got badly sunburned and, feeling sick and sore, hurried back up north. Before we left, I spent a ghastly night near Toulon on a stony beach beside a main road and railway line, with a rotating lighthouse-beam flashing in my sleepless eyes every thirty seconds. Towards the end of the trip we abandoned the tent in favour of simple hotels. In Paris we went to a strip-show. It was the first time I had seen nude women in the flesh, and the experience doubly surprised me by being amusing and unerotic.

A little earlier, probably around Easter 1958, four of us rented a cruiser on the Norfolk Broads for a week. That holiday too was less than a resounding success. The weather was poor, and, being young and foolish, we rushed around at full throttle and so missed seeing all sorts of interesting things. There were disputes as to who should be at the helm, and we ran aground twice. I remember Beccles only for going to the cinema on a wet afternoon. No strip shows there!

I had passed my driving test in January 1958 at the first attempt, despite having had no professional driving lessons. During the school holidays, even before I was seventeen, the minimum age for driving on the public road, I had obtained a fair amount of practice on farm tracks and especially among the tree plantations on Sturt. Sturt had been used by the army for training during the Second World War, and some well-surfaced tracks remained. But I also benefited greatly from the suspension, from 24 November 1956 to 30 September 1957, of the requirement that a learner driver must be accompanied by a qualified driver. This measure, which would be unthinkable today and is not often recalled, was introduced on account of the fuel shortage brought about by the Suez crisis and the suspension of driving tests for several months. I benefited from it from my seventeenth birthday on 26 April 1957 and was able to put in a lot of practice on public roads all through the following summer holiday, often on farm business.

I took my driving test in Ludlow, Shropshire, a historic market town about fourteen miles distant from Silligrove. The day before the test, the foreman of a local timber merchant with whom Henry had done business accompanied me to Ludlow. He was not a professional instructor, but he knew the course and showed me round it. Ludlow, like almost everywhere else, had very little motor traffic at that time, but there was one potentially tricky thing about the test: it started in those days on a very steep street with one's vehicle facing uphill. Woe betide any candidate who allowed the car to roll back! The lightness of traffic in the late 1950s is illustrated by the case of Birmingham. One could drive into the city centre and park almost anywhere, even outside premises in New Street, Corporation Street, and Colmore Row, for example.

I sailed to Dublin from Liverpool and returned by the same route for the Christmas vacation, but the crossing was a long one, the second class sleeping accommodation was sordid, and, on the eastward journey the vessel carried cattle, which were noisily landed at Birkenhead at an unearthly hour of the morning. After that, I favoured the Holyhead (Caergybi)–Dún Laoghaire crossing, as being much shorter and quicker. Typically I would depart Birmingham New Street around 10 p.m., change trains in Crewe, and catch the boat sailing around 3.25 a.m. I did not take a cabin and, if the sea was rough, as it often was, I used to lie on the life rafts on a partly screened area of the deck. It was cold, but airy, and I reckoned that I would be well placed if the ship foundered! The two regular vessels were the "sisters" *Cambria* and *Hibernia*, but, if one of them were out of service, the substitute was *The Princess Maud* – older (1934), much smaller, and, having no stabilisers, notorious for plunging and rolling. One's heart sank if one found that she was doing duty. Later in my time in Dublin, I sometimes flew with Aer Lingus from Birmingham in a Fokker-F27 Friendship. To obtain the student discount, one had to submit a form signed by one's tutor. He was not in Classics, and I do not recall visiting him for any other purpose.

For my first two terms I had accommodation in Koinonia House, a Methodist hostel at 33 Harcourt Street off the south side of St Stephen's Green. Many of the other inmates were Africans studying medicine at the nearby Royal College of Surgeons. The place was adequate, but unexciting except when Desmond the handyman absconded to London after emptying the warden's safe. The previous day he had said he would teach me to telephone-tap, but his departure meant that I never received the promised tuition. What a narrow escape I had from a life of criminality! I have often wondered what happened to him.

I do not remember much of interest in Harcourt Street apart from the Georgian architecture and the extraordinary gents' hairdresser's premises. There was nothing unusual about the cutting and trimming. What was remarkable was that the hairdresser, whose name may have been Michael McDonagh, had a bookshelf of Irish poets (Clarence Mangan, Oscar Wilde, W.B. Yeats, et al.) and, as the spirit moved him, would read extracts from them for the entertainment and enlightenment of his customers. A visit to him was an unmissable experience, provided that one had an hour or two to spare.

The walk to Trinity College on College Green took one close to the Hotel Russell on the south side of St Stephen's Green. Sadly demolished about fifty years ago, it was one of four luxury hotels in the city, the others being The Shelbourne on the north side of St Stephen's Green, The Royal Hibernian on Dawson Street, and The Gresham on O'Connell Street. Noted for its fine dining, it received many famous guests, including Virginia and Leonard Woolf in 1934. Proceeding along the west side of St Stephen's Green, one passed the Royal College of Surgeons, and then walked down narrow Grafton Street, home to famous stores like Switzer's and Brown Thomas, and Bewley's café from which the most delicious aroma of coffee always emanated. Arrived at College Green, dominated by the Bank of Ireland and the Palladian west front of Trinity, one passed between the statues of two eighteenth-century alumni, Edmund Burke and Oliver Goldsmith, before entering the vestibule which leads to the cobbled Parliament (or Front) Square, with the Corinthian porticoes of the Chapel on the left matching those of the Public Theatre (or Examination Hall) on the right, before the square opens out to reveal the Dining Hall on the left, the 1937 Reading Room on the right, and the Campanile straight ahead. The Campanile stands in the middle of the west side of Library Square, the other sides of which are occupied by the (Old) Library (south), the Graduates' Memorial Building or GMB (north) with the area known as Botany Bay behind, and the Rubrics (east). My walk to the School of Classics would take me alongside the Library and then the Museum Building to the southeast corner of New Square, where the School had rooms on the top floor of no. 40. The approach to the College and the walk through it were an architectural and historical treat, which lifted one's spirits. I was to enjoy a similar experience when I went to teach in Durham thirty years later.

At this time few who were not staff or students entered Trinity. Notable exceptions were the tourists who trooped in to view in the Library what we irreverently called Kelly's Book – the Book of Kells, an illuminated Latin text of the four Gospels executed in the ninth century – and a few minutes later trooped out again. The number of undergraduates was about 1,500 – far fewer than today. It was a good size for a university in the old sense, from the Latin *universitas*, of a "society", "community", or "corporation". At the same time, it was an institution with a big problem, the problem being that it was a Protestant university in a predominantly Roman Catholic country. It is all very different now, but in those days RC parents sent their children to Trinity under pain of mortal sin, and the Archbishop of Dublin, John Charles McQuaid, had refused to appoint a resident chaplain to cater for the spiritual needs of the hundreds of RC students, although a local parish priest was permitted to do that to the best of his ability. The College authorities, on the other hand, had taken steps to attract Roman Catholics and make them feel welcome. For example, they had recognised the RC Laurentian Society and provided it with rooms. The hostility of Irish Catholics to Protestants around 1960 is illustrated by a joke that was doing the rounds then. A young woman returns from working in London and tells her mother that, in order to pay the bills, she had become a prostitute. Her mother, who is hard of hearing, faints with shock. When she comes round, the daughter repeats that she had no choice but to become a prostitute, to which the mother responds with: "A prostitute, you say? What a mercy! I thought you said a Protestant".

One of the attractions of Trinity for me was its four-year course, which really did mean four years, because the degree examinations were taken in October, at the end of the summer vacation. Another was the shortness of the three terms, just seven or eight weeks each, which allowed ample time for working on one's own. A still more important attraction was its staff. The Regius Professor of Greek, (William) Bedell Stanford, was internationally recognised as a leading authority on Homer and Greek tragedy. A striking and rather formidable presence, he was a stimulating teacher, who took a dim view of anyone missing his classes. He was one of Trinity's elected representatives in the Irish Senate. The Chair of Latin was occupied by Donald Ernest Wilson Wormell, a fine Latinist whose main interest was Latin poetry, but who had collaborated with his colleague Herbert William Parke in producing a major two-volume work on the Delphic Oracle, the first volume giving the history of the oracle, the second the oracular responses. British, but with a doctorate from Yale University, he was the most civilised of men and an inspiring teacher, and I was fortunate to have him not only in my undergraduate years, but also as the supervisor of my postgraduate thesis on Lucretius. Parke, who was Vice-Provost and Librarian as well as Professor of Ancient History, gave his classes much entertainment as well as enlightenment. He tended to arrive a bit late and in a state of some sartorial disarray. From the teaching room we could see him approaching from the direction of the Library, steering a sometimes-erratic course as he sorted his notes. On arrival, he would execute an inelegant ballet act as he donned his academic gown. I recall especially vividly his illustrated lectures on Greek art, including the words he used to describe early Greek statues: "Stylised hair ... archaic smile ... full lips ... weak navel". He had an inexhaustible fund of anecdotes and stories about other scholars. The professors were assisted by several other staff. I mention two. John Victor Luce taught a range of topics, including Plato and Juvenal. We thought him a bit pedestrian at times, but later he blossomed into an authority on Homer and the Heroic Age. He also became Trinity's Public Orator (1971). Alfred Edward Hinds apparently had a stellar undergraduate career, but, although a competent lecturer, did not light any sparks and did not seem to publish much. A business meeting of the College Classical Society in about 1962 voted the following gifts to the three professors: Stanford, a bottle of blue hair-rinse; Wormell, a bottle of syrup of figs; Parke, a voucher for use at Prescott's the dry cleaners.

My classmates in Michaelmas Term 1958 included Edna Broderick, Heather Mellish-Oxley, and Ann Ross (all Ancient and Modern Literature), Michael Longley, Juliet Maguiness, Robin Miller, and Foster Murphy (all Classics). Ann was to marry Trinity classicist John Killen; Edna, brilliant critic, married Michael Longley, brilliant poet; and Heather married Trinity agriculturalist David Bird. We were a lively bunch, and five of us were to be elected scholars – Ann, Edna, Robin, Foster, and I. Juliet's father was the classicist William Stuart Maguiness, a Trinity contemporary and friend of Samuel Beckett, who I believe became Juliet's godfather.

In January 1959, towards the end of the Christmas vacation, we sat our first examinations. I returned to Dublin in late December to revise for them, promising myself as a treat, to be enjoyed only on completion, to see the film *South Pacific*. I certainly worked hard and hoped to do reasonably well, but, when the results of the Classics candidates were posted up, I was dismayed not to see my name anywhere at first. To my genuine surprise, it was at the top of the list. After celebratory visits to the Adelphi Cinema and the restaurant of the Wicklow Hotel, I continued my studies with greater confidence.

I had joined the Hist. – the College Historical Society, claimed to be one of the oldest debating societies in the world, founded in 1770. Like the other main society, the Phil. or Philosophical Society, it had premises in the GMB. At this time it still admitted men only. The University had first admitted women to its degree courses in 1904, but in several areas continued to discriminate against them, excluding them from fellowships and foundation scholarships and requiring them to be off the College premises by 7 p.m.

Outside the walls of Trinity, there were endless attractions and distractions. This was a time when Dublin still had no very tall buildings, although that was soon to change. Just walking the streets, crossing the Liffey at O'Connell Bridge, and exploring the quays, were entertainments in themselves, the people being an important part of the experience. Even before leaving the College, one could smell the St James's Gate Guinness brewery, and, emerging on to College Green, one was likely to see, among the traffic, horse-drawn vehicles laden with casks of stout. Sometimes one would catch sight of a celebrity. I remember encountering Brendan Behan, playwright and poet, coming out of New Books on Pearse Street, crossing the street, and making off in the direction of his favourite McDaid's pub in Harry Street. The theatres included the famous Abbey, which, since the fire of 1951, had moved to the Queen's in Pearse Street, and the Theatre Royal, Hawkins Street, for variety shows, made extra-special by its veteran resident organist Tommy Dando with his signature tune "Keep your sunny side up, up!" Among the cinemas, the Astor specialised in continental films: I remember particularly Ingmar Bergman's *Wild Strawberries*. Dublin has a long and proud musical tradition. It is where Handel's *Messiah* was first performed on 13 April 1742. The tradition continued, with all tastes catered for. It was always fun browsing in the bookshops, notably Fred Hanna in Nassau Street and George Webb on Crampton Quay. For free enlightenment and enjoyment, one could visit the National Museum of Science and Art in Kildare Street or the National Gallery of Ireland in Merrion Square or listen to a parliamentary debate in Dáil Éireann in Leinster House. As for pubs, my favourite for lunch was Neary's in Chatham Street. The mixed meats and fresh salmon salads were excellent value at 3/6 and 4/- respectively, and the accompanying drink was a bottle of Guinness. My preference was for bottled stout at lunchtime, draught in the evenings. In 1958 the cost of a pint of draught Guinness was 1/6, the cost of a half-pint or "glass" was half that, i.e. ninepence, but soon the cost of a half-pint was raised to tenpence, while the cost of a pint was left unchanged. It was a cunning move, which of course encouraged drinkers to order pints. On a winter's evening, in freezing weather, a visit to Mooney's for a dock (very large!) glass of its no. 1 port (2/-) was very comforting. A favourite restaurant, reasonably priced, was the Trocadero, owned by a Greek Cypriot, in Grafton Street, then in St Andrew Street. There was some excitement when one of Dublin's first Chinese restaurants, the Universal, opened in Wicklow Street in 1961. Many of its earliest customers ordered chips rather than rice with their curries. Its highest-priced item cost 6/-: topped with a fried egg, it was called the "Universal Special". The finest restaurant was French – Jammet's in Nassau Street. For economic reasons, I only visited it twice – first as a guest of Colin, secondly, when Henry hosted a lunch party there the day before my wedding. It used to be said that a sure sign of a restaurant's quality was the presence of priests, and they certainly patronised Jammet's and, for example, the dining room of the Shelbourne Hotel.

During my first year, I continued to do cross-country running, as a member of the Dublin University Harriers' second VIII, but the Phoenix Park, where the home fixtures and most of the training took place, was a two-mile bus-ride from Trinity, and I found it all too time-consuming. Instead, I played tennis on the courts in Botany Bay and occasionally cricket. Although I never enjoyed playing rugby, I did enjoy watching the international matches at Lansdowne Road, which were attended from 1959 by President Éamon de Valera.

On arrival in Dublin, I was still a practising Quaker, although out of curiosity I sometimes attended Sunday services at Christ Church Cathedral or St Patrick's Cathedral instead of at the Friends' Meeting House in Eustace Street, but I soon stopped going to any of them, the main reason being that my study of Lucretius and the philosophy of Epicurus which he followed convinced me that there is no life after death and no divine providence. Since then, I have not wavered in my atheism, although I have continued and developed my taste for religious music, especially baroque. Like A.E. Housman, I consider myself a high-church atheist. At this point it needs to be mentioned that, although Epicurus did not believe in divine providence, he did believe, rather curiously, in divine beings who, composed of the finest atoms, live in the spaces between the infinite number of worlds in the universe, enjoying perfect peace of mind and never intervening in our affairs.

At the end of my second term, I moved from Koinonia House into College. Conveniently, my first rooms, shared with two other students, Old Salopian Timothy Stephens and Old Shirburnian Simon Shirley, were in no. 40 on the same floor as the School of Classics. (We were one another's "wives" in Trinity parlance.) So there was no excuse for being late for a class. The accommodation was quite spacious, but hardly luxurious. There was no running water. To find that, and it was cold water only, one had to go to a sink one floor down. There was one WC cubicle, without a washbasin, on the ground floor. There was no shower or bath nearer than the bathhouse – a splendid facility, a gift of Lord Iveagh, opened in 1924: it provided huge baths, endless hot water, and excellent acoustics for singing. The drawback was that it was in Botany Bay, up against the Dining Hall, so at a considerable distance from no. 40. We had a gas-ring for boiling up water for hot drinks and shaving, but, unlike a Ugandan student in the rooms below ours, the smell of whose slow-cooked curries penetrated our floorboards, we did not do any serious cooking. Lunch was usually the buffet in the Dining Hall and dinner a formal meal there for which one wore an academic gown, as one did also for classes and any visit to a member of the academic staff. To assist us in keeping our rooms in order, we had the services of a male "skip" or servant, the equivalent of a "scout" at Oxford. I remember Doherty and Knocter. Neither worked to a high standard of hygiene or efficiency, and Knocter had an economical but distasteful habit of emptying hot water bottles into the kettle.

In August-September 1959, I visited Italy and Greece for the first time, taking an Ingham's guided tour, which was seriously educational, well organised, and economical. The tour leader was the Czech architect Walter Bor. There was no flying. We travelled to Venice by train and spent two nights there before proceeding by sea, aboard the *Agamemnon*, to Piraeus for Athens. Among the party were two sisters from Bishop Auckland. I got on well with the younger one, Trish (Patricia), especially when we took a gondola together the first evening in Venice. I was nineteen, but it was the first time I had kissed a girl, and it was an intoxicating experience. I hoped the romance would continue and was heartbroken when Trish called it off just before we embarked on the ship. Her elder sister, inappropriately (I thought) called Joy, had reminded her that she had a boyfriend back home and told her to behave herself. It occurred to me that Joy may have been a bit jealous. In any case, I would gladly have pushed her into the Adriatic. In the evening of our first day in Athens, there was a full moon and several of us went up on the Acropolis to admire it. Trish stayed in the hotel because Joy had a headache, and at breakfast the next morning I told her what a wonderfully romantic experience it had been. I did not add that I missed her dreadfully.

In Greece we visited many of the key sites in Attica and the Peloponnese, plus Delphi. We also made a quick trip by sea to Crete, to see Knossos. On the way home we sailed from Patras to Brindisi and stopped for two nights in Rome. For me the tour was a good introduction, which brought alive my studies of ancient history and culture. In the four following years I was to make independent travels to broaden and deepen my knowledge of the Classical World.

I again topped the Classics Honours class in October 1959 to win a prize, and in 1960 entered for and gained two prestigious awards. The first, in the Hilary Term, was the Tyrrell Memorial Gold Medal, awarded for the translation of lengthy passages of English prose and verse, set by the professors of Greek and Latin, into Greek and Latin prose and verse. Hearing of my success in the late afternoon, I did one of the most stupid and shameful things in my life. There was some excuse for having a celebratory drink with friends in a pub that evening, but there was no excuse for becoming legless and having to be carried in through the Front Gate of the College and on to my bedroom. The next morning I was in no state to attend Stanford's class and hear him make some laudatory comments on my award-winning compositions. Needless to say, the pain of the hangover far outweighed, both in length and intensity, the brief pleasure of drinking the whiskey, and the incident taught me a lesson which I never forgot. Moreover, my behaviour was contrary to the wise advice of Epicurus.

The other award was of a Foundation Scholarship in Classics. A long series of examination papers was sat. In view of my results in January and October 1959, I knew I must have a fair chance of success, but I took nothing for granted. The announcement of newly elected fellows and scholars was made by the Provost from the steps of the Public Theatre at an appointed time (10 a.m.) on Trinity Monday, 13 May 1960. I was so nervous that I got up at about 6 and spent hours pacing the quays alongside the Liffey. Arriving back in College, I waited at the back of the crowd, hoping for the best, fearing the worst. It was a great relief to hear that I was first scholar in Classics, and I was pleased that my friends Robin Miller and Foster Murphy had also obtained scholarships. Edna Broderick and Ann Ross were made scholars too, but, because they were women, non-foundation ones. The rest of the day was busy. Various formalities to do with our election were required before I could go to the historic General Post Office on O'Connell Street to send a telegram to Barbara and Henry. In the evening there was a formal dinner in evening dress in the Dining Hall for the scholars of the decades – 1960, 1950, 1940 etc. The next day the results were printed in *The Times* and, much more extensively, in *The Irish Times*.

Becoming a Scholar of the House was an honour, entitling one to use the post-nominal "Sch.", and valuable in other ways. It entitled one also to free accommodation in College, free evening meals, and a waiver of tuition fees. It also made one eligible to be a "waiter" with a remuneration of £16 a year. The waiter's duty was to recite the College's lengthy Latin graces before and after dinner in the Dining Hall. Some found the requirement too difficult, especially if they did not know Latin, but also if they did not like speaking from a pulpit before several hundred people. The pulpit was near the High Table, which was much frequented by John Luce's father, the Berkeleian philosopher A.A. Luce. He took a close interest in the correct recitation of the graces, but on one occasion I won a bet from fellow-scholar Robert Hunter that I would not dare alter the beginning of the grace after meat from *Tibi laus, tibi honor, tibi gloria, O beata et gloriosa Trinitas*, to *Tibi Luce, tibi honor, tibi gloria* ... A favourite prank on a Saturday evening was to ring up A.A., ask "Is that Luce?" and, when he replied in the affirmative, say "Well, I am tight". I cannot remember whether I ever actually did that, or merely contemplated doing it.

A kind of prank which I definitely perpetrated at least twice was writing a letter to the Republican newspaper the *United Irishman* under the name of Seamus O'Donovan, which on the first occasion the editor abbreviated to S.O'D. No doubt I deserved to be called that. After the first letter was published, someone who was not a great fan of mine approached me in the Hist. and said: "Have you seen this *marvellous* letter in the *United Irishman*?" He was a bit deflated when I told him I had written it.

After the end of the Trinity (Summer) Term, I moved from the shared rooms in no. 40 to single but quite spacious accommodation in no. 25, in the Rubrics, Trinity's oldest surviving building, dating from around 1700. The rooms were on the ground floor. There was still no running water, but the WC was also on the ground floor, and cold water was fetched from an outdoor tap just a few yards away across the cobbles. What luxury! I revelled in having rooms to myself. It is true that they were a little further from the School of Classics, but they were more convenient for the bathhouse, the GMB, the tennis courts, the Dining Hall, and the Reading Room. Moreover, they had an exciting history. It was on an upper floor of no. 25 that a Fellow named Edward Ford was shot dead in a student disorder on 7 March 1734. The students had broken his windows with stones, whereupon he fired his pistol at them. They then returned with firearms and murdered him.

In early July (1960) I had a visit at Silligrove from an Italian man, Lucio Cipollini, whom I had met on the Milan-Venice train in 1959. An employee of a Milan bank and in his mid-twenties, he was highly educated and well travelled in Europe and the USA, but he had been making his first visit to Venice and he had never been to Rome or Naples. He was agreeable company and had a good sense of humour. He brought with him his attractive sister, Bianca. She was seventeen and spoke virtually no English. At the end of their trip Lucio went to see a friend in Leeds, leaving Henry to take Bianca to a train for London. I was already in London, in readiness for my next expedition to Greece. I was in the bath in an aunt's flat when the telephone rang. Lucio had been delayed, and I was to meet Bianca at Paddington Station and look after her until late evening. I took her to a cosy restaurant in Soho with a small dance-floor. We managed very little conversation, but smiled a lot, and, when we started to dance, she surprised me by throwing her arms round my neck, kissing me, and holding me tight. I doubt if she ever fully described the evening to her brother, and I certainly did not. I never saw her again, but have always fondly remembered her.

A day or two later, on or about 12 July, I departed for Greece, this time travelling on my own, visiting new areas, and going on to new countries. I made the long train journey, without a couchette, on the Tauern Express from Ostend to Thessaloniki, chief city of northern Greece, before making my way down to Athens via Volos and the island of Evia (Euboia). In Athens I rented a flat at 62 Odos Omirou and used this as a base for exploring Athens, Attica, and places further afield. All went well except that I was plagued with a series of heavy nosebleeds. I was lucky to find a competent specialist, who treated me with cautery. One of my expeditions was to the island of Aigina to see the splendid Doric temple of Aphaia. The place was deserted until four Greek youths came on the scene. They did not offer any physical violence, but their body language and words were unmistakeably hostile. Assuming that I was British, they attacked me for what they perceived to be my government's bad behaviour in Cyprus. When I told them that I was actually a university student in the Republic of Ireland, the whole atmosphere changed instantly to one of friendliness, and we parted common victims of British imperialism. Hostility to the British was not uncommon in Greece at this time, and British visitors were not yet numerous. When the Ingham's tour party disembarked at Piraeus the previous year, there was quite a crowd of curious onlookers on the quayside, and one of the few things I disliked about Athens was the way so many of its citizens stared at me. It was a relief to find, as I did very soon, that Turks did not do that.

After a fortnight in Greece, I headed for Istanbul. I had hoped to go by sea, but there were no sailings at that time. So I took the train, scheduled to take 44 hours to reach its destination. That was long enough, but the journey was to take much longer, because, on arrival at the Turkish frontier at Edirne, the carriages were shunted into a siding and left without lights, without water, without refreshments, and without any coherent explanation, for about twelve hours. I spent an uncomfortable night – tired and increasingly hungry. Part of the problem was that I did not yet have any Turkish currency. I never discovered exactly what the problem was, but assume it was connected to the upheavals that arose with the overthrow on 27 May of the government of Adnan Menderes by the military, led by General Cemal Gürsel. On arrival at Sirkeci Terminal, Istanbul, I cashed travellers' cheques, deposited my baggage, and hastened to the nearby Golden Horn, where I sat at a trestle-table to enjoy, at minimal cost, a delicious meal of fried fish and fresh bread. Hunger at last satisfied, I proceeded across the Galata Bridge to the Beyoğlu district, where I took a room at the Otel Ali Baba with a fine view of its back yard and dustbins. I am pretty sure that I went to bed early that first night.

This was my first experience of Turkey, and I had only a few words of Turkish. I was not to know that it was the first of very many visits, and that the country was to be more important than any other for my scholarly career. In 1960 I had five or six days to get to know Istanbul and took full advantage of the time, assisted on one occasion by the Turkish Army. Soldiers were ubiquitous, but seemed to have little to do. I was studying a city-plan in a park, when a young officer asked me if he could help. When I said that I was looking for the Archaeological Museum, he ordered two of his men to escort me to its door. Highlights for me included: Justinian's great church, St Sophia (Ayasofya); The Blue Mosque (Sultan Ahmet Camii); the Grand Bazaar (Kapalı Çarsı); and a ferry trip to Üsküdar on the Asian shore of the Bosporus. There were no bridges then.

On 5 August I departed Istanbul on the Simplon-Orient Express. I had obtained from the Hungarian Consulate in the city a transit visa that would allow me to spend two days in Budapest. So I needed to change trains in Belgrade. On the way there I shared a compartment with a group of muscular Turkish wrestlers. At times they practised their art – only among themselves, fortunately. They were very friendly to me. One of them spoke some English, and we shared white cheese and black olives. When the train stopped in Sofia for an hour or two, we all got off to stretch our legs. Near the station we conversed briefly with a young Bulgarian woman. She spoke French, but not English or Turkish. The English-speaking wrestler said to me: "Ask her where we can find a public house". I assumed he meant a pub or café, so I put the question to her. But I was wrong: he was having a bit of fun and meant a brothel, the Turkish for which, *genel ev*, literally means "public house".

The overnight train from Belgrade to Budapest was uncomfortable, the second-class seats being wooden slats. It was going on to Warsaw and East Berlin. Emerging from Budapest's Keleti Railway Station, I passed a group of young women who were so well dressed that I guessed that they were western tourists, but they were locals, and it was a great surprise, less than four years after the 1956 revolution in Hungary and its suppression by the Soviet Union, to see so many signs of material prosperity.

My visa allowed me only one night in Budapest. I spent it in the Hotel Duna, centrally situated on the left bank of the Danube. It was blissfully comfortable after two nights seated in crowded trains, and I remember a dinner that included a delicious starter of mushrooms. I did a lot of walking, visited the Hungarian Parliament building, still pockmarked with bullet-holes from the 1956 revolution, and Pest Castle among other places. I patronised a traditional tavern, and from a news-kiosk I bought a copy of *L'Albanie Nouvelle*, an eye-opening magazine from one of Europe's least-known countries. The overnight train to Vienna was almost empty and quite plush even in second class. From Vienna I went straight back to London and, after a day or two at Silligrove, on to Dublin, where I needed to prepare for the sessional examinations. I must have done the preparation conscientiously, for again I came out top of the Classics class, but I did not devote all my time to revision. There were two main distractions.

The first distraction was the wish for a regular girlfriend. From time to time I had taken Trinity girls out, notably an attractive blonde classmate – a North Londoner, whose family lived next door to Edmundo Ros, the famous Trinidad-born musician and bandleader. But none of the friendships really "clicked", and I began to think that I should try my luck outside the College. So I went twice to dances at the Metropole and once to Clerys, both of them on O'Connell Street and now gone. They were reckoned to be good dating-venues. On my first visit to the Metropole my partner and I were told off for "two-arm embracing", which suggests that we were getting on quite well, and I cannot remember why no date followed. The second time there, I did not dare engage in any such intimacy, but I did find a partner who wanted to see me again and again. Her name was Elizabeth ("Betty") Mary Dempsey (Plate 8). Vivacious and attractive, she was 25, five years older than me. She was one of seven surviving children, including two sets of twins, of whom she and her brother Harry were one. At the time I met her, two of her brothers were working in England, but she and her other siblings – two sisters and two brothers – lived at home with their widowed mother, Moira, in quite a small house at 25 Clarence Mangan Road, near the South Circular Road. The whole family was extraordinarily welcoming to me, and the brothers especially had a keen sense of humour. Betty worked as a legal secretary in the old-established solicitors' firm of D. & T. Fitzgerald, at 30 Anglesea Street, close to the Bank of Ireland on College Green. The firm is named in Joyce's *Ulysses*, and I was very proud of that. I should add that Betty's typing and shorthand skills were invaluable to me. She remained my girlfriend for the rest of my time in Trinity, except when a problem arose early in 1961.

The problem was that she, as a strict Roman Catholic, was far from wholeheartedly approving of my second distraction, which was an increasingly militant commitment to the peace movement and socialism. She could tolerate my membership of CND, but not my membership, begun on 1 January 1962, of the Irish Workers' League (IWL), the Republic of Ireland's Communist Party. So for a short while we did not see one another. Given her upbringing, I could understand her disapproval of the IWL, even though she knew little or nothing about its people and policies, but I hoped she would judge me by any personal qualities I had rather than by my membership of a political party. After a while, a sort of truce was tacitly agreed, which was not very satisfactory because it meant that discussion of politics was severely curtailed. Discussion of religion was pretty well a no-go area too. Another troublesome area was sex. I do not mean sexual intercourse, which, as Philip Larkin affirms, had not yet been invented:

> Sexual intercourse began
> In nineteen sixty-three
> (Which was rather late for me) -
> Between the end of the "Chatterley" ban
> And the Beatles' first LP.
> *(Annus Mirabilis 1–5)*

8) Dublin: Betty and Martin exiting the Metropole,
O'Connell Street, ca. 1961

It was rather late for me too. I respected Betty's refusal to have premarital intercourse, but I found her objections to any form of intimate touching throughout the four years between our first meeting and our marriage a considerable strain. I mention all these disagreements and difficulties, because they may help to explain why our marriage was not to last. At the same time I acknowledge that my own inadequacies, including my lack of maturity, were contributory factors. Nevertheless I did love her, and we had a lot of fun together not only in Dublin, but also elsewhere in Ireland and abroad. It helped that in 1961 we had the use of a car, a Volkswagen "Beetle". It belonged to my uncle Tom Smith. While he and his wife made an extended visit to

New Zealand, he garaged the vehicle at Silligrove and told Henry that I was welcome to use it when I was at home on vacation. Rather impertinently, I asked him if I might take it to Dublin and use it in term-time as well. He generously agreed, enabling us to drive to all sorts of places, including County Kerry, Connemara, and Donegal. Earlier I owned a pre-war Austin 7, which needed a lot of work done on it. I agreed to employ a friend's landlord, who was said to be an excellent mechanic. What I was not told was that he had a big problem with drink, and, when I collected the car, its engine blew up with a big bang as I was driving into Trinity. I think he had forgotten to lubricate the big end. Anyhow, that was that.

The contents of my Trinity scrapbook and file show that 1961 was a busy year for me. In February I wrote in opposition to the week-long Mission conducted in Trinity by Michael Ramsey, Archbishop of York and Archbishop-elect of Canterbury. I set out my views in a letter to *Trinity News* and a short article in another student publication called *Joculator*. I was invited, along with several others, to have tea with him. On the rare occasions that I could hear what he was saying, I found him deadly dull. At Easter I joined the CND peace march from Aldermaston (near Reading) to London. I had not done so in 1960 because I was occupied with Scholarship examinations. Being a Quaker, Barbara was happy for me to march. Henry was not. I carried a banner inscribed in Irish: "May we be alive this time next year!" On the way into London, a bystander called out: "Is that Chinese, mate?" On 28 April I bought a one-way train ticket to Belfast to compete with twenty others in a foot-race to Dublin. The first prize was a barrel of Guinness. We set off from City Hall at 11 a.m. on Saturday the 29th. The distance is 103 miles. At 17 miles I was lying third, and I was still in that position at the half-way checkpoint, a café in Dundalk, reached around 10.30 p.m. The last few miles had not been pleasant on account of steady rain and quite heavy traffic as cinemas closed. I sat down to rest and refresh myself with food and drink and then got to my feet to carry on towards Drogheda and Dublin. But disappointingly I found that my feet were so sore and my legs so stiff that I could hardly walk. I hobbled across the road to a simple hotel and, the next morning, took a train to Dublin and needed taxis to convey me the short distances to Dundalk Railway Station and from the station in Dublin to Trinity. Only two competitors managed to complete the race. A few days later a reporter from *Trinity News* interviewed me about the Aldermaston march and the Belfast-Dublin walk and wrote a well-informed article, "The Mystique of the March".

In May, I clashed with Michael Longley, in the columns of *Trinity News*, about the message and interpretation of D.H. Lawrence's *Lady Chatterley's Lover*, discussing it from a Marxist standpoint. In the same month my Marxism was highlighted in two articles in Trinity publications. The first is a report, in *Trinity News*, of the Fabian Society elections, in which I was unsuccessful. Trinity's Fabian Society was more left-wing than the name might suggest. Most of its leading members, including Victor Blease and Michael Downing, were CND supporters or members. On one occasion some of us hurried out to the French Embassy in Ballsbridge to protest against French nuclear testing. The Embassy had a long drive, so we had to telephone it, as well as Radio Éireann, to make known our presence. On another occasion we were attacked, as we crossed Parliament Square with our placards, by Count Nikolai Tolstoy and others, whom we labelled Fascist thugs. I was similarly attacked when I competed in the Walk event at the College Races carrying a Ban-the-Bomb placard. Admittedly that was asking for trouble. The second report, in May 1961, in the magazine *T.C.D.* under "Vanity Fair: People and Parties", describes the "surprisingly liberal party" held by Marxist Martin Smith at which

> An excellent selection of drinks was served to a motley gathering of classicists, Fabians and nuclear disarmers. Victor Blease abducted Linda Stephenson, just to annoy Michael Downing. Bill Pedoe and Meryl Lucas, Maureen Brush and Isobel Swain lent an air of distinction to the proceedings, while Derek Mahon and Robbie Brown lent *un soupçon de je ne sais quoi* – the one falling cherubically asleep and the other mislaying half a tooth somewhere. Mike Dibb managed to get to the theatre, Tony Taylor managed the Commons Grace against all odds, and Robert Hunter finished off with a glorious though vain attempt to walk through the Pearse Street Gate (which had, of course, been shut at least an hour beforehand).

Like Michael Longley, Derek Mahon was to be recognised as one of the best poets in Ireland in recent times. The last time I saw him was one evening in the Trinity Reading Room in September 1962, when it was packed with students revising for examinations. He came into the room holding a brick aloft and announced: "I am now going to make a symbolic gesture". He then dropped the brick and walked out. An earlier occasion I remember is when I called at Longley's rooms in Botany Bay and disturbed him and Mahon working on a poem. Mahon swore in frustration, but quickly realised that I was not to have known what they were doing. I have sometimes wondered what embryonic poetic masterpiece I may have aborted.

Between mid-June and mid-July 1961 I made a solo tour of Italy and Sicily, mostly by train. My previous experience had amounted to just two days in Venice and two in Rome with the Ingham's party in 1959. Now I filled in some of the important gaps, including Florence, much more of Rome, Naples, Vesuvius, Pompeii, Herculaneum, and Paestum. From Naples I took a boat to Palermo, where I admired the fine architecture, but was appalled by the sight of some of the worst slums in Europe. I had been given an introduction to the Communist journalist Marcello Cimino, editor of *L'Ora*. He kindly invited me to dinner and was a mine of information, including about other places I was intending to visit in Sicily and about the Mafia. The first place was Partinico, a small town about twenty miles west of Palermo. Although its population was then only about 15,000, its murder-rate was about three a fortnight. Most of the killings were perpetrated by the Mafia. On arrival there the next morning, I learned that the stationmaster had had his throat cut on the platform the previous evening. I made my way into the town and asked a road-sweeper to direct me to the building occupied by the internationally renowned social worker Danilo Dolci, sometimes called "the Gandhi of Sicily", and his organisation. The man was too frightened to speak to me, but luckily at that moment a car drew up, and the woman driver said she was one of Dolci's colleagues and would give me a lift. Still more luckily, it chanced to be the one day in the month when all his helpers in impoverished areas of Sicily assembled to give their reports and discuss future action. It was a privilege to attend the meeting, and an eye-opener.

Taking a train in the direction of Trapani, I stopped halfway to view the fine Doric temple and theatre at Segesta. Both of them are in lofty situations among grand scenery. As I began to walk back down, dark clouds were gathering and threatening rain. I just made it to the station café before the heavens opened. While the rain poured down, I was served a simple meal which I bracket with the one by the Golden Horn as exceptionally satisfying – a hunk of fresh bread, delicious cheese, and a large glass of red wine.

I viewed more fine temples at Agrigento before proceeding to Siracusa, Catania, and Taormina, with a day devoted to Etna. I then took a train to Milan, where I needed to change trains, and did something stupid. The train for Calais was waiting, but I could see that I had plenty of time to go the station buffet and buy food for the journey. I left my luggage in a compartment, carefully noting the position of the carriage alongside the platform. But, when I returned with my pizza slices, I could not find the compartment, and it became increasingly obvious that my train had departed. There were in fact two trains going to Calais, one of them apparently unscheduled. That would not have mattered, if I had my luggage – and my passport, which I had unwisely left in the luggage. I spent an anxious twenty-four hours, cursing my stupidity, wondering if I would ever see my luggage again, and having to explain to customs officers why I had no passport. On arrival in Calais, I went to the stationmaster's office, and there was my suitcase. Phew!

In the October sessional examinations I again came first in Classics, and for this I was awarded the Mullins Classical Exhibition to add to my scholarship. In all the examinations I sat during my four years as an undergraduate, translation of English into Greek and Latin was required, and in each paper two pieces were to be attempted – the first into prose, the second into prose or verse. For the second, unlike the great majority of other candidates, I always chose verse. It was more challenging, and there was the risk that the composition could go badly wrong, but, if the result were good, it would probably receive very high marks. I remember composing one piece in which inspiration came very late in the allotted time, and I only just managed to write down the last ten or so lines before "time's up" was announced by the invigilator. Strangely, although neither the subject nor my thoughts were erotic, the completion of the piece was accompanied by an orgasm. Presumably my brain generated a confused signal, producing the wrong climax. I mention this in case it is of interest to psychologists!

On the political front, I started collecting signatures for a ban on the sale of Outspan South African oranges for buffet lunches in the Dining Hall, but abandoned the campaign when Arab students pointed out that they would probably be replaced with Israeli Jaffas. A successful campaign, publicised in *Trinity News* in November and December, was to improve the very lax and sometimes non-existent fire precautions in residential areas of the College.

My membership of the Irish Workers' League brought me into contact with its Chairman, Seán (Johnny) Nolan, who presided also over New Books, and its General Secretary, Michael O'Riordan, a warmer man, a veteran of the Spanish Civil War, and later the recipient of an honour from Fidel Castro. They kept in close touch with Moscow, where the situation had recently changed: Stalin had died (1953) and been denounced by Khrushchev (1957), and there was now a developing rift with Mao Tse-tung. Not all IWL members were happy with all the changes. One proudly showed me his watch, which he told me was a personal gift from Stalin.

In March 1962 there was concern that Ireland would join the European Economic Community (Common Market) and get drawn into NATO. I joined a protest march from St Stephen's Green to the Parnell Monument in O'Connell Street, carrying an amateurish copy I made of a cartoon in *The Daily Worker.* It showed a prosperous-looking pig carrying a briefcase marked "N.A.T.O.", and the title was "THIS LITTLE PIG WENT TO COMMON MARKET". Plate 9 shows me and Michael Downing leading the demonstration, with the philosopher Alasdair MacIntyre, who must have been visiting, immediately behind. At Easter, I again did the Aldermaston March. But political campaigning did not occupy all my time. I was also committed to the College Classical Society. After serving as assistant secretary, then secretary, I was elected auditor or chairman for 1961–1962. One of my duties was to preside over the Auditorial Meeting in May 1962 and to invite other speakers to address it. My first choice for principal visiting speaker was

9) Dublin: Anti-NATO march, Michael Downing and Martin (with placard) leading, Alasdair MacIntyre behind, March 1962

George Thomson, professor of Greek at Birmingham University and expert on parallelisms between Greek and Irish. A further attraction for me was that he was a Marxist, and I was disappointed when he declined. My second choice was the Cornishman H.D.F. Kitto, professor of Greek at Bristol, who accepted and offered "Thucydides' Irony". He came by air, and it was arranged that Robin Miller and I would meet him at the Busáras (Bus Station). Before we set off, we asked Professor Parke what Kitto looked like. After only a moment's thought, he replied: "He looks just like a cockatoo". The airport bus arrived ahead of schedule, and Robin and I were still on our way, when we espied a short man who did indeed resemble a cockatoo coming towards us. The lecture was rather disappointing, but Kitto was good company and preferred to be with the students rather than with the staff.

Also good company in a very different sort of way was an elder brother of Henry, Fr Reginald ("Regie" or "Regi") Smith of the Anglican Community of the Resurrection – the one who called Barbara "a Martha". He was spending a few days with the nuns of the Community of St John the Evangelist, quite a way from the city-centre. Henry asked me to entertain him for a day and show him some of the sights. He also gave me enough money to cover lunch for two at the Shelbourne Hotel. A tall man, wearing a cassock, Regie was an impressive presence, and everywhere we went, he was mistaken for a high-ranking RC priest. One incident was when we were walking by a busy road and he brought a bus to a screeching halt between stops; another was in the Shelbourne dining room where the waiters gave him extraordinarily attentive and respectful service; others were on O'Connell Street, where strangers doffed their hats and wished him good afternoon. He lapped up all the attention. Whether he realised that it was all or almost all based on a misunderstanding, I am not sure.

I returned to Italy in 1962 with Betty. Thinking that Barbara and Henry might like to meet her, we stayed at Silligrove for a few days beforehand. It was a mistake. While Barbara was welcoming, Henry was furious with me for going away with a woman who was not my wife. He insisted that I stay not at Silligrove, but in Edith Trow's spare room in Silligrove Cottage across the road. The only time I remember him speaking to me was when he ambushed me in the farmyard and asked if I was "contemplating matrimony". I replied that matrimony was a possible outcome sometime in the future, but had never been discussed with Betty, let alone proposed to her. I cannot remember if I added that Betty's Catholicism guaranteed that we would not be sharing a bed. What I do remember is that I did not remind him of his attitude at this time, when, three years later, he took a much more than avuncular interest in one of his nieces by marriage. The hypocrisy was so obvious that there was no need.

Before the Italian trip, I moved from the Rubrics to a bed-sitter on an upper floor of the GMB, with a view across Library Square. Here, in no. 30, I had running water – hot as well as cold – for the first time in College. There was a kitchenette-cum-washroom, and a shower and WC along the landing. Trinity had a scheme whereby resident students could hire, for a small charge, an original work of art. I chose a large canvas by Patrick Scott. The artist had painted a whitish strip along the top, to represent sky, and the rest brown, except that he had flicked small spots of white paint here and there. He called it *Bog Cotton*. When it was hung, I asked my female skip what she thought of it. Not wanting to hurt my feelings, she gave the memorable reply: "Well, it's in a lovely frame".

In August and September I planned to be very busy with revision for the degree examinations in October. I was indeed as busy as possible, but my work was impeded by significant eye problems. I saw a specialist, who advised me to give my eyes a complete rest, which was not very useful in the circumstances, and Colin came over for a weekend to see if he could do anything to help. I never told my professors about the problem. Nor did my friend and fellow-scholar Robin Miller tell them that he had spent many weeks in hospital after a diagnosis of multiple sclerosis. I often thought of Robin's case when during my teaching career students asked for much more minor events to be taken into account. I managed to sit all the papers and, although not as well prepared as I had hoped, obtained a "first" and, through heading the list of Classics candidates, was awarded the Brooke Moderatorship Prize.

While I was awaiting my results, I joined Barbara, Henry, and Carol for a few days of holiday in Cornwall, but my participation in it soon came to an abrupt end. On 22 October the Cuban Missile Crisis began, and President Kennedy announced a naval blockade to prevent delivery of missiles from the USSR to Cuba. Henry had heard the news and relayed it to Carol and me during an afternoon walk. I queried whether Kennedy was not in danger of contravening international law. Henry's reaction was so unpleasantly violent that I went back to our hotel. When I told Barbara about the incident, she was appalled, and we agreed that I should leave for Dublin the next morning. I do not recall any peace-making gesture on either side before I departed, but Henry was probably mollified when my degree examination results were announced.

Betty and I may well have celebrated the success in Alfredo's Italian restaurant at 14 St Mary's Abbey. It was a favourite place of ours, especially after an evening at the cinema or theatre. One made a booking by telephone and, on arrival, was inspected through a spy-hole before being admitted. The food, cooked by Alfredo Vido's wife, was good, as was the wine-list, and he played the piano pleasantly – to dance to if one wished.

I had originally intended to take a Classics Method Teaching course at Oxford University after graduation, with a view to becoming a schoolteacher, and had been accepted for it. But in the light of my degree results, I decided to study at Trinity for the degree of Master in Letters (MLitt.). The subject of my thesis was *Lucretius: The Man and His Mission*. I had first encountered the Roman Epicurean poet in the Upper Sixth form at Shrewsbury, but my interest in him was first inspired at Trinity by Donald Wormell. His admiration for him was primarily as a poet. For me, his Epicurean philosophy was at least as important.

I got down to work straight away, but was rather surprised when my supervisor said he expected me to submit my first chapter after three weeks. But he was quite right to insist that I got something down on paper early on. Finding that many items relevant to my research were not available in Dublin, I went to London immediately after Christmas 1962. My stay there, generously funded by Henry, was in Bloomsbury in the old-established Bonnington Hotel on Southampton Row, within easy walking distance of the two libraries in which I needed to work – the historic Reading Room of the British Museum in Great Russell Street and the excellent modern Library of the Hellenic and Roman Societies at 31–34 Gordon Square up towards Euston Station. I worked my socks off and recall only two brief recreational incidents – the singing of "Auld Lang Syne" with strangers in a pub on New Year's Eve and a very mild flirtation with my Irish chambermaid, a redhead from Co. Carlow, who revealed all sorts of hotel secrets – for example, that the carafes of fresh drinking water in the bedrooms were all filled from the tap.

Mention of New Year's Eve 1962 reminds me that a year or two earlier Colin invited me to see the New Year in with him and a Birmingham friend of his in an establishment called the Oxford Club in Moseley. The name has a respectable ring, and, when at breakfast the following morning I told my mother where we had been, she exclaimed: "Oh, how very nice! Was that

Barrow Cadbury's club?", naming a recently-deceased Quaker relative who had been committed to teetotalism. "I am pretty sure it wasn't", I replied, sparing her the painful supporting information that the barman was in drag, and that the celebratory drink was not cocoa, but champagne from a bottle bearing a label which we peeled off to reveal a second label underneath carrying the legend "Produce of Spain".

In June 1963 my first cousin Miranda made a visit, timed to coincide with the Trinity Ball in College. I already had a partner, Betty, so I had the tricky task of finding one for her. A friend recommended a friend of his who was partnerless. He was a decent guy, who turned out to be much more interested in her than she was in him, with the result that she had to decline a request for her contact details. I met her off the boat from Liverpool early in the morning and, as a sort of show-off, took her straight to a pub, one of several that were open at that hour to serve the needs of dockworkers. One evening I took her to the 55 Club in a basement on O'Connell Street. We were eating and apparently drinking wine after hours, when there was a great commotion. The staff, who had been given a minute's forewarning of a police raid by the doorman at street level, hurriedly moved all the bottles behind the scenes. The police were good natured and treated the raid as a big joke, especially when they found an opened bottle of wine on the floor and were told it must have fallen there. After a few minutes they departed and the bottles were returned to the tables. One day I hired a car and drove Miranda, Betty, Robin, and his girlfriend into the Dublin mountains. Miranda was always the best of company – cheerful and amusing. She was also intrepidly enterprising. A year or two later she visited Kenya and got involved with Joy and George Adamson and the making of the film *Born Free* (1966), starring Virginia McKenna and Bill Travers, about the rearing of the orphaned lion-cub Elsa and her return to the wild. While there she had a flattering offer of marriage from a Kikuyu tribesman, who reckoned she was worth several head of cattle.

A few days after Miranda's visit, President Kennedy arrived in Dublin for a four-day visit to Ireland (26–29 June 1963). I had a fine view of him and his motorcade from a high-up window in Trinity as he passed through College Green. It would have been a good position for an armed assassin, but there was no sign of any security.

Although my MLitt thesis was far from finished, I applied for several university teaching posts in the spring and summer of 1963. I was interviewed at Magee University College (Londonderry), Exeter, Hull, and Edinburgh.

I was unsuccessful in each case. Betty and I had booked a sixteen day trip to Greece (her first) in August (by-passing Silligrove this time!), and I was resigned to there being no further job-seeking until after we returned. But at short notice I was invited to an interview at the University College of North Wales, Bangor, and there was just time to fit this in before we departed.

I cannot close my reminiscences of Trinity without mentioning Robert Brendan McDowell. A brilliant Irish historian, he was also a character of such extraordinary wit and eccentricity that he became a legend in his lifetime. With his horn-rimmed spectacles and strange, multi-layered attire, including, whatever the weather, a scruffy overcoat, a long scarf, and a pork-pie hat squashed down on his head, he was instantly recognisable. He walked purposefully, often muttering to himself and shaking a large bunch of keys. From 1956 to 1969 he was Junior Dean (JD) and therefore responsible for discipline. I think I only went to see him once – to request permission for my drinks-party, to which of course I invited him. We all tried to imitate him, but nobody succeeded half as well as the actor Terence Brady. One would think that the JD's appearance was unique, but during our Greek trip in August 1963 Betty and I had a strange experience. We were sitting in an outdoor café in Corinth when a man *looking exactly like him* went by. We gaped at one another in astonishment and were so convinced that he was the JD that we followed him round the square and into a neighbouring street. It was only when he disappeared into the police station that we concluded that he was probably not the JD, but the JD's Greek double.

6

Wales and Turkey 1 (1963–1973)

I was lucky to land the Bangor post, an Assistant Lectureship in Greek and Latin, rather than one of the others for which I had applied because it alone had the two advantages of involving the teaching of both Greek and Latin and of being a permanent appointment, subject to satisfactory completion of the probationary period of three years. Also, Bangor is well placed for access to Dublin and London and has the mountains of Eryri (Snowdonia) and other scenic areas, including the island of Anglesey, close by.

Prior to the Bangor interview, the candidates were entertained to lunch in the Castle Hotel. I had arrived at breakfast time after travelling on the overnight boat from Dún Laoghaire to Holyhead. I used the morning to acquaint myself with the city and its history, with special attention to its ancient cathedral and to the University College, established in 1884 as a constituent college of the University of Wales. Bangor was one of five colleges with a Classics department, the other four being Aberystwyth, Cardiff, Swansea, and Lampeter. Just before going to meet the professors of Greek and Latin, I called in at a pub for a quick vodka and then had the kudos of saying that I was happy not to have a drink in the bar before the meal. I was anyhow more relaxed than I had been at the earlier interviews, and not just on account of the vodka. It was perhaps partly because I was better rehearsed, partly because I was almost resigned to not being successful – at least not before I had returned from the trip to Greece with Betty. For whatever reasons, the interview, chaired by the Principal in the Council Chamber, went well.

My starting salary was to be £1,000 p.a. which Barbara thought extraordinarily high. No accommodation in the College was available, so I placed an advertisement in a local newspaper. Much the best offer came from the College's Catering Manager, who with her husband ran a waterside establishment on Anglesey called The Moorings Club, on the outskirts of Menai Bridge, on the road to Beaumaris. The club operated at weekends and especially on Sundays, when pubs were closed in northwest Wales. Out of earshot of the club and having a separate entrance was an upper-floor apartment consisting of a good-sized room overlooking a creek of the Menai Strait – very scenic when the tide was in, less so when the tide was out. There was also a double bedroom, a bathroom, and a gas cooker on the landing. There was no parking space, but I was able to rent a shed from a blacksmith whose forge was not far away. The small town of Menai Bridge was within easy walking distance, and the College, reached across Thomas Telford's graceful and historic Menai Suspension Bridge (1826), was a few minutes' drive away. I had a few days of being carless before Barbara and Henry generously gave me their Morris Minor.

After returning from Greece in mid-August, I stayed in Dublin, working not on my thesis, but on the preparation of my classes in Bangor. I might say "over-preparation", for I had not realised that the expected standard of work was lower than in Trinity, so that (for example) it was not appropriate to talk about the textual tradition of Plautus or the lyric metres of Sophocles. For the most part, the students needed help with the translation and interpretation of the prescribed texts. Nevertheless some of the Honours students were really good. One, Michael Vickers, who graduated in 1964, became Senior Assistant Curator at the Ashmolean Museum in Oxford and Professor of Archaeology in the University of Oxford. As well as a variety of Greek and Latin texts at different levels, I taught Ancient Philosophy from the Presocratics to Plato and Aristotle; also Greek and Latin language, including prose composition and, occasionally, verse composition. At this time there was frequent and sometimes acrimonious debate among classicists as to whether prose composition was still a worthwhile exercise. Since 1960, Oxford and Cambridge had no longer required entrants to have passed O (Ordinary) Level Latin. Naturally the number of students studying Latin in other universities fell sharply, and there was a move to make courses more "relevant" to the modern world. Closely associated with the decline of Latin and Greek was the introduction of "Classical Studies" courses, in which there was no study of the languages, although provision was often made for beginners' Greek and Latin to be made available, frequently as subsidiary courses. One forum for debate was the Joint Association of Classical Teachers, of which I became a founder-member in

1964. But the first debate in which I took part was at a gathering of University of Wales Classics staff at Aberystwyth in December 1963. The proceedings were interminable and inconclusive, and my only positive recollection is of Willie Smyth, a TCD graduate at Swansea, and me sneaking out of the stuffy room and running downhill to the Coopers Arms before it closed. The view I took is that, if one is to make a serious study of any language, ancient or modern, translation into it, as well as out of it, is a necessary exercise.

The commencement of my employment in Bangor (1 October 1963) was closely followed by the publication of the Robbins Report on Higher Education (24 October 1963), which recommended an expansion of university education to enable all who wanted it to get it. It was ironic that, in the case of Latin and Greek, contraction was occurring just when most subjects were expanding, and it was almost inevitable that most universities found it necessary to provide service courses for other departments, like English and History, to partner Classical Studies with other subjects in Joint Honours courses, and even to establish Classical Studies Single Honours courses with compulsory linguistic elements.

I joined an establishment of six full-time staff, including myself. There were separate departments of Greek and Latin, each with its professorial head. The rest of us taught in both departments. Richard Ernest Wycherley, "Wych" to friends and colleagues, had occupied the Chair of Greek since 1945. A modest, amiable man, he was an expert on Greek architecture, who had published *How the Greeks Built Cities* and was collaborating in the publication of American discoveries in the Athenian Agora. The Latin professor, Martin Lowther Clarke, had been appointed in 1948. A man of small stature with a big brain, he spoke little unless he had something significant to say. I remember how, after a lecture he had given to the local Classical Association, a member of the audience put to him at great length a suggestion of hers that seemed to me far-fetched and irrelevant, concluding: "Do you think, Professor Clarke, there is anything in what I say?" All he said in reply was "no". A fine Latinist, who had won many prizes when he was a student in Cambridge, he had written books on the history of classical scholarship in England as well as *Rhetoric at Rome* and *The Roman Mind.* Richard ("Dickie") A. Browne, Senior Lecturer, was also a good Latinist, one of his specialities being British Latin. I crossed with him for just one year before he took retirement and always found him friendly and amusing. Irish and a bachelor, he was full of bright ideas – well, ideas which he thought were bright. Often they were investment tips for stocks and shares. I never followed them, especially after hearing from his friends stories of his past failures. One was that during the Second World War he formed the opinion that, as soon as hostilities ended, there would be a great demand for second-hand typewriters. So he bought scores of them, but the expected demand never materialised with the result that he had to dump them. About my own career, he gave me two bits of advice – to stick to and develop my areas of expertise, and to start applying for promotion immediately. Perhaps he reckoned it a good thing always to go quickly, for he had a reputation for being a fast driver. On one occasion he terrified Martin Clarke by driving him and an external examiner across Anglesey at high speed. John Richard Thornhill Pollard and John Ellis Jones had the rank of Lecturer. The latter, a Welsh-speaking local, was a Greek and Roman archaeologist and historian. I did not meet him and his Luxembourg-born wife, Renée, during my first term because he had contracted jaundice. He was friendly and full of energy and enthusiasm, but in his lecturing so enthusiastic about details that he had a habit of not covering the complete course for his students. He did excellent work as secretary to the Bangor and North Wales branch of the Classical Association and as curator of the Museum of Welsh Antiquities. John Pollard's career had been interrupted at an early stage by the Second World War throughout which he served as an Army Captain. He had been appointed in Bangor in 1949 and published *Journey to the Styx*. This book was soon to be followed by *Helen of Troy* and *Seers, Shrines and Sirens*. All three books are entertaining and popularising rather than groundbreaking works of scholarship. In teaching, he held students' attention in a schoolmasterly manner. On one occasion I remember him outraging Martin Clarke by suggesting, as a lecture-title, "Was Virgil Welsh?" He had many extra-curricular interests, including ornithology, country sports, and driving his daughters and their mounts to equestrian events around the country. He and his wife, Shirley, were friendly and amusing company. They were hospitable too, and it was at a Sunday-morning party they gave at their house the day before the start of the autumn term 1963 that I first met them and several other colleagues whom I was to come to regard as friends. One of these was the Revd Charles Whitley, an Old Testament scholar in the Department of Biblical Studies. After the party he gave me a lift to the Moorings Club, my surprise at being driven by a tipsy clergyman being diminished slightly when I learned that he was a TCD graduate.

My first term as a university teacher was negotiated without serious incident, and I began to develop some of the tricks of the trade – for example:

"When in doubt, shout like hell!" Small classes were usually taken in the room I shared with Paul Davies, who had just joined the Department of English. That was in Penrallt, on the top floor of a formerly-residential house. There was just one telephone, in the hallway on the ground floor. Our room afforded a grandstand view of the new extension to the Arts Library, including its research rooms. Paul was no timewaster: having noticed a dishy young woman working in an English research room, he hurried over to chat her up. Soon they were living together, then married. I did not notice any dishy women in the Classics research room. Its most frequent visitor was the Revd Chancellor J.W. James, whose non-stop talking about St David, deadly dull at any time, was intolerable if one was rushing to prepare for a class. Larger classes took place in a lecture room in the main, castle-like building, which, completed in 1910, occupies a prominent position overlooking the town. Below the top corridor, in which professors had their rooms, were two corridors of lecture rooms, including the ones for Greek and Latin.

Betty's first visit to me in Wales was a brief one: she arrived from Dublin in the evening of Friday 25 October and departed on Sunday the 27th. She stayed with me at the Moorings Club most reluctantly. I thought that she had agreed on the telephone, but, a few days before her arrival, she expressed her unhappiness and even hinted that she might not come. On her arrival, she raised an objection to the double bed, although it was very wide and I promised that she could have half of it all to herself. I even suggested that we could put something down the middle, as Colin had done when he and I were compelled to share a double bed on a family holiday and he used fire-irons to demarcate the border between us. The next day I showed her Bangor, the College, and Beaumaris, and on the 27th I drove her to Caernarfon and on to the Llŷn Peninsula. It was a breezy and chilly afternoon, but we had a walk along the pebbly beach at Pwllheli, and there I proposed to her, somewhat on impulse and in the hope of ending what I perceived to be her prudery. My proposal was accepted. We celebrated with a drink in a nearby refreshment room. She never touched alcohol, so her drink was a soft one. Since it was a Sunday, my drink ought to have been non-alcoholic too, but, on hearing about our engagement, the waiter happily broke the law.

The news of the engagement was well received by both families, but a major hurdle remained to be crossed. To marry a non-Catholic, Betty needed to obtain a dispensation from Archbishop McQuaid – the same man who had refused to appoint a chaplain to serve the needs of Catholics in Trinity.

His permission was not given until 7 March 1964, only four weeks before the wedding. Before then, I was required to undergo a course of instruction from the Catholic chaplain in Bangor, Fr Michael Richards. A member of Opus Dei, he looked as though he was following St Paul's advice to mortify one's members. I found him totally lacking in warmth or a sense of humour. We tolerated one another until he raised the matter of transubstantiation. I told him that I did not believe in either supernatural conjuring tricks or cannibalism. At that point, to my great relief, he gave up. I signed a document promising that any children of the marriage would be brought up as Catholics. But after all this, Betty and I were not allowed a full wedding ceremony, just a brief one at a side-altar. I did not mind, except for Betty's sake. But one who was very displeased was my aunt Jean Smith. She had converted to Catholicism in 1933, and her brother Jim Smith had followed her lead in 1934. In November 1934 the two of them were received in a *private* audience by Pope Pius XI, and in 1953 Jim was created a Papal Knight in recognition of the support he gave Catholic organisations in Nigeria, where he was a colonial administrator. Jean told me, the day before Betty's and my wedding, that, if only she had known about the problems, she could have used her influence to dispel them. When Fr Richards committed suicide in 1977, the sad news did not come as a complete surprise to me.

An engagement party was held at Silligrove on Saturday, 23 November 1963. The event was as cheerful as could be expected the day after the shocking news of President Kennedy's assassination in Dallas, Texas. Jean made tasteful menu cards decorated with a red dragon above my initials and green shamrock above Betty's. The three-course luncheon menu was: Smoked Scotch Salmon; Roasted Shropshire Turkey and Danish Ham with Potatoes and French Peas; Fruit, followed by Coffee.

I spent most of the Christmas vacation in Dublin, staying in Trinity and preparing, as well as the next term's lecture courses, a lecture to a one-day school in Classics arranged for 24 January by the Education Department for sixth formers in North Wales schools. This was an important event for me, being my first real opportunity to show the heads of my departments what I could do. I chose as my title "Lucretius and the Modern World". The lecture received an enthusiastic reception not only in the packed Powis Hall, but also in the written report of the Education Department's organiser, who singled it out for praise, commenting that it was exceptional in the way it showed the relevance of antiquity to the world of today. I was immediately asked to give a repeat performance to staff and senior pupils at Rydal School in Colwyn Bay.

Betty was continuing her secretarial work in office hours, but we had plenty of time to see one another, and on Christmas Day I was invited to have lunch with her family. The lunch was excellent and I was more than ready for it, for it was served two or three hours later than the estimated one o'clock. Punctuality is not in my experience a prominent Irish virtue. Despite her now being my fiancée, Betty's prudishness continued along with her fidelity to the Church. After we were married and she first started meeting British Catholics (for example, our Bangor friends Christopher and Bernadette Allmand) in Wales, she was amazed at how liberal-minded many of them were. In Ireland she had never encountered anyone who was prepared to voice any criticism of the Catholic hierarchy. It was of course to emerge that the Church was far from perfect. Witness the cruelties of the Magdalene Laundries; witness the hypocrisy of Bishop Eamonn Casey, whose fathering of a son gave rise to the slogan, printed on T-shirts, "Wear a condom – just in Casey!"

In the Spring Term of 1964 I had a very heavy teaching load and struggled to do all the necessary, not helped by the meetings with Fr Richards, the delay in granting a dispensation, and the various arrangements for the wedding and honeymoon. Also, I was trying to get items of my research into print. I succeeded first with a text-and-interpretation article on a passage in Lucretius book 5, accepted by the Dublin University journal *Hermathena*.

The marriage took place on Saturday 4 April 1964. Because of the delayed granting of the Archbishop's dispensation, none of the churches in the city of Dublin was available, and the ceremony was held in a southern parish of the diocese in the Church of our Lady of Victories, Sallynoggin, close to Dún Laoghaire and about six miles from the city. The reception, a sit-down luncheon, was held in the nearby Victor Hotel. Betty's family was present in force, and a surprising number of my relatives – aunts, uncles, and cousins – accepted invitations. Several of my Trinity friends, including Robin Miller, were also present. Colin was my best man, and Betty's elder sister, Marjorie, was her bridesmaid. Marjorie was keen to find a husband for herself and had caused a mixture of amusement and outrage (mainly amusement) by claiming that, when I made visits to the family home, I was really more interested in seeing her than Betty.

Two or three weeks before the wedding, Henry asked me to obtain from two Dublin city-centre hotels quotations for our guests' accommodation.

I did this in what I thought was clear handwriting, signing myself "M.F. Smith (Mr.)". When one of the hotels replied to Mr. M.F. Suritu, my reaction was: "What idiots! Fancy not recognising a common name like Smith!" But I had to revise my opinion the next day, when I received a letter from the other hotel addressed to Mr. M.F. Suritee. Since then, I have either typed my name or written it in capitals.

So as to ensure solitude and freedom from parties and pranks, I spent the night of 3 April alone in the Regent Hotel on D'Olier Street, a city-centre hotel so basic that none of the guests would be likely to have chosen it. Only Colin knew my location, and he promised to keep it a secret. He came round after breakfast and received the wedding ring from me. I drove us to Sallynoggin in a hired car. On arrival, we found that a sizeable gypsy encampment had been established close to the church and Victor Hotel. Betty and her nearest and dearest were outraged, while I and the whole British contingent were enchanted by what was seen as a traditional manifestation of Irishness. I do not remember much about the ceremony, apart from Betty and Marjorie looking beautiful, and Colin and me respectable (Plates 10–11), except that, as photographs of us kneeling reveal, I had holes in my shoes – perhaps a nod to another Irish tradition! In his speech at the reception Colin alluded to my left-wing views, which might have caused alarm in certain quarters, if his meaning had been fully understood. So far, the day had gone smoothly, but this was soon to change.

We were to start our honeymoon in London, and I had booked seats on a plane which I reckoned we would be able to catch comfortably. But I miscalculated. Betty, Marjorie, and their younger sister, Terry, disappeared into the hotel's bridal changing-room, and, despite increasingly frantic messages being passed to them, did not emerge until long after the comfortable departure-time. Colin rang Aer Lingus to tell them we would be checking in late, and I had to drive hell for leather to the airport, for which we were on the "wrong" side of Dublin. We just made it, despite a minor collision, when a vehicle I was overtaking swerved slightly and removed one of our wheel-hub caps – just a graze, and there was no time to stop. It was a nerve-wracking start to our marriage, and the prioritising of sister-talk about the wedding over prompt departure with one's new husband seemed odd to me. But it was nothing like as odd as what was to happen immediately after I got married for the second time.

10) Sallynoggin, Co. Dublin: Betty and Martin on their wedding day, 4 April 1964

11) Sallynoggin: Martin (L) and Colin, 4 April 1964

In London I had booked a room in the Strand Palace Hotel, and, a few days before the wedding, I had delivered my car to a nearby garage. Henry had given me £100 towards the costs of the ten-day honeymoon, and it just about covered them. The highest charge, for the Strand Palace room, was three guineas a night. Betty had not seen much of London before, so we did some traditional sightseeing as well as going to the theatre. After four nights in London, we made our way along the south coast, making one-night stops in Brighton, Bournemouth, and Torquay before spending the rest of our time in Cornwall, staying in the Mullion Cove Hotel on the Lizard, an area which I had loved as a child and was eager to share with Betty.

After we arrived in London, we wondered how things went in Dublin after our departure. Barbara, Henry, and my aunts and uncles had a quiet evening before returning to England the next day, but the younger guests, including Colin, Carol, Nigel, and Miranda had a very lively and even hilarious time with Betty's siblings not only in the evening, but all through the following day. It was rather heart-warming to hear that the two groups, who had not met one another before, shook down so well together.

Our honeymoon over, married life proper began in Menai Bridge. We wanted a place of our own, but needed time to find one. The Moorings Club apartment was small for a couple, but not unbearably cramped. At least now there were no more arguments about sharing the double bed! I was busy with teaching and examining. By the way, in my early years in Bangor there were classes on Saturday mornings as well as on weekdays. I suspect that the practice was abandoned after the completion of the New Arts Building in 1969 eased timetable problems. Betty did not drive, but the shops in Menai Bridge provided almost everything we needed, and in those days no expeditions to supermarkets were made because there were very few, if any, supermarkets. Conveniently for Betty, the town also had a Catholic church.

Anglesey and the neighbouring county of Caernarfon, in which Bangor was then situated, had a high proportion of Welsh speakers. At present all was calm, but later there was to be much unhappiness, manifested in sit-ins and other actions, that Welsh culture and language were being diluted and sidelined by the expanding University College, whose entrants were predominantly not Welsh speaking. The unhappiness was very understandable, although something overlooked by most of the demonstrators, some of whom made much of the way local quarrymen had contributed generously to the appeal for funds before the College was founded, is that many donors had been less interested in the promotion of the Welsh language than in the preparation of students for service in the kingdom and empire. There was no foundation chair of Welsh. For several years I made no serious attempt to learn Welsh, reasoning that it was more important for me to improve my knowledge of languages I needed in my research, notably German, Italian, and Turkish, and that I might not be in post in a Welsh establishment for much longer. I came to regret my decision and realise that not taking advantage of residence in what was in effect a giant language-laboratory was a wasted opportunity. In 1974 I started to make amends with the BBC course *Dewch i Siarad / Let's Speak Welsh*. Later I took the intensive Welsh course known as *Cwrs Wlpan* and a course in local Gwynedd Welsh, and I attended summer schools. So I made an effort, but without managing to achieve fluency. What I could do was introduce visiting speakers bilingually and, in general, demonstrate respect for the Welsh language. I could not condone all the actions of Welsh-language supporters, which included tearing down any notices (e.g. of essay titles) not written in Welsh or, if bilingual, not displaying the Welsh above or to the left of the English. The nadir of their protest-actions was reached when some of them broke into the Arts Library and dumped in a wet quarry the index cards which formed the catalogue of non-Welsh items in the College's collections. This was sheer vandalism and philistinism. Betty was one of those who volunteered to work long hours without pay to help restore the catalogue. When locals were not speaking Welsh, they might be speaking English with idioms literally translated from Welsh. It could be quite startling to hear somebody say: "Did you know Mrs Jones has been in bed with the doctor for three days"?

Even in our short time and restricted quarters at the Moorings Club we managed a bit of entertaining, although more often we were entertained by others, either to dinner or at parties. Much entertainment was to be found in the College in music and drama. There were frequent concerts, and in the early years several departments, including French, German, and Classics, staged plays. There was no theatre until the opening of Theatr Gwynedd in 1975, and, although I do not have the statistics to prove it, my impression is that dramatic activity was more widespread in the College before that event than after it. There were productions of seven Classical plays in the years 1965–1970, six of them in English, one in Welsh. There were also play-readings, including those given by a group of staff, mainly from the English and Classics departments, who performed, sometimes behind a screen, in the Senior Common Room.

I was a regular participant, and remember a very challenging occasion when I had to read my part while helping to carry Heracles off on a stretcher at the end of Sophocles' *Women of Trachis.* One of the problems with acting Greek tragedy is that it can so easily become comedy as one character after another is bumped off. This was the case with a Classical Society production of Sophocles' *Antigone* about 1980, in which the deaths, and the ancient sofa wheeled on to display the corpses, aroused much merriment. A.E. Housman exploited the comic possibilities of such scenes in his brilliant parody *Fragment of a Greek Tragedy* – one of the funniest pieces of writing known to me.

In the summer of 1964 we bought our first home, 44 Lon y Bryn, a semi-detached house in a modern estate called Cae Tros Lon, opposite Ysgol David Hughes in Menai Bridge. It was small – a sitting room and kitchen downstairs and two bedrooms, a boxroom, and a bathroom upstairs. There was a garage, and a back garden large enough to grow a few vegetables. The asking price was £3,250, and we did not dare offer less because the vacation was well advanced and we were told that a schoolteacher from Amlwch was interested. Whether this gentleman's alleged interest was real, or invented to encourage us to settle, we never discovered. In any case, we were able to buy the house thanks to the great generosity of Barbara's sister Lou, wife of John Cadbury.

The retirement of Dickie Browne in 1964 necessitated the appointment of a new member of staff, and I derived a small measure of satisfaction when the successful candidate turned out to be the person who had obtained the Londonderry post for which I had applied a year earlier. Our new colleague was Dr Joan Haldane, a graduate and postgraduate of London University, a specialist in Greek tragedy and Greek and Roman poetry. She was also a poet herself, author of *Pattern of Words* (1964). A gentle soul, she was very thin. I expect we would have found this more worrying if she had not been very thin all the time we had known her, and, on the quite frequent occasions we entertained her, she seemed to eat well, and she enjoyed discussing food. But, after ten years or so, it emerged that she was suffering from anorexia nervosa, and she had at least one spell in a psychiatric hospital. However, her condition continued to deteriorate, and in the Autumn Term of 1976, she was admitted to the Caernarfon & Anglesey Hospital, Bangor. I visited her frequently, and on one of my visits she asked me if I could get her a small container in which she could lock her cash and valuables. Finding that such an item was quite expensive to buy, I asked the College's Finance Department if it could help, and it kindly lent a suitable metal box. It was only after Joan's death that I learned that she had been using it to hide her food. She died in the late evening of 23 December 1976, an hour or two after I had been with her and recited in Latin the opening passage of Lucretius' poem, his address to Venus. She had been unable to speak, but was conscious and nodded her assent when I asked if she would like to hear it.

At the beginning of Autumn Term 1964 I was allocated several "moral tutees". All but one of them were new arrivals. The exception was a young man, a classicist, who was severely autistic. Sometimes he had managed to produce good written work, sometimes nothing at all. His previous tutor, the professor of Psychology no less, had more or less given up on him and thought he might be more responsive to someone who was much younger. I did my best, but the outcome was an aegrotat degree. I managed better with a young woman who was in one of my classes, but not actually one of my tutees. She approached me in a state of distress and depression about her work and life in general, and I was very afraid that she might do herself harm. I think it possible that I saved her from attempting suicide. I think that because she told me so.

I have mentioned that much of my early school-education was significantly impeded by poor eyesight. I suspect, but cannot prove, that imperfect hearing may have been another impediment. But it was only in October 1964 that the deficiency came to light. Interviewing a moral tutee, I enquired whether he had come straight from school or taken a gap-year. I understood him to say that he had spent time in the Dominican Republic. "How very interesting!", I commented. "Was it hot?" The student looked puzzled and made me aware that he had spent a year as a novice in the Dominican Order, without divulging whether the experience was either interesting or hot. A few years later there was a rather similar incident, coincidentally also involving a Latin-American country. I was a regular customer of a small branch of Lloyds Bank in Upper Bangor, near the College. The clerk who usually handled my cheques had been absent for several weeks and, when he returned, I greeted him warmly: "David, how good to see you back! Where have you been?" "Panama", I heard him say. "Gosh, how very interesting!", I exclaimed. "Was it hot?" "Not particularly", he replied. "I was posted temporarily to our branch in Penmaenmawr", naming a village a few miles up the coast.

To compensate perhaps for my defective eyesight and hearing, I am endowed with an unusually keen sense of smell. So, when she was younger, was Lucinda, and we used to joke about offering our services to the Gas Board, to detect leaks. My ability to detect smells that elude others has been a mixed blessing, and I will spare my readers unsavoury examples.

Throughout my time in Bangor I taught a wide range of subjects at Honours, Pass, and subsidiary levels. They included: Greek and Latin language; Greek history; Greek and Roman philosophy; Greek and Roman literature, including epic, lyric, tragedy, and comedy. Long ago I used to hear talk of "narrow-minded classicists". I do not think that I could be described as one. Membership of quite a small university department practically guaranteed that one was obliged to teach in all sorts of areas. My classical research has involved not only literature and philosophy, but also archaeology, history, and epigraphy, and I have written several books on modern writers, artists, and social reformers (ch. 13).

On 9 July 1965 I submitted my MLitt thesis on Lucretius. It was examined by Donald Dudley, Professor of Latin at Birmingham University, who liked it so much that he reckoned it deserved a PhD. Betty and I went to Dublin for the degree ceremony on 2 December. Barbara and Moira were present too (Plate 12). In May, I had given a talk on "Lucretius' Interpretation of the Plague" to a gathering of Classics staff at Gregynog, home of the famous private press of that name. It was derived mainly from my thesis and contributed material to my article "Some Lucretian Thought Processes" (1966). The 750-acre Gregynog estate, near Newtown in Montgomeryshire, was bought by sisters Gwendoline and Margaret ("Daisy") Davies in 1920. They were enthusiastic supporters of the Arts & Crafts Movement and gave every encouragement to art and music. In 1960 Margaret Davies bequeathed Gregynog to the University of Wales to be used as a conference centre. If one were a senior member of staff, one would be allocated a huge room in the old part of the house. Otherwise one might be accommodated in a modern extension which advertised itself bilingually as

RHANDY
ANNEXE

– inevitably converted in conversation to "Randy annexe". The Davies sisters had been teetotal, and in the beginning there was no bar. Conference guests were allowed one glass of sherry before dinner. But, as soon as the evening session was finished, most of us would pile into the Faculty minibuses in which we had travelled from our colleges and seek out the nearest pub several miles

12) Dublin (TCD): Martin before receiving degrees of MA and MLitt, with Barbara (L), Betty (centre), and Moira (R), and the Rubrics behind, 2 December 1965

away. The meetings were usually held in late May, when undergraduates were occupied with final revision for examinations and the rhododendrons were at their best. I can still hear the soporific drone of a motor mower competing with the drone of a lecturer during a postprandial session.

In August 1965 Betty and I took the Morris Minor on a trip through France and northern Italy. We saw fine scenery and interesting places, but there were two flies in the ointment. One was my poor health. I was twice struck down by feverish illnesses – first as were driving south from Grenoble, then, two or three days later, at Capo Mele in northwest Italy. The second attack was particularly severe, and Betty's anxiety was increased when, in a delirium, I recited all 193 verses of Milton's *Lycidas*, a poem which I had learned at Shrewsbury when I was fifteen. The other problem was the weather in parts of Italy, where we were pursued or preceded by torrential rainstorms. The worst occurred in Siena, south of Florence, the day before the August Palio. The morning was fine, but after lunch we watched from our bedroom window at the back of the hotel as the whole area became a lake. There was no flooding at the front, where our car was parked, but, when the rain stopped and allowed an inspection, we found that masonry dislodged from the hotel's roof had fallen and caused significant damage to the bonnet and wing-mirrors. A high point of the trip for me was visiting Sarsina, birthplace of the comic playwright Plautus (254–184 BC), and finding the main square named after him and a monument in his memory.

As soon as I finished my thesis, I turned my attention to my next substantial piece of work. One idea was to write a book about Lucretius, and, upon the recommendation of R.M. Ogilvie, I was approached by Batsford the publishers and offered a contract. But I preferred to do other things. The first was to produce a prose translation of the whole of Lucretius' poem *De Rerum Natura (On the Nature of Things)*. There was already the Penguin Books version by R.E. Latham, but I agreed with Benjamin Farrington that Latham was too much inclined "to jolly the argument along with breezy colloquialisms". I thought I could do better. I also thought that making a translation would help me in my endeavour to understand Lucretius: translators are in a sense the fullest form of commentators in that they have to reveal the meaning of every word. At the same time I began making what may well be the largest collection of Lucretius editions and translations in private ownership anywhere in the world, ranging in date from 1486 to the present.

In April 1966 I sent a sample of my translation to the New English Library. Despite a favourable reader's report, the editor found one excuse after another for not accepting the book. But I continued with my work, and in March 1967 signed a contract with Sphere Books after acceptance of it by Richard B. Fisher. I had everything finished in summer 1967, but there was then a delay of two years before publication. That was bad enough. What was worse was that Sphere made little effort with promotion and publicity, and, in violation of the contract, remaindered the unsold copies without informing me. Nevertheless during its short first life the translation brought Lucretius to the attention of some who would not otherwise have known him. A notable example is Stephen Greenblatt of Harvard University, who in his book *The Swerve: How the Renaissance Began* (2011) describes how it opened up a whole new world for him. In 2001 a revised version of the translation, with an extended introduction and notes, was published by Hackett Publishing Company, Indianapolis, and, thanks to the enthusiastic support of Hackett's brilliant editor, Deborah Wilkes, has been very successful, with tens of thousands of copies sold. While Sphere was dilly-dallying with my Lucretius, I hastened on to my next project – a project that was to take me many times to a ruined hilltop-city in Turkey and occupy me for the rest of my life.

Betty's mother, Moira ("Ma Dempsey"), died on 9 March 1966, aged sixty-five, from the respiratory illness she had suffered from for many years. No doubt it had been exacerbated by her smoking, which her doctor allegedly encouraged her to continue for the sake of her lungs. She was a delightful lady, possessed of the good sense of humour that characterised her children. She was always very kind to me, and wholly approved of Betty's marriage to me. Although a Catholic, she had a Protestant background, which perhaps partly explained her tolerance.

In early September 1966 Betty and I moved from our little house in Menai Bridge to a very large one in Bangor. Derwen Deg ("Fair Oak") occupies an elevated position on the east side of the Menai Strait, looking across to Anglesey (Plate 13). The partly-wooded grounds extend to nearly three acres, and the property is just a few minutes' walk from the main College building. As for the house itself, we and our cat, Pushkin, had at our disposal four reception rooms, four main bedrooms, three secondary bedrooms, three bathrooms, kitchens, and five cellar rooms. The views and the gardens were lovely, but the property, which we bought from Mrs. Winifred Wartski, widow of Isidore Wartski, a prominent Bangor businessman and former mayor, was absurdly beyond and above what we needed and could comfortably manage. On our first viewing, we were amused to find that from a rocky and wooded eminence above the house, there was a grandstand view of my senior colleague John Pollard's garden. Our time there was often happy, but punctuated by several worrying incidents, including a murder in a nearby house, nocturnal intruders in the gardens, airgun pellets fired through a bedroom window, gunshots fired by a cantankerous retired army-officer neighbour, and the collapse of a rockery after heavy rain. After two years we had had enough.

Betty was expecting a baby, and Fr Michael Richards was keen to buy Derwen Deg with Opus Dei money and use it as a hostel for Catholic students. At least we were not adversely affected financially by the purchase and sale. In fact we made a modest profit.

13) Derwen Deg, Bangor, ca. 1955

One who spent two years (1968–1970) in Derwen Deg after it became a hostel – her final year of Latin Honours with subsidiary Greek, and her year taking the Postgraduate Certificate in Education – was Jane Cupello, a model student and a person of great character, charm, and culture. I was sorry to lose touch with her after she left Bangor and I was delighted to renew her acquaintance when I moved to Durham, where she was living with her husband, Richard Abram, and their three children.

After two years in a house that was too small, and two in a house that was far too large, we moved in the summer of 1968 into a medium-sized modern house, called Penrhiw ("Hilltop"), with two reception rooms, four bedrooms, and a quite spacious but manageable garden. Situated in Penrhosgarnedd on the southern outskirts of Bangor, it looked across to Anglesey. As I went to bed on the night of 23 May 1970 I could see a fire coming from the direction of Robert Stephenson's tubular bridge which had carried the railway lines over the Menai Strait since 1848. It never occurred to me that the bridge itself, being made of wrought iron, could be on fire.

Betty and I were in Scotland together for the first time in late August and early September 1967, travelling round central and northern parts clockwise. We went over to Skye, staying in the Cuillin Hills Hotel, Portree, where our dinner was disturbed by what sounded like an airlock in the plumbing system, but turned out to be an expatriate Scot attempting the bagpipes on the terrace. Then, during the night, we were awakened by a disturbance below our bedroom window. In the morning Betty remarked on the incident, but I had no recollection of it and questioned whether she had dreamed it. She denied that and quoted me as having said at the time: "Don't worry, it is probably just a member of staff playing a prank". When we were paying the bill, we asked the manager to settle the argument. "Oh", he said, "I am so sorry you were disturbed. It was just a member of my staff playing a prank". An even greater excitement awaited us in the Caledonian Hotel, Ullapool, where we found our fellow-guests included Lord and Lady Boothby on their honeymoon. She (Wanda Sanna) was a raven-haired Sardinian and about thirty-three years younger than him. Their marriage in Caxton Hall on 30 August 1967 attracted much public attention. The next morning we saw him at the harbour talking to mackerel fishermen. On the subject of weddings, Carol married George Arrowsmith on 11 March 1967. The reception was held in the Union Club, Birmingham. When she and George attended Miranda's marriage to Sean Overend in 1965, the announcer who had been hired to call out guests' names at the reception got a bit mixed up. Carol having told him "Carol Smith and George Arrowsmith", he announced "Carol Smith and Arrow Smith".

In the spring of 1968 came tragic news of my first cousin Catharine ("Kate"), younger daughter of Barbara's brother Joe Tangye and his wife, Elisabeth. A lovely person in looks and nature, she had married Ranieri di Carpegna, an Italian employed by the European Commission. The wedding took place at historic Harvington Hall. On 11 May 1968 Kate gave birth to a healthy baby daughter, Isabella, in a Brussels clinic. The joyful news was communicated to her parents in Worcestershire, and the champagne was uncorked. But a few hours later they heard that Kate had died, of a massive haemorrhage. She was 25.

The last weeks of Betty's pregnancy were problematic. High blood pressure meant that the doctors wanted her in hospital weeks before the birth, which was to be by caesarean section. She was admitted on or about 9 October. No doubt the caution was well advised, but it created a bit of a problem. Partly for superstitious reasons, we had not yet purchased the essentials for the new baby, and the pram and nappies chosen by Barbara were decidedly old-fashioned. The birth took place on Thursday, 14 November, in St David's Maternity Hospital, Bangor, at about 3.30 p.m. As was common practice at the time, the father was not present, and my absence was not noticed by Betty, who was unconscious. I was taking a class from 3 p.m. and discovered the outcome after it by telephoning the wife of a mature student who was a nurse in St David's. I had been very nervous, and it was a joyous relief to hear that all had gone well, with the baby weighing 6 pounds and 11¾ ounces and with Betty safe too. I was allowed to view the baby and returned to the hospital after going home to telephone family members. We had decided to call our daughter Catharine Lucinda Ferguson, but it was a few days before we agreed to prioritise Lucinda over Catharine (Barbara's second name). For Betty's sake, mother and child remained in hospital for a few days. Each time I visited, I gently stroked Lucinda's head, prompting her mother to make the heart-warming observation that, as soon as I left, the baby started crying. Betty did not breast-feed Lucinda, again in accordance with frequent practice at the time.

Lucinda was christened on Sunday 15 December in St Mary's Catholic Church on Bangor's High Street. The building is now J.D. Wetherspoon's Black Bull Inn. Afterwards there was a celebration at Penrhiw, where the guests ate the christening cake and drank Veuve du Vernay Brut. We stayed at home for Christmas, which was just as well, because Lucinda was unwell and running a temperature. Her parents' ignorance did not help. When our doctor visited from Menai Bridge, the first thing he did was throw open the bedroom window with the words "babies are not pot-plants". The fresh air soon worked wonders.

I return now to my research and the new project I embarked on after completing the translation of Lucretius. Most classical scholars spend their time studying Greek and Latin texts that have been known for many centuries. But, when I was an undergraduate, I was thrilled by stories of those who have discovered new texts, whether manuscripts unnoticed in libraries, papyri preserved in the sands of Egypt or the volcanic ash of Herculaneum, or inscriptions. I formed an ambition to follow in their footsteps – an ambition which over a period of nearly sixty years I have fulfilled beyond my wildest dreams.

During my postgraduate studies of Lucretius, I had encountered scattered references to Diogenes of Oinoanda, who, probably early in the second century AD, expounded the philosophy of Epicurus in a gigantic Greek inscription carved on the wall of a stoa (colonnade) in his home-city in northern Lycia, in the mountains of southwest Asia Minor (Asiatic Turkey). Eighty-eight pieces of the inscription, of varying sizes, had been discovered by French and Austrian epigraphists late in the nineteenth century, but no serious attempt had been made to find more, or even to re-examine the pieces already discovered despite the recent scholarly interest of Alberto Grilli and C.W. Chilton. Both had published editions of Diogenes – Grilli in 1960, Chilton in 1967, and in 1962 the latter had made a visit of a few hours to Oinoanda, but reported no new discoveries and the disappearance of most of those already made. I decided that I should do some serious work on Diogenes and obtain a firsthand acquaintance with Oinoanda.

My present estimate is that the inscription originally contained about 25,000 words, which makes it much the largest inscription known from the ancient world. It is unique also in presenting a complete system of philosophy. Diogenes tells his readers that he is "at the sunset of his life" and wishes, before he dies, to share with them "the medicines of salvation", by which he means the philosophical "medicine" devised by Epicurus to cure the moral sickness that afflicts most human beings, by eliminating their unnecessary fears and desires and so enabling them to achieve the perfect peace of mind in which perfect happiness consists. He addresses not only his contemporaries, but also generations to come ("for they belong to us, although they are not yet born"). Moreover, he wants to benefit foreigners as well as Oinoandans – or rather

> those who are called foreigners, although they are not really so, for … the whole compass of this world gives all people a single country … and a single home, the world. (Fr. 30)

His philanthropic and cosmopolitan message, addressed *urbi et orbi* (to the city and the world), is remarkable and highly relevant to our age, as is his (and Epicurus') conviction that scientific knowledge, properly applied, can rid us of fear, especially of the gods and of death.

The wall that carried the inscription no longer stands. In late antiquity the stoa was either destroyed by an earthquake or deliberately demolished, and the blocks of the inscription were re-used as building material over a wide area of the city, which means that recovering Diogenes' work is an exercise rather like that of assembling a massive jigsaw puzzle, with the extra difficulties that many of the pieces are damaged or missing.

The inscription occupied several (probably seven) horizontal courses of the wall, with the courses differing from one another in height, but each course consisting of stones of roughly equal height. It is not a single treatise, but contains several writings. The longest were Diogenes' epitomes on *Physics* and *Ethics*, both carved in small letters because they were at or close to eye level. The *Physics* was meant to be read first, the study of physics, including epistemology, being the necessary means whereby the ethical goal is achieved. It occupied the second lowest course, while the *Ethics* was in the lowest course. Both writings were carved in fourteen-line columns, but through the lower margin of the *Ethics* ran, in somewhat larger letters, a continuous line of Epicurean ethical maxims, many of them known from other sources. Above the *Physics*, also in fourteen-line columns of small letters, were letters of Diogenes on a variety of topics to do with physics and ethics, and perhaps also, despite their larger letters and shorter columns, his *Monolithic Maxims*, so called (by his recent researchers) because there is no overflow of the text onto a second stone. In the middle course – the fourth from the bottom and fourth from the top – are the so-called *Ten-Line-Column Writings*, carved in medium-sized letters, containing writings of Diogenes and, possibly, a letter from the youthful Epicurus to his mother, making an unusual request for a son writing to a parent – not to send him any more money. Carved in eighteen-line columns of large letters and occupying the three topmost courses was Diogenes' discussion of *Old Age*, carved in large letters because the writing was above eye-level.

My first visit to Oinoanda took place in July 1968, just before we moved from Derwen Deg to Penrhiw. It and my second visit in June-July 1969 were amateurish affairs. I took photographs, but did not yet make epigraphic "squeezes" – impressions of inscriptions made by using a brush to beat wetted filter paper into the indentations on the stones. In the winter of 1969–1970 I caused occasional puzzlement by practising the technique in North Wales churchyards. Nevertheless the first two expeditions yielded worthwhile results – the rediscovery of many of the fragments recorded in the nineteenth century and four new pieces (Plate 14). I continued my independent investigations in each of the years 1970–1973 and was particularly successful in 1970 and 1972. By the end of 1973 the score was 51 rediscovered fragments and 38 new ones. The new ones added some 1,250 words to the known text of the inscription.

Highlights included a passage of the *Ethics* in which Diogenes looks forward to a time when humanity has followed Epicurus in embracing wisdom:

> Then truly the life of the gods will pass to human beings. For everything will be full of righteousness and mutual love, and there will come to be no need for fortifications or laws or all the other things we devise on account of one another. (Fr. 56)

He adds that there will be no slavery, and the necessities of life will be provided by co-operative farming in the intervals of studying philosophy together.

Although I found the work at Oinoanda exciting and deeply satisfying, I never found it easy, and the development of a serious illness made it more difficult. Oinoanda is remotely situated on the saddle-ridge of a wooded hill north-east of Fethiye, at an altitude of 1,400 metres (ca. 4,600 feet), roughly the height of the summit of Ben Nevis. The scenery, which includes mountains that rise to 3,213 metres (10,541 feet) is magnificent (Plate 15). Even today, the area is little visited, but the coastal parts of southern and western Turkey are now major international tourist destinations served by big airports that receive many thousands of charter flights every year, and there are now fine roads running into the mountains, including one which passes close by Oinoanda. But in the 1960s and 1970s things were very different. Izmir and Antalya received domestic flights from Istanbul and Ankara, but there were no other airports in the region and most of the roads were rough and unasphalted. The tourists were mainly Turkish. Fethiye, which now has about 163,000 inhabitants, had a population of 7,500 in 1968, and the nearby resort of Ölü Deniz ("Dead Sea") was totally undeveloped. My practice was to fly to Izmir via Istanbul and proceed to Fethiye in a Hertz hired car. For most of its distance, the road from Fethiye to İncealiler, the small village from which one begins to walk and climb to Oinoanda, was very difficult, and so either I used Fethiye as a base for very long and tiring day-visits to the site or I rented a bare room above a shop in Seki, a village about six miles from İncealiler. If the latter, I slept on an air mattress, fetched cold water from the grounds of a mosque, and had the most primitive and economical of sanitary arrangements – a hole in the floor over a cowshed. It amused me to contrast the Seki facilities with those in the bathroom in Izmir's Büyük Efes Oteli ("Grand Ephesus Hotel"), where the seat of the spotless WC carried the printed assurance "sanitised for your protection". Reaching the air-conditioned comfort of that luxurious hotel after a gruelling spell of work at Oinoanda, and knowing that one would be flying from Istanbul to London in a Pan Am round the world clipper the next day, was sheer bliss. But it was also bliss arriving from Seki at Fethiye's simple but clean Kaya Hotel, taking a shower, and dining at the excellent Rafet Restaurant by the harbour. On one occasion, queuing in the bank, I bumped into Sybil Williams, wife of Eric Williams, author of *The Wooden Horse*. She invited me to come aboard their boat-home, fittingly named *Escaper*, but I was in a hurry to depart for Izmir. She said that Fethiye was one of their favourite ports.

Each year I had the company and assistance on the site of one of the sons of "Baba" ("Father") Ali Işıklı, who had no shortage of children – fourteen by two wives. On one occasion my helper, married with one child, wrote a question for me on a piece of paper. I did not understand it at the time, and, only when I rediscovered it two years later, saw that it asked if I had any information about birth control. By then he had fathered two more children.

Despite this unfortunate lapse, I had the privilege of enjoying an affectionate friendship with the whole family and other villagers too. Of the others, I single out for special mention Sami Işık, a one-legged farmer, whom I first met on the site, where he and his formidable dog were watching over his sheep and he was playing his panpipes (Plate 16). On many occasions thereafter he gave me hard-boiled eggs when I went up the hill of Oinoanda in the morning and flowers from his garden when I came back down. When I published a big edition of Diogenes' inscription in 1993, I dedicated it to the villagers, calling their friendship "one of the most precious things in my life". Betty visited Oinoanda with me in 1973, in advance of the Tenth International Congress of Classical Archaeology in Ankara and Izmir – a gathering to which I will return shortly. She was an excellent assistant, who located more of "our" seven new fragments than I did.

Each year between 1969 and 1973 I was busy with the decipherment and editing of new and newly-rediscovered Epicurean texts from Oinoanda, which were published in the *American Journal of Archaeology* (two articles), *Journal of Hellenic Studies*, an Austrian Academy monograph, and *Hermathena*. In 1969 there was also some work to be done in advance of the Annual Conference of the Classical Association, which was held in Bangor between 7 and 10 April 1970. Some of the work was administrative, since I was the Hon. Treasurer of the local branch, but mainly it was focused on preparation of my lecture, which it had been agreed would be the opening one of the conference. I chose

14) Oinoanda: Martin with Diogenes NF 1, July 1969

Above L: 15) Oinoanda: view S from theatre, 1994
Above R: 16) Sami Işık of İncealiler, ca. 1970

as its title "Philosophy and Philanthropy in the Mountains of Lycia: The Inscription of Diogenes of Oenoanda". It was illustrated with colour slides. Few members of the audience were likely to know much, if anything, about Diogenes, and I was determined to show that he and Oinoanda were worthy of attention. The message of the lecture, which Barbara and Henry came to hear, was not only well received by the audience, but also reported and discussed at some length in *The Times* the following morning (8 April) in an article entitled "Monumental Old Carver Is Brought to Life". At that time only four new pieces of the inscription had been brought to light. The following month, the number rose to sixteen, and the making of squeezes of all the known fragments – "old" as well as "new" – was under way. The squeeze-making programme continued apace in May 1971, when just two new fragments were found, and in late April and early May 1972, when thirteen new Diogenes texts came to light and I recorded also at nearby Kemerarası what remained of an important Hadrianic inscription, 117 lines long, about the establishment of a music festival called the Demostheneia. Unknown to me, it had already been recorded, by a German epigraphist, but was unpublished. The documents quoted in the inscription are dated AD 124 and 125. They contain much information about Oinoanda and its territory, but what startled me most when I first set eyes on the inscription was the extraordinarily close similarity of its style of lettering to that of Diogenes' inscription – identical really, except that the lettering of the Demostheneia inscription is smaller. Hitherto Diogenes' work had been dated ca. AD 200. Henceforth it would be dated by most scholars to the reign of Hadrian (AD 117–138).

In 1973 I was promoted Senior Lecturer at the fairly young age of thirty-three. John Ellis Jones, promoted at the same time, was just over ten years senior to me. The International Congress of Classical Archaeology (23–30 September), which I attended with Betty in September after visiting Oinoanda, was my first opportunity to present my research to an audience outside the United Kingdom and to bring it to the attention of scholars in Turkey. The congress began in Ankara, which I had not visited before. This was Betty's first time in Turkey, and it got off to an unfortunate start. We had just disembarked on arrival at Izmir Airport from London, via Istanbul, when her suitcase was run over and flattened by a Turkish Airlines vehicle as it was being transported from the plane to the terminal. The suitcase was a write-off, but damage to the contents, mainly clothing, was slight. I cannot remember if I restrained myself from saying that it was lucky that her suitcase was run over rather than mine, which contained various items required for the work at Oinoanda. The main annoyance was that there was a delay to our departure the following morning while we accompanied an airline employee to the bazaar to choose a replacement.

After five days at Oinoanda, we drove east to Antalya and used it as a base to visit Termessos, an impressive mountainous site, which was the mother-city of Oinoanda (also known as Termessos-at-Oinoanda or Termessos Minor), and the ancient cities of Aspendos, Perge, and Side, all with fine monuments – almost deserted in those days, now heaving with tourists. We then drove to Ankara. After a tour of the city and an excursion to Gordion, the proceedings of the conference got under way with two days of papers. But I did not attend any part of the programme, least of all the evening entertainments – a Turkish Government reception and a visit to the ballet, to both of which Betty went unescorted. Much as I had been at Capo Mele in 1965, I was in the grip of a feverish sickness. I was still feeling very unwell early on 26 September, when we were scheduled to board a coach for the 370-mile journey to Izmir. I took a cocktail of drugs – analgesics and pills for travel sickness and stomach disorders – and hoped for the best. After an hour or two I came out in a drenching sweat and knew I was going to be alright. At Afyon, where the convoy of coaches stopped for lunch at the museum, everyone was presented with a cardboard lunch-box tied up with pink ribbons. I did not need to open mine to tell that the contents, a cold chicken salad, had gone off. So had everyone else's lunch. The coaches made a second stop – to view the American excavations at Sardis – in the late afternoon. It was good to get back to Izmir, to the air-conditioned comfort of the Büyük Efes Hotel, with two days to complete my recovery before reading my illustrated paper on "Oinoanda: The Epicurean Inscription" in the morning of 29 September.

In the paper, for which only twenty minutes were allocated, I included an assessment of the prospects for further finds and emphasised the need for a scientific excavation – a matter which I had already taken up with Norwegian and Austrian scholars. At the end of the conference-session I was approached by David H. French, the newly-appointed director of the British Institute of Archaeology at Ankara (BIAA), who said that the Institute must seek permission for a survey of Oinoanda to be carried out under the direction of its new Honorary Secretary, Alan Stirling Hall of Keele University, who was also at the conference. I had not met either French or Hall before, but welcomed the suggestion that BIAA come in on the investigation of the site. In my solo efforts I had already achieved far more than I ever thought possible, and the Turkish Government's introduction of a new antiquities law in September 1973 meant that I could not have continued without a permit. Moreover, at various times during my work I had emphasised the desirability of involving more people and more expertise. Hall's field of interest was epigraphy, and I hoped and expected that he would be a congenial colleague and collaborator. Sadly, my hopes and expectations were to be bitterly disappointed.

Diogenes and Oinoanda are two of the great loves of my life, and I have particularly happy memories of the early years of my engagement with them, when, except in 1973, I was exploring on my own with just the company of a local villager, undisturbed by any sound except the tinkling of goats' and camels' bells, the gentle rustling of tortoises, and the music of Sami's panpipes. The peace, loneliness, and beauty of the site were perfection, despite the need to be wary of snakes and scorpions. The presence of Diogenes' inscription was a powerful contributor to the atmosphere. The inscription is special for several reasons. First, because of its Epicurean message. Secondly, because of the closeness to Diogenes engendered by it: when we read the inscribed stones, we have the very unusual experience of reading an ancient author's writings exactly as they were seen by their first readers. It is true that they no longer form the wall of the stoa, but they remain close to their original home, on the ground Diogenes and his contemporaries walked. The thrill of discovering pieces of the inscription and being the first to read them for perhaps 1,700 years is very great indeed. A third reason for attraction is, somewhat paradoxically, the fragmentary state of Diogenes' work. It presents the challenges and appeal (as well as the frustrations) of an unfinished jigsaw puzzle, with which, as I have suggested above, it has much in common. Particular satisfaction results when two or more pieces of the puzzle can be joined up, as happened more than once in my early years and has happened many times since. The making of any addition to the text, large or small, always arouses excitement.

Very important though Oinoanda and Diogenes are to me, an even greater love of my life is Lucinda, and that has been the case since the day she was born, soon after my first expedition. Unfortunately, that far from equates to perfection in fatherhood: as in my own life, so, in respect to hers, I have made bad mistakes – some to do with her education, others to do with my at times irregular private life and the breakdown of my marriage to Betty. I can only apologise and beg forgiveness, pleading *humanum est errare*, even though Oscar Wilde's Lord Illingworth does not encourage me to expect success:

> Children begin by loving their parents; after a time they judge them; rarely, if ever, do they forgive them.
>
> *A Woman of No Importance*

Betty died in 1997, so is sadly not available to testify for or against me or to comment on her relationship with Lucinda, but my perception is that she was a devoted mother during our marriage and remained so after it ended, but that, not being a saint, she sometimes allowed her annoyance with me to impact our daughter.

From the beginning, both she and I did all we could to promote not only Lucinda's well-being, but also her education. We spent much time talking and reading to her, and encouraging her to read. I expect that many parents attribute remarkable talents to their young children, and I was and am no exception. In speaking, reading, and writing she was a very early developer. By the time she started school in St Catherine's, the junior section of St Gerard's Convent School, in Bangor in September 1971, when she was aged two years and ten months, she had astonished Colin by reading him an article in *The Times* and had started learning Greek, introduced to it by me as a bit of fun. Sometimes she was able to help her form-mistress, Mrs Harris, with origins of words. When the teacher was unable to explain why "hippopotamus" is so called, Lucinda piped up that it comes from the Greek words for "horse" and "river"; and when she was stumped by the origin of "rhododendron", her very young pupil explained that it is a combination of the Greek words for "rose" and "tree". Betty and I were naturally proud of our daughter as well as rather sorry for Mrs Harris, who was good at her job – at least those parts of it which did not require a knowledge of Greek! At the same time there was some relief when, during a pantomime at the Winter Gardens in Great Malvern, Lucinda whispered to me: "Daddy, I don't want to be a professor of Greek. I want to be a princess".

I have lived for most of my life, including the last forty-four years of it, without a television, and I am glad of that. But in 1969, when I was about to make my second visit to Oinoanda, a set was hired to enable Barbara, who was coming to stay with Betty and Lucinda during my absence, to watch the Investiture of the Prince of Wales at Caernarfon Castle. After her departure, the set was retained, and it came in surprisingly useful: Betty and I enjoyed Mike Yarwood's impersonations, and Lucinda enjoyed "Magic Roundabout" and, from late March 1971, "Sesame Street", the latter being particularly educational.

An acquisition in 1971 was a new white Volkswagen campervan, a "Dormobile" conversion. None of the family was as pleased to ride in it as Lucinda, because for the first time she could travel by road and see not only out of the window, but also over the tops of walls and hedges. It was often used for short breaks in Britain, and twice for long journeys abroad.

7

Wales and Turkey 2 (1974–1988)

For several months in the summer and autumn of 1973, and probably for longer, I had a bad cough and night sweats. On 10 January 1974, the first day of the College's Spring Term, I made an overdue appointment to see a doctor. The following morning he told me that I had pulmonary tuberculosis and must go into hospital immediately. When I asked him if it was curable, he said: "Good heavens, yes". When I told Betty, she exploded with the Dubliner's curse-avoiding expression "Janey Mack!" Fortunately she was now a qualified car-driver, for the hospital, called Bryn Seiont, was on the far side of Caernarfon, about ten miles from Penrhiw. It was to be my home for nearly two months, from 11 January until 4 March. After my discharge, I was instructed to take four weeks' sick leave, and the treatment with powerful drugs lasted for about eighteen months. Lucinda, now aged five, was not permitted to visit me, so Betty took her into the hospital's car park, enabling her to exchange waves and blown kisses with me.

There is no way of knowing for sure where and when I picked up the infection, but it is a fair guess that it was during my work at Oinoanda, when I was sometimes living in primitive conditions, not eating proper meals, and getting very exhausted – not least so in May 1970. The days I spent at Oinoanda that time were exceptionally successful, but, not long before I left home, I had an operation for the removal of my wisdom teeth. I was in hospital for two days and emerged in a surprisingly-weakened state with significant weight-loss. I had not completely recovered before I went to Turkey.

Bryn Seiont Hospital served two purposes – as an isolation unit for those with infectious diseases and as a home for the terminally ill. Most of the inmates were elderly. Many of those in the isolation unit had been quarrymen and were suffering pitifully from pneumoconiosis, and some from TB as well. It was a dismal place, brightened only by the kindness of some of the staff and the stoicism and good humour of many of the patients. One of the three senior nurses went out of her way to be unpleasant and was much disliked by her junior colleagues as well as by her patients. There was speculation that she had an unsatisfactory sex life. One young nurse told me her senior colleague had upset her so much that she had just placed her letter of resignation on the matron's desk. I managed to persuade her to retrieve it. During the British general election campaign in February 1974, the supposedly sex-starved sister missed the deadline for submitting applications for patients' postal votes, so causing mass disenfranchisement. We wondered if she had done it deliberately. In the event, most of us got the result we wanted, which was the election of Dafydd Wigley of Plaid Cymru as Member of Parliament for Caernarfon. He was a frequent visitor to Bryn Seiont and campaigned tirelessly for the rights of pneumoconiosis sufferers to be granted compensation.

The hospital's standards of comfort and hygiene left much to be desired. Male patients shared two WCs without locks on the doors. After going downstairs and using a ladies' WC with a lock, I was soon caught and reprimanded. So I organised a system whereby the position of a chair outside the door signalled whether a WC was occupied or vacant. At breakfast time the staff had an economical arrangement whereby they combined the delivery of the food with the removal of the urine bottles, reminding me of the way adult starlings combine the delivery of titbits to their nestlings with removal of waste matter from the nest.

One good thing, for which I was very grateful, was that I was given a two-bed ward for single occupation. I was warned there was no guarantee that I could keep it indefinitely, but I never had to share it. The room looked across the hospital's drive to the single-storey wing which housed terminally ill patients. I always knew when one of them had died because I could hear the comings and goings of the trolley that conveyed the corpses to the mortuary, further along the drive.

Hospitalisation meant that I was spared taking any classes in the Spring Term 1974. But I still had plenty of work to do, and I went into Bryn Seiont with two typewriters – one of them Greek – and a stack of books. Eric Warmington, editor of the famous Loeb Classical Library series, published by William Heinemann and Harvard University Press, had invited me to revise the Lucretius volume, originally edited by W.H.D. Rouse. This involved re-editing the text, rewriting the introduction and most of the notes, revising the translation to make it accord with the new text and sometimes to meet the requirements of modern English, and making a new index. Warmington did ask me whether I thought Rouse's version could be retained: if I had known at the time that Sphere had remaindered my 1969 translation, I would have asked if it could be used instead of Rouse's in the Loeb volume, but they had neglected to tell me, so I assumed my version was still in print. In the hospital I worked on the new Loeb, which was published on 21 July 1975, and also on the presentation of the new Diogenes texts I had found in 1972, published by the Austrian Academy of Sciences (1974). In addition, I improved my knowledge of German and read many books.

Since our conversation in Izmir about BIAA's future involvement in the investigation of Oinoanda, I had been in frequent touch with David French and Alan Hall, communicating information about the site and discussing what needed to be done. French went down from Ankara to have a look at Oinoanda and speak to the locals, who gave him a heartwarmingly-favourable report of me and my eccentricities, and convinced him that I must be present "to bless the waters" when the work started, even if I were not physically fit enough to participate in it. Defying medical opinion that it was inadvisable to go to Oinoanda while still recovering from my illness, I did go in July 1974.

On 30 September Richard Wycherley and Martin Clarke retired from the chairs of Greek and Latin and were replaced by Bryan Peter Reardon, who had been appointed to a new chair of Classics, and Gordon Thomas Cockburn, who was appointed lecturer. Bryan, whose main speciality was the ancient novel, was British, educated in Glasgow and Cambridge, but had taken his doctorate at Nantes and had held academic posts in Canada, latterly as professor of Classics at Trent University, Ontario. At Bangor he was a breath of fresh air, introducing new ideas and courses, although he resisted the recommendation of an American academic to boost recruitment by prefixing the name of every course, e.g. Greek Tragedy and Roman Epic, with the words "Sex and Violence in". He and I got on well, although he only stayed for four years. The same is true of Gordon, who came from Edinburgh and was to be a colleague of mine, first in Bangor, then in Durham, for twenty-six years. I first met Bryan a few days before leaving for Turkey, and two days later Betty and I were visited from the USA by Diskin and Jenny Strauss Clay. They brought with them their young daughter Andreia, who was excited about meeting Lucindarella. Diskin was much interested in Diogenes. He had published an article about him, and we had corresponded. He was to join in the work at Oinoanda in 1975.

I decided to go to Oinoanda in 1974 by road, in the Dormobile. It was a difficult decision. Among the cons, I had not yet driven the vehicle outside the UK and I would have no passenger for company, let alone a co-driver; the 6,000-mile round trip was bound to be exhausting; I would be going contrary to medical advice; and the dangers of the road through Austria, Yugoslavia, and Bulgaria, used by Turkish and Greek guest-workers in Belgium and Germany racing to get home for their summer holidays, were well known. The pros were that the team would have an extra vehicle at its disposal during the season, and that I would be able to take out, as well as squeeze paper and other equipment, all sorts of provisions, allowing me to be independent of the dreadful dirty restaurant beneath the primitive apartment which BIAA had rented in Seki. I could also, if need be, sleep in it. Lucinda lent me Tiny Ted to look out of the windscreen and bring me home safely.

On the planned day of my departure (15 July), I was shaving in the bathroom at home, when I heard on the radio that a crisis had developed over Cyprus, threatening war between Greece and Turkey. The Cypriot National Guard, with support from the Greek ruling junta, overthrew the democratically-elected President Makarios and replaced him with Nikos Sampson, a former terrorist. Five days later, on 20 July, Turkish troops landed in Cyprus. Alan Hall had already gone to Turkey, and two of the four young surveyors from the North-East London Polytechnic were on their way there in a BIAA Land Rover. I thought it would be imprudent if I set off before I had received advice from Ankara. So that day I drove only as far as Silligrove (the family home in Shropshire). I spent two nights there before proceeding to Dover on the 17th, and it was only after my arrival there that I received a telegram advising me to set off. So, that evening I crossed to Ostend and spent the next four days driving across Europe in heavy rain, stopping for the nights at Greding in Bavaria, Zagreb, and Niş, seeing the results of numerous road accidents, and crossing into Turkey near Edirne in the evening of 21 July. All this time I had no news whatsoever, but it was not encouraging that vehicles were only being allowed to enter Turkey if their lights were blacked out. The following day I crossed the Dardanelles and spent the night in the Tusan Motel near Çanakkale. I was the only guest, all the tourists having fled, and I ate dinner and went to bed by candlelight, a strict black-out being in force. But Nature is no respecter of black-out orders, and during the night there was a violent thunderstorm with frequent lightning flashes illuminating the whole area.

The weather cleared by dawn, and I made a short diversion to see for the first time the ruins of Troy, arrival at which was signalled by the Helen Casino, a wooden horse, modern murals, and a bust of Homer. Like Byron, who visited in 1810 but was spared the Helen Casino, I was unimpressed. Moreover, the swarms of flies, revelling in the warm sunshine after heavy rain, meant that I ran round the walls faster than Achilles. I was glad to be back on the road, heading south past Assos and Bergama to Izmir and on to Selçuk, where I spent the night. The following day I drove to Fethiye and on to Seki, where Alan Hall was too busy to welcome me, but I met Osman Özbek, our delightful *temsilci* (Turkish Government representative), and two of the surveyors, Maureen Healey and Andy Slade. Maureen and Andy had flown out and arrived ahead of their two colleagues, Graham Cooper and David Stephens, who had taken the Land Rover to Ankara for repairs. Its road unworthiness had been demonstrated in Bulgaria, where on a downhill stretch Graham and David had the unusual motoring experience of being overtaken by one of their own wheels. Just after its arrival in Seki, the Dormobile was twice wounded in combat – first when I reversed it into a small electricity pylon on the village square, secondly when, on a return journey from Fethiye, it collided, on an uphill stretch of single-track road, with an overloaded lorry, which appeared round a corner and, having defective brakes, could not stop. Fortunately neither collision affected the running of the vehicle. In Seki the surveyors and I were accommodated in classrooms of a primary school, high above the village. We did not live in luxury, but conditions were much more salubrious than those in the mouse-ridden apartment rented by Alan Hall, where the kitchen and toilet were separated only by a flimsy curtain and the occupants kept succumbing to illness.

Pleasure at having reached Seki and being back at work at Oinoanda turned to dismay when, after I had been on the site for just one day, an order to stop was received from Ankara. The Cyprus crisis had eased a little. When it had been at its peak, the authorities had been too busy to bother with foreigners working far from the likely scene of any military action. Now they were less busy. This first ban on our work lasted eleven days. A second ban was imposed on 16 August and not lifted before I set off for home on 29 August. The curious thing was that the bans only applied to work at Oinoanda itself. We were welcome to go anywhere else we wanted, and did so (Plate 17).

17) Martin solo-dancing to gypsy music at wedding near Ölü Deniz, 24 August 1974

During my twelve days on the site, I recorded twenty-three new pieces of Diogenes' work. Most of them were small, but several were significant in size and content, especially two pieces of the *Physics* (fr. 20, 21), which are part of his argument, directed against the Stoics, that the gods did not create the world either for themselves or for human beings (Plate 18). One of his points concerns the sea, which occupies so much of the earth that

> it makes a peninsula of the inhabited world. It is itself also full of yet other evils and, to cap all, has water that is not even drinkable, but briny and bitter, as if it had been purposely made like this by the god to prevent human beings from drinking. (Fr. 21 II 1–10)

18) Oinoanda: Diogenes fr. 21 (NF 40), 48.5 x 88 x 35+ cm

During the stay in Seki I produced drawings of all the known pieces of the inscription, and not just of the new discoveries, to accompany Osman Özbek's report to the authorities – a laborious and time-consuming task.

Alan Hall's direction of the epigraphical and topographical survey of Oinoanda left much to be desired. He was an epigraphist and Roman historian, but not an architect or archaeologist, and he had little knowledge of the largest inscription on the site, that of Diogenes, and little understanding of its importance. His knowledge of Turkish was poor, at least at the beginning, as was his management of his team, several members of which he upset greatly. Whereas my relations with the locals had always been harmonious, all sorts of difficulties cropped up when he was in charge. He did not conceal his dislike for me. I suspect that the root-cause of it was jealousy: I was nine years his junior, but academically more successful; I had worked at Oinoanda for six years before he came on the scene; I was popular with the locals; and I had the privilege of the support and friendship of Professor Terence Bruce Mitford of St Andrews University, a distinguished specialist in the archaeology and epigraphy of Cyprus and Southern Turkey, with whom (I gathered) Alan and David French had crossed swords over work-permits. One thing I did admire about Alan was his ability to climb the hill of Oinoanda and move about the rugged site despite a significant disability: when he was a child, he contracted tuberculosis in his left leg, and during the treatment the left leg stopped growing, with the result that it was significantly shorter than the right leg and necessitated the wearing of a special boot. He used to say that in Turkey the boot was a great conversation-opener, because people were often curious to know what the problem was. Despite his unfriendliness to me, I always treated him with respect until the occurrence of an unpleasant incident in 1975, which I describe later.

During the troubles in Cyprus, supplies of petrol were prioritised for the Turkish military, and on several occasions I was concerned that the Dormobile's tank would run dry. Once I made a round trip of thirty miles to procure thirty litres from a filling station that had recently been resupplied. But, by the time I left Seki for home, on 29 August, the situation had improved. The previous evening, Seki had experienced a terrific thunderstorm with torrential rain. Five agricultural workers, on their way home, were swept away in a flash flood and died. And yet, at İncealiler, just five miles away as the crow flies, there was not a drop of rain.

I crossed into Bulgaria late on the 30th after waiting four hours for formalities to be completed on the Turkish side of the border. I celebrated my arrival in Bulgaria with an omelette in the frontier restaurant, served by a waiter who bore a striking resemblance to Norman Wisdom. Afterwards I had a tricky encounter with an inebriated passport officer, who wanted me to give two friends of his a lift to Sofia. I told him (truthfully) that I was heading not for Sofia, but for the nearest campsite. The next day, on the way to the Yugoslav border, I was twice stopped by traffic policemen. The first one just wanted to look round the Dormobile and was thrilled to see the cooker, sink, fridge, cupboard, wardrobe, bed, and bunks. The other alleged that I had exceeded the speed limit at a crossroads. As Henry had taught me to do when stopped by the police, I got out of my vehicle. I pretended I did not know what the problem was, gave a friendly smile, and showed my driving licence and passport. The tactic worked, helped by the timely arrival of a Turkish motorist, who had been stopped by another policeman and was arguing angrily with him. "My" policeman waved me off and hurried to assist his colleague. The rest of my journey went smoothly until I reached the Strait of Dover. I spent the nights of 31 August and 1 September at campsites near Belgrade and at Radstadt in Austria, and in the evening of 2 September, after a drive (that day) of 663 miles, I reached Ostend and boarded the 10.20 p.m. sailing for Dover. I had a light meal and dozed in a chair, intending to spend the second half of the night in the Dormobile at Dover. But it was not to be.

During the crossing a terrific storm blew up – the same storm which wrecked British Prime Minister Edward Heath's boat *Morning Cloud III* off the Sussex coast with the loss also of two members of its crew. The ferry could not get into Dover harbour until 9.20 a.m., meaning that the crossing took eleven hours instead of three and three quarters. I was completely exhausted by the ordeal at sea on top of the longest drive I have ever made on a single day. At about 5 a.m. I managed to get a cabin and slept a little, but I was still very washed out when I reached Silligrove in the early evening. I never drove to Turkey again.

The continuation of the BIAA project at Oinoanda had already been discussed in Seki, and there was much further discussion of it after the team's return to the UK. Fund-raising was one concern. My independent work had been financed partly by myself, partly by the University College of North Wales. After the 1974 season I suggested to Alan Hall and David French that I be given the title of Co-Director or Assistant Director, to give me more say in how things were done, and more clout in my endeavour to raise funds. My suggestion was bluntly rejected, without any reason being given: "We decided that things should stay as they are" (letter from Alan Hall, 4 October 1974). One consequence of their exclusion of me was that no funds were forthcoming from two uncles of mine, who, in the belief that I was involved in the direction of the work, had generously offered to support it.

In contrast with the coolness of relations with Alan and David was the warmth of the reception I received at L'École française d'Athènes in Athens in April 1975. Betty and Lucinda came with me – to Athens, that is, not to the School. We flew out on the 5th and back on the 20th. My purpose was to examine the squeezes of Diogenes fragments made by the young Frenchmen who had been the first discoverers of the inscription between 1884 and 1889, and the notebook kept by Georges Cousin, Diogenes' first editor, in 1889. Cousin had not published drawings or photographs or given measurements, so there were many unanswered questions about the French discoveries, especially about those stones which had not been rediscovered by the Austrian epigraphists Rudolf Heberdey and Ernst Kalinka in 1895 or during the recent British investigations. My researches were very productive and resulted in the publication of an article, "Diogenes of Oenoanda and L'École française d'Athènes", dedicated to the eminent epigraphist Louis Robert and published in *Bulletin de Correspondance Hellénique* (1977). Just before I went to Athens, I was elected FSA – a Fellow of the Society of Antiquaries of London (26 March 1975).

To join the work at Oinoanda in 1975, I flew London-Istanbul-Antalya on 4 August. On the way to London by train on the 3rd a passenger attempted suicide in a toilet, and boarding of the plane to Antalya was delayed by an elderly lady who refused to mount the aircraft steps and was carried, screaming, aboard. If I had been superstitious, I might have regarded the incidents as unhappy auguries, and unhappiness was soon to come. As in 1974, I was accommodated in the school with four young surveyors – not the same ones, but equally competent and pleasant. After a few days Diskin Clay joined us. Alan Hall's hope, never realised, was that Diskin would attract American money. Jim Coulton of Edinburgh University, later of Oxford University, a delightful modest man and an authority on ancient architecture, was already doing valuable work during his first days on the site, and in future years he was to do much more, first at Oinoanda and later at neighbouring Balboura. I am one of those who benefited greatly from his expert advice. Diskin was cheerful and amusing company. When we went down to Ölü Deniz for a brief break from the work, he and I fantasised about discovering Epicurus' lost *Letter to Idomeneus*. Also, drinking wine under the Milky Way and wishing for female company, we coined one or two new Turkish verbs.

So far as the discovery of Diogenes was concerned, the season was disappointing. Although the total of forty-three new pieces sounds impressive, only two of them bore any complete lines of text. The tally would have been more impressive had it not been for an incident in the afternoon of Monday, 25 August. I was with the surveyors on what had come to be known as Martin's Hill on account of the large number of finds I had made there. They were plotting the position of Diogenes fragments on their plan and asked me about the block I was standing on. I had not realised that it was inscribed, but there, poking out of the soil, were several letters. In accordance with practice we believed to have been approved by the government representative, Sırrı Özenir – a practice followed by Alan Hall with regard to the inscriptions he had found, we immediately started to uncover the text, and were assisted in the task by Alan, who offered advice about how best to do it and, as revealed in a photograph taken by Diskin Clay, actually participated in the work. All was going well, until Sırrı bey came on the scene with a black look on his face and told Alan he wanted to speak to him. Alan returned and said to me: "Martin, this time you have gone too far. You must apologise to Sırrı bey. And you must cover up the stone". Well, of course I did apologise, while also pointing out that we thought we were working within agreed guidelines. In retrospect, it is a pity that we had not sought the representative's approval for exposing the stone, but clearly Alan did not think this necessary, and to my mind it was despicable that, despite his involvement in what we did, he made me the scapegoat for the whole incident. Six years were to pass before I was permitted to expose and copy the very well preserved and interesting text, fr. 19 (Plate 19), which is about wrong and right ways of representing the gods in literature and art: it is wrong to represent them carrying weapons or being angry; instead

> we ought to make statues of the gods genial and smiling, so that we may smile back at them rather than be afraid of them.

For the sake of the project, I bit my lip, but in May 1976 the matter was brought to the attention of the British Academy and the Council of BIAA not by me, but, entirely on his own initiative, by Terence Mitford. To cut a long story short, a committee was set up to investigate the complaint and

19) Oinoanda: Diogenes fr. 19 (NF 115), 47 x 64 x 35+ cm

others which were brought to its attention. The Honorary Secretary of the British Academy, Dr Neville Williams, was sympathetic and concerned, and I was strongly supported by my colleagues in the University College of North Wales. The committee declined my request that Alan Hall be replaced as director of the Oinoanda project and expressed the hope that I would be willing to continue my collaboration in it. Alan was now hoping that a large-scale excavation, directed by Richard P. Harper and funded from America, would take place, but that never happened. Instead, various experts, including Jim Coulton, studied Oinoanda's buildings and water supply. In the course of this work some more pieces of Diogenes' inscription were found in 1976, 1977, 1981, and 1983. Because of his opposition to my participation, I was only present in 1981, but published the finds made in the other years as well. Alan died on 12 December 1986, and several years were to pass before work at Oinoanda was resumed.

I was not quite back from the 1975 season at Oinoanda, when the shocking news came that Betty's twin brother, Harry, had been killed in a car crash on 29 August. He lived in Southampton with his wife, Mary. I liked him very much, but of course my loss was nothing compared with Betty's. The two of them were very close, and I think that some part of her died with him, that she lost some of her sparkle, and that this may have adversely affected our marriage. Anyhow, I felt that something was missing. All through the years of the Oinoanda project I had given illustrated lectures on it around the country and also in France and Ireland, and a lecture tour I made of north-east Britain in December 1975 took in Edinburgh, St Andrews, and Newcastle. The audiences were exceptionally appreciative, and I met a woman who attracted me physically and intellectually. No significant "relationship" developed, but Betty and I agreed to separate, and this happened for just four or five weeks in June-July 1976, when I went to live in Llandegfan on Anglesey. The address was 19 Mill Lodge. It was a surreal experience: the weather was scorching hot, and for several days I was so heavily involved with a conference on the ancient novel organised by Bryan Reardon that I spent little time in the house. Back at Penrhiw, where Betty had redecorated my study, we resumed married life, and I think we both felt that our marriage had been refreshed by the brief separation.

Lucinda's welfare and happiness, and our shared love for her, were major reasons for our decision to get back together. She was now seven, led a busy social life, and continued to do splendidly at school. Soon she would be receiving her tuition in Greek not from me, but from Mrs P. ("Pat") M. Jones, Classics teacher at Friars School, Bangor. In June she made her first communion and looked perfectly beautiful (Plate 20). Another consideration for me was family pressure: Barbara was upset about Betty's and my separation, and on 21 July her beloved brother Chris had died suddenly while on holiday in Connemara. It was put to me that she could not cope with two pieces of bad news.

In 1976 I was promoted Reader, and in 1977 to a Personal Chair. On 10 March 1977 I had been offered the Chair of Classics at the University of Wales, Aberystwyth. My referees included two eminent authorities on Ancient Philosophy – G.B. Kerferd of Manchester and W.K.C. Guthrie of Cambridge. One reason for Keith Guthrie's keen interest in my research was that early in

20) Penrhiw, Penrhosgarnedd: Lucinda attired for her first communion, 20 June 1976

his career he too had done epigraphical work in Turkey. Moreover, he had been my host when I gave a talk on Diogenes to the Cambridge University Ancient Philosophy Society ("B Club") in 1975. Because of Aberystwyth's remote location, the interview took place in the Great Western Royal Hotel at Paddington Station in London. I asked if I could have a few days to consider the offer, and this was agreed. There were good reasons for my hesitation. One was that there was no school for Lucinda in Aberystwyth as good as St Gerard's in Bangor. Another was the upheaval there would be for all three of us. Also, the existing staff in Aberystwyth, all known to me from colloquia at Gregynog, were teaching most of the things I liked teaching, so that I would either have had to push them about or taken on courses less congenial to me. But there was a further consideration: Bryan Reardon, Head of Classics at Bangor, had been offered a post at University of California at Irvine and had accepted it subject to his being able to obtain a visa. Knowing that Bryan was likely to go, Sir Charles Evans, Bangor's Principal, wanted me to stay and take Bryan's place. That is what happened, but there was a blissful academic year (1977–1978), when I had a chair but relatively few administrative duties. While I was considering Aberystwyth's offer, its Principal, Sir Goronwy Daniel, telephoned me twice to offer salary increases. That was flattering, but the salary was not the problem.

A day or two after the start of the Autumn Term 1977 Betty, Lucinda, and I flew to Istanbul. I had been invited by l'Institut français d'études anatoliennes d'Istanbul to participate in a colloquium on Ancient Lycia organised by the Institute's director, Henri Metzger, famous for his excavations at Xanthos and Letoon in Lycia. We stayed in the somewhat-decayed splendour of the Pera Palas Hotel, famous for, among other things, being where Agatha Christie, author of *Murder on the Orient Express*, had been a guest. I gave an illustrated talk on "Oenoanda and Its Philosophical Inscription" and, later, an unscheduled shorter paper on Georges Cousin at Oinoanda, revealing some of the results of my work in Athens in April 1975. The second paper caused much amusement with its descriptions of Cousin ardently proclaiming and reiterating his love of France as well as his love of knowledge, and giving a catalogue of his misfortunes – the difficulty of finding accommodation and food in İncealiler, being swindled by his host, falling from his horse, stomach trouble, fever, and sleeping out of doors because of weevils. "*La mauvaise chance me poursuit*" ("I am dogged by bad luck"), he wrote. Betty and Lucinda did not attend the colloquium, but they were invited to the colloquium dinner, at which Lucinda was seated in a place of honour, beside Madame Metzger. While in Istanbul I visited the German Archaeological Institute, and the three of us made some interesting visits and excursions together.

Mention of Henri Metzger and Xanthos prompts me to mention next an article of mine published in 1977 by the Turkish Historical Society. It is entitled "An Association Copy of Charles Fellows' 1838 Journal". Fellows was an explorer and antiquary best known for his travels in Asia Minor, especially Lycia. Xanthos was one of the ancient cities he discovered in 1838. In 1842 and 1844 he supervised the removal of the Xanthian marbles, including the sculptures of the Nereid Tomb and Harpy Tomb, to London and the British Museum. My article is about a copy, in my possession, of Fellows' journal of his first journey. It is the copy he gave to his sister, inscribing it:

> To Mrs. Pearson, London
> My dear Maria
> In the countries in which
> I have been rambling, it was well
> said "that in order to Educate a people,
> you must instruct Mothers." If by
> any information contained in this
> Journal, which was kept at your
> suggestion, I contribute to the infor-
> mation of your Children, I shall be
> amply rewarded, knowing that they
> will be happier, in having fewer
> prejudices, than had their Uncle,
> and your sincerely attached
> Brother,
> Charles Fellows
> 20 Russell Square
> May 1839

Inside the book is an autograph letter, dated April 1857 and written soon after his sister's death, to a Miss Oldham, who had looked after her during her last illness. He asks her to accept the book and others containing inscriptions. I ended the article by expressing the wish that the Xanthos sculptures be returned to Turkey – a wish consistent with my long-held belief that the Parthenon Marbles be returned to Greece.

Among those to whom I sent a copy of the article was Dame Freya Stark, of whom Harold Nicolson wrote:

> She has written the best travel books of her generation and her name will survive as an artist in prose.
>
> (Blurb on jacket of *Alexander's Path*)

I thought the article might interest her because she had written about Lycia, Xanthos, and Fellows in *The Lycian Shore* (1956) and *Alexander's Path* (1958). In the latter book she had described her visit to Oinoanda. She replied with a letter postmarked Asolo, 10.5.[19]78:

> *Via Canova,*
> *Asolo; Treviso.*
> *Tel. 52732*
>
> Dear Professor Smith,
> I am so grateful to you for your paper which interested me very much – especially the change of mind about the Turks, which is so natural for a traveller with a Greek background. I have just been staying with an old Armenian friend who is (not surprisingly) very anti-Turk; but I believe he would agree with me if he ever stayed long among them, for what one notices so much is their kindness. I have a perfectly unsupported suspicion that most of those terrible massacres were done by Kurds (mostly in Kurdish areas?) – but no evidence sufficient to hold a theory.
> Thank you so much
> yrs sincerely
> Freya Stark

In response (22 May 1978) I praised Dame Freya's books about her travels in Turkey and mentioned my work at Oinoanda and the BIAA project there. She replied (9 June [19]78):

> Dear Mr Smith
> I must tell you how much I envy your working in Oenoanda. It seemed

to me the place I would like best in all the world to work in – the beauty, the loneliness, the untouched country round it, and only its own history to be thought of in its ruins – I do wish you many good finds –

Yours very sincerely,

Freya Stark

In March 1978 Betty, Lucinda, and I visited Albania together. It was the first of five visits I made to that country between 1978 and 1985. They are described in the next chapter. A second holiday we took in 1978 was to Scotland – a second country in which traditional male dress includes a kilt! Much of the holiday, in early September, is a blur for me, because of a shocking piece of news received during it. We stayed on Mull, in the Western Isles Hotel. It was my first time on the island since the family holiday in 1952. On that occasion the weather did not allow a visit to Staffa and Fingal's Cave, but this time we were blessed with a calm sunny day and had several hours ashore – more hours than expected because a problem with the boat from Mull meant that it was very late collecting us. The next evening, we were having dinner when Betty was told there was a telephone call for her. She returned to the table visibly shaken. One of her younger brothers, Charlie, twin of her sister Terry, had been killed in a car crash in Australia, where he had been living with his wife, Gillian, and children. The awful news, coming almost exactly three years after the death, also in a car crash, of Betty's twin, Harry, not only spoiled our holiday, but also knocked the stuffing out of her. How right the Greek tragedians were to think that, when troubles come, they often come in clusters rather than singly!

In 1979 the three of us made a three-week trip to Italy and Sicily in the Dormobile, leaving Bangor on 18 August and returning on 8 September. It was Lucinda's first time in Italy and indeed in France and Switzerland as well. It was also Betty's first time in southern Italy and Sicily, which were the main focus of the trip. On the way to Italy, we stopped a night near Chamonix. Reluctantly, since I do not have a good head for heights, I agreed to accompany Lucinda on a chair lift to a glacier. We started off skimming low over a delightful meadow, but soon found ourselves suspended high above a deep valley, looking down on the tops of pine-trees. She rather enjoyed the fifteen-minute ride, but I was terrified and refused to accompany her on the descent, so that Betty, having seen off husband and daughter, saw only daughter return.

We did not loiter on the way to Sicily, the thinking being that, if we did loiter, we might never reach it. One of our main aims in Sicily was to go up Etna. We managed it on 25 August, when the weather was clear (which it had not been on the 24th), but too windy for the cable-car to operate. I was not unhappy about that, remembering that on my visit in 1961 the cable-car ride had been quite unnerving, not least when a Maltese lady screamed in terror. So from the cable-car station we took a four-wheel-drive bus, which was in fact the only way to get right to the top, because the upper section of the *funivia* had been destroyed by the lava. Very warmly dressed, we walked up to the central crater, taking care not to be blown into it by the fierce wind and coughing with the sulphurous fumes emanating from it. We were lucky to visit when we did, for seventeen days later, on 12 September, the volcano unexpectedly exploded, killing nine people and injuring twenty-three. Earlier in the year I had survived a severe natural disaster in Albania, and we were soon to avoid a terrible accident on the *autostrada* south of Naples, so there was much to be thankful for.

I noticed many changes in Sicily since my first visit. Thanks mainly to European Union money, the roads had been much improved, and the terrible poverty observed in 1961 had been much reduced. We visited the fine ancient sites of Segesta, Selinus, Agrigento, Syracuse, and Piazza Armerina, the last famous for the wonderful mosaics, including "the Bikini Girls", in the great imperial villa. We also made a fascinating visit to the small town of Piana degli Albanesi, the most important and influential Albanian community in Sicily, established in the fifteenth century. It is situated just south of Palermo. It was a thrill to speak Albanian with the locals in the Shqipëria [Albania] Bar. After leaving Sicily, we visited, in Calabria, two other Albanian communities, at San Demetrio Corone and Spezzano Albanese.

On the *autostrada* about thirty miles south of Salerno, we came upon the scene of a horrific accident. It involved two lorries and at least four cars. One of the lorries had gone down an embankment, and the other, laden with gravel, had crossed the central reservation. The cars were severely damaged. Both carriageways were blocked, so everything was at a standstill – except for a hearse that came through the traffic behind us, tooting its horn. A little earlier we had stopped for a cup of coffee, and we did wonder if that might have saved us from involvement in the accident. It was with great relief that we reached a seaside campsite at Vico Equense, near Sorrento.

If we had needed any discouragement from motoring to our next destinations – Pompeii, Herculaneum, and Naples – the accident would have provided it. But the obviously most sensible transport was the Circumvesuviana railway. The nearest station to our campsite was Seiano. Both Pompeii and Herculaneum were overwhelmed in the eruption of Vesuvius in AD 79. Pompeii is the better known and more visited of the two, but, whenever I offer a recommendation to intending visitors, I advise them not to skip Herculaneum. Pompeii is amazing, but it is also shadeless and can be exhausting and overcrowded with tourists. So it was on our visit, which occupied a whole morning (four and a half hours). Herculaneum, where we spent about two hours in the afternoon, is more compact and better preserved, attracts fewer tourists, and is less tiring. Our visit was prefatory to an important engagement we had in Naples the following day. Herculaneum is home to the Villa of the Papyri, discovered in 1752, and so called because it contained the charred remains of an extensive library of ancient texts, many of them by Epicurean authors, including Epicurus himself. The author most frequently represented in the surviving collection is Philodemus, an Epicurean of the first century BC. The texts are written in columns on papyrus scrolls. The state of their preservation varies enormously, and work on their decipherment, begun just after their discovery, continues.

Our engagement on 1 September was to meet Dr David Sedley at the Office of the Papyri (Officina dei Papiri) at the National Library (Biblioteca Nazionale) in the Palazzo Reale (Plate 21). David, a Fellow of Christ's College, Cambridge, was (and is) an expert on both ancient Greek philosophy and the Herculaneum papyri, and had edited and translated one of the most important texts, Epicurus' *On Nature*, Book 28, for his doctoral dissertation at University College, London, in 1974. He was now staying in Naples with his wife, Bev, and their young daughter. He was an excellent guide, showing us a selection of the papyri and other items, including the ingenious machine for unrolling papyri made in the 1750s by Father Antonio Piaggio. As an Epicurean scholar, I would have been interested in the Herculaneum papyri in any case, but my interest was all the greater because Diogenes' writings, although carved on stone, imitate papyrus texts in the way they are presented in columns, also in respect of rules about syllable-division and the methods of punctuation used.

After the guided tour of the Office of the Papyri, Bev and David kindly entertained us to lunch in the apartment in which they were staying, and then introduced us to its owner, Dr Francesca Longo Auricchio, another Epicurean scholar and papyrologist, destined to have a long and distinguished career in both capacities, and someone with whom I have been privileged to share scholarly collaboration and friendship for over four decades.

The day after seeing the papyri, a Sunday, we "did" Vesuvius (tame compared with Etna) and the fine Doric temples at Paestum. The next afternoon, we met up with the Sedleys again and went with them to visit Marcello Gigante and his wife. *Gigante* means "giant", which sometimes caused amusement because Marcello was a man of small stature. But in the story of Epicurean studies and especially the study of the philosophical papyri he was truly a giant figure. As well as doing much valuable research himself, he founded in 1969 the International Centre for the Study of the Herculaneum Papyri (Centro Internazionale per lo Studio dei Papiri Ercolanesi, abbreviated to CISPE), which still flourishes today, more than twenty years after his death. He established and directed a collection of Herculaneum texts under the title "La Scuola di Epicuro" ("The School of Epicurus"), and two of my editions of Diogenes were to be included in this important series as supplements. It was at our meeting on 3 September 1979 that he invited my collaboration. Henceforth Diogenes was unofficially considered an honorary citizen of Herculaneum.

21) Naples: Officina dei Papiri: David Sedley studying a Herculaneum papyrus, 1 September 1979

When I was a pupil at Shrewsbury School, several of my contemporaries who had arrived there with the best knowledge of Latin and Greek had been boarders at Packwood Haugh, a preparatory school for boys aged 8–13 at Ruyton-XI-Towns near Oswestry. Its headmaster was Edward Pease-Watkin. One afternoon in mid-July (1979), while waiting in Bangor to collect Lucinda after a school trip, I got into conversation with another parent, a lady who had a daughter in Lucinda's day-school and, she told me, a son at Packwood. Furthermore she told me that Pease-Watkin was still headmaster, that Latin and Greek were still prominent in the curriculum, and that the school was now co-educational. The matter was discussed with Betty and of course with Lucinda, who at the time sounded keen on going to Packwood, so within days it was fixed that she would start in September. Academically, she continued to be successful there, but she was far from entirely happy, mainly on account of the unacceptable way in which Pease-Watkin treated the children, or some of them, in his charge. Like my headmaster at The Downs, he was not averse to administering corporal punishment. In February 1981 she was awarded a Classics entrance exhibition at Wycombe Abbey School, High Wycombe – a remarkable achievement, given that she had studied Latin for only four terms. Later, the exhibition was to be converted into a sixth form scholarship.

Sometimes Lucinda accompanied me on walks and scrambles in Eryri (Snowdonia). My experience of the area went back to 1952, when, asked by Henry what I would like to do on my birthday, I said that I should like to climb the highest mountain in Wales that does not have a railway running up it. That meant Carnedd Llewelyn. On that occasion I climbed it with Colin. In the late 1970s and early 1980s Lucinda and I ascended it and most of the other peaks, including the highest, Yr Wyddfa (Snowdon). She was an excellent companion. Fortunately, she was away at school when, one winter's day, I nearly came to grief on Y Garn, a mountain just over 3,000 feet high in the Glyder range. Betty dropped me off at Llyn Ogwen, and my plan was to go over the top of Y Garn, descend to Llanberis, and telephone her when I was ready to be collected. I was well equipped except that I did not have an ice-axe. The summit of the mountain was hidden in mist, and I arrived at a snowfield which, very unwisely, I started to climb, believing that the summit was very near, and that I could easily manage the less steep descent on the other side. After a few minutes I stopped, realising that I was in a difficult and dangerous position. Then a miracle occurred. I heard the muffled sound of voices and clanking ice-axes coming down through the mist. It was a party of young climbers with an experienced leader. I asked the leader about conditions higher up. He told me that they were bad, and that I should go no further. I was happy to take his advice. He lent me his ice-axe and saw me safely off the snowfield and out of the mist. I was very lucky, and I learned a lesson which I never forgot. The next day I bought an ice-axe, and a few days later I climbed Y Garn in clear conditions.

In 1981 Betty and I separated again, this time permanently. I moved into 2 Bryn Gwyn, Upper Bangor, a ground-floor apartment in a late Victorian house owned by the University College. It suited me well, and I got on splendidly with two elderly ladies who lived in apartments above mine – Elsie Williams, a widow, on the first floor, and Mona Price, a spinster, on the second. They were pleased to have a man on the ground floor, and I was able to perform manly tasks for them, like carrying their heavy shopping upstairs. Lucinda had her own room, but was with me all too infrequently.

Betty petitioned for divorce on the ground of my "unreasonable behaviour", and the decree nisi was made absolute in January 1982. At one stage she suggested that I had wanted Lucinda in boarding school to clear the way for our divorce. That was definitely not the case. The decision to send her to Packwood was a joint one. But it is probably true that Lucinda's absence from home removed some of the glue that kept her parents together. What is certainly true is that the separation and divorce were painful for all of us. There was another woman in and out of my life for a while, but that relationship was tempestuous, the episodes of happiness during it were brief, and I felt much guilt. I regret my selfishness and folly, and more and worse folly was to follow.

In the early 1980s I expressed some of my feelings in several poems. One of them, "The Waterfall", was inspired by a bitterly-cold winter afternoon's walk to Aber Falls, between Bangor and Llanfairfechan, and finding the water

> crystallised –
> A pellucid tapestry suspended
> Silent lifeless brittle barren frigid,
> Forgetful of true destiny, devoid of true reason and purpose.

The frozen waterfall was beautiful, but somehow artificial, and the poem's last lines describe its return to its true nature:

I came to the waterfall again.
And as I watched, I saw the stream released from its bondage,
Purposeful and free, laughing and singing and dancing
As it ran on its fertile course to the goal in the summer sea.

Implicit is the hope that I too might be similarly released – released from emotional imprisonment, and, through love, find my better self.

Another poem, "The Day I Slept", expresses blindness to what might have been and the squandering of opportunities:

I didn't see the sunrise,
    I didn't see the dawn,
I didn't see the early dew
    Bejewelling the lawn.

I slept throughout the morning
    And all the afternoon;
I slept until the evening –
    And then awoke too soon;

For I awoke at sunset
    And saw the blood-red sky;
Yes, I awoke and saw the light –
    Only to watch it die.

After Bryan Reardon's departure from Bangor for California in 1978, I was first Acting Head, then, from 1979, Head of Department. Also in 1979, the Department's establishment was augmented by the appointment of John L. Moles as Lecturer. A native of Belfast, he moved to Bangor from a post at Queen's University, Belfast. He was extraordinarily brainy. He had published two books on chess tactics and been Ulster Champion and Irish Champion of chess. He displayed similar genius in his academic work, his main fields of interest being Greek and Roman Historiography and Biography, and Cynicism. He and I were colleagues at Bangor until 1987, then again at Durham from 1988.

John Moles had just turned thirty when he took up his post in Bangor. At the other end of the departmental age-scale was Constance ("Conny")

Bullock-Davies, recruited in 1977 to assist with the teaching of Latin and special-subject courses. At that time she was 77, and she was to continue teaching for another ten or eleven years. She was extraordinarily erudite across a wide range of languages and cultures. She took her first degree and doctorate in English, and began by lecturing in that. Later she supervised trainee teachers of Classics and Modern Languages. She learned Welsh after moving to Bangor. Her research interests were wide, but chiefly focused on Arthurian and medieval literature and society. She was always wonderful company, and her pupils loved her.

In both 1980 and 1981 I went out to Turkey. The 1980 visit (13–28 September) was a private one, not made as part of the BIAA project. I had not been to Oinoanda since 1975, and I wanted to see with my own eyes what, if anything, had changed, and I wanted to have discussions with Turkish friends and colleagues and with the authorities in Ankara. The day before my flight out, there was a military coup in Turkey, led by General Kenan Evren, and not for the first time I experienced curfews, road-blocks, and fuel-shortages. As often before, I rented a car in Izmir. I spent just a day at Oinoanda, accompanied and chaperoned by Melih Arslan of Fethiye Museum. I then made quite an extensive tour of other Lycian sites, prioritising ones which I had not visited in earlier years. Finally I drove to Ankara to report to BIAA on my travels and researches and to discuss the future of Oinoanda at the Directorate-General of Museums and Antiquities.

The 1981 visit (10 July-6 August) was "official" – the one during which I was permitted to record the piece of Diogenes' inscription that involved so much unpleasantness in 1975. The day I flew out, I had the strange experience of leaving the UK married and arriving in Turkey divorced. I went to Ankara and, at the request of Alan Hall, drove him, Jim Coulton, and Eric Stenton, an expert on fountains and aqueducts, in a long-wheel-base Land Rover to Fethiye, a distance of nearly 400 miles. Alan seemed to be more trusting and approving of me as a chauffeur than as an archaeological colleague! A few days later he reprimanded me for infringing on his territory by having discussed the history of Oinoanda in my paper to the Istanbul colloquium, and without his permission. In Fethiye we met up with our government representative, Edip Özgür, an agreeable man with whom I shared a mouse- and bat-infested room in the wretched apartment rented by BIAA in Seki. So far as possible, I avoided eating in the restaurant, with the result that, unlike Alan and Eric, I was not taken ill. As well as recording seven new pieces of Diogenes, I found an interesting sculpture buried in a wall. It is a votive relief portraying two rustic gods with axes over their shoulders (Plate 22). The stone is broken on the left, and parallel representations suggest that there were originally three gods, and that each was carved with a snake rising from the ground. In the broken panel only one snake is preserved. The relief was entrusted to Edip Özgür, in the expectation that he would deliver it to the Fethiye Museum and publish it, but it seems that he did neither of these things, and eventually Nicholas Milner and I published it and several other votive reliefs from Oinoanda (*Anatolian Studies*, 1994). The whereabouts of the piece are, to the best of my knowledge, unknown.

In 1981 Dr Pavel Oliva, a distinguished ancient historian in Prague, held a visiting fellowship at the University of Oxford. After he had arrived in England, I invited him to visit Bangor and give a lecture. He enthusiastically accepted the invitation, and his visit was a great success. Although I did not know it until after he arrived, he did not approve of his country's communist regime. He begged me, as he had begged colleagues in Oxford, to attend the 16th International Eirene Conference in Prague in 1982 (31 August-4 September). I agreed and gave an illustrated talk on Diogenes entitled

22) Oinoanda: votive relief portraying rustic gods,
31 x 27.5 x ca. 10.5 cm, July 1981

"Epicureanism in a Stoa". The title was meant to be a bit startling because the Stoics were, in Diogenes' time, the Epicureans' chief philosophical opponents, but Diogenes himself tells us that his inscription was in a stoa (colonnade). On the last evening of the conference there was a *Festabend* in a fine room at the Academy of Sciences. It was hosted by Pavel and his wife, and they used their control of the guest-list to exclude most of the participants from the USSR and its satellites. After the conference, I took the opportunity to do some sightseeing and make some excursions, including to the spa city of Karlovy Vary, which was as dead as a doornail at that time. In Prague I sometimes had as a guide a friend of the Czech wife of a Bangor colleague, Frank Bradbrook. Frank's wife, a fine scholar of Czech literature, was Bohuslava ("Bohunka") Bradbrook. She had fled Czechoslovakia in 1952 and was not free to return. Her Prague friend, Dr Maria Ullrichová, was very welcoming and an excellent guide. She had a forceful way of speaking English – for example: "You *will* admire this magnificent garden". One would not have dared not admire it! When we parted, after she had taken me to church, she gave me a quantity of poppy-seed for Bohunka. It was to make a special Czech cake, but I did wonder whether there might be a problem at Customs.

After seven years in print, my edition of the Loeb Classical Library Lucretius was doing so well that a reprint was required. It was said to be in the top ten of best sellers in the series. The reprint appeared in 1982, and the changes I made to the 1975 version were so numerous and substantial that it seemed reasonable to call it a "second edition". But the editor of the series, for reasons that were so unconvincing that I cannot remember them, declined to do that. E.J. Kenney, former Kennedy Professor of Latin at Cambridge University, called it "the best and most widely accessible of the editions available". I was amused to hear that it was chosen by former British Prime Minister Boris Johnson to be part of his holiday reading in Scotland in August 2020. If he actually read it, he seems not to have been influenced by Lucretius' condemnations of political ambition and power.

In 1982 and 1983 Lucinda and I holidayed on the Inner Hebridean island of Colonsay, situated between Mull and Jura, staying each time in the excellent hotel and being looked after by its proprietors, Kevin and Christa Byrne. We enjoyed it enormously as our repeat-visiting implies, and Lucinda returned with her young daughter, Ciara, in June 1994, on which occasion Kevin memorably sent me her bill with a remarkably high figure for "sundries", which turned out to be mainly her gin and tonics. With its small population and few vehicles, the island was beautifully quiet. We explored it and neighbouring Oronsay (or Oransay), joined to it at low tide by The Strand and home to a ruined priory, on foot and by bicycle. The scenery, including the distant views of Mull and Jura, was beautiful; there were remnants of Caledonian forest; and the wildlife was abundant. On one walk we were high up the highest hill and resting below a ridge when a Golden Eagle soared just above us and very close. On our first visit Lucinda sighted her gym mistress on the ferry from Oban, and she was relieved to find that she was not staying in the hotel. A delightful and most interesting couple who were staying in it on our second visit were John and Hilda Padel, and we greatly enjoyed their company. He was a distinguished psychiatrist and Shakespearian specialist, who told us that he had new ideas about the dating of the *Sonnets*. She, fittingly for one who was a granddaughter of Charles Darwin, was (among other things) a biologist and conservationist. Their daughter is the poet and scholar Ruth Padel.

In 1983 Lucinda also accompanied me on a more exotic trip – to Albania. That is described in the next chapter. In the same year I edited the last batch of new Diogenes texts found in Turkey during the work directed by Alan Hall. There were three of them, and remarkably and also alarmingly they had been used as building material in a village several kilometres from Oinoanda, apparently having been removed from an ancient site at the bottom of the hill in the 1960s. I say "alarmingly" because the three may not be the only ones to have been carried off, and others may have been destroyed.

One of the external lectures I was invited to give in 1983 was to the Hibernian Hellenists, a body formed of Classics staff in all the universities in the island of Ireland. The meeting I addressed was a colloquium in the hotel at Ballymascanlan, just south of the border with Northern Ireland. John Luce drove me up from Dublin. It was winter, and dark when we arrived, so we had no opportunity to go off for a walk and perhaps encounter, as colloquiasts had on past occasions, IRA soldiers on training exercises. Four years later a huge cache of IRA weapons was found nearby. The proceedings began with drinks, followed by a substantial dinner and more drinks. My illustrated talk was given after dinner in a comfortable lounge, and, when the lights were dimmed for the slides, many members of the audience struggled to stay awake, and at least one failed.

In 1984 the University College of North Wales celebrated the centenary of its foundation (Plate 23). The Department of Classics participated in the fund-raising effort and organised various activities, both work-related and social. One of my personal contributions was to give a demonstration of epigraphic squeeze-making in the main assembly hall, taking appropriate measures to avoid water-damage to the parquet floor. It aroused a good deal of interest. Just before the centenary, Sir Charles Evans resigned as Principal and was replaced by Eric Sunderland, Professor of Anthropology at Durham University. Sir Charles's retirement was welcomed by many. One big problem was that, although able to speak Welsh, he declined to do so. I discovered his hostility to the language when, as Head of Department, I sounded him out about the possibility of appointing a Welsh-speaking member of staff who could partner our existing Welsh-speaker (John Ellis Jones) in providing courses through the medium of Welsh. I was taken aback by the negativity of his response. Eric, a native of South Wales, was happy to speak Welsh and encourage Welsh-speaking. He was also a sociable man, who made a favourable impression both on staff and students in the College and on external bodies and individuals with whom he had dealings. I got to know him and his wife, Pat, quite well, partly because they were near neighbours of mine.

Soon after welcoming a new Principal from Durham, three of the Classics Department's four remaining full-time staff departed – *to* Durham! The future of such a small department could not be rosy at a time when money for universities was in short supply and mergers, closures, and early retirements, euphemistically called "rationalisation", were being discussed and encouraged. In this situation, on the brilliant initiative of Tony Woodman, Professor of Latin at Durham University, and with the support of his university and the University Grants Committee, three of us received an invitation to join the Durham University Department of Classics and Ancient History, which was twice the size of our department, but badly needed augmentation in order to remain viable. The invitation did not include John Ellis Jones, whose talents, including as a Welsh-speaker, were not needed in Durham. Moreover, as well as being a "local lad", he was the one nearest to retirement, and it was agreed that he would join the Bangor English Department and provide subsidiary courses in Classical Studies. The rest of us agreed to accept the invitation. The transfer was made in three stages: Gordon Cockburn went in 1986, John Moles in 1987, and I in 1988. It was fitting that the captain of the ship should have been the last to leave.

The above account gives no idea of the extraordinary amount of stress generated by the discussions and negotiations to do with the merger. Gordon

23) Bangor: Martin at centenary of UCNW, 1984

and John (Moles) had wives and their jobs to consider, and there was much opposition to the move in the University College. Most troublesome of all was the agreement that a substantial number of Classics books in Bangor be transferred to Durham as part of the deal: predictably, the Bangorians thought they were losing too many items, while the Durham folk complained that they were getting too few. Consequently I was attacked from both sides, and returned home from many a long meeting of the Arts Faculty Board or Senate feeling severely battered and bruised and badly in need of a stiff drink. My other, more healthy, solace was music. I was a frequent concert-goer and an especially ardent lover of baroque music with a growing collection of tapes and compact discs. I had valued friends in the Bangor Music Department, including its distinguished Head, William ("Will") Mathias, and his wife, Yvonne. I first got to know them when Lucinda and their daughter, Rhiannon, were in the same school and class until Lucinda went to boarding school. Will, famous for, among other things, the anthem he composed for the wedding of Prince Charles and Lady Diana Spencer in 1981, sometimes sought my advice when he was setting Latin to music, wanting to be sure of the quantities and stress carried by certain words.

In 1982–1984 I had been an external examiner in Classics at the University of Newcastle upon Tyne, and my links to it were to continue – first through Lucinda, who, while still in the sixth form at Wycombe Abbey, was offered a place to read Classics after being interviewed by the Professor of Latin, David West, on 21 June 1985. David was an unusual person as well as an unusually stimulating teacher, and as I left after accompanying Lucinda to the department, I saw him take her by the arm and prance and dance with her down the passage in apparent imitation of Eric Morecambe and Ernie Wise. After the interview with the colourful professor, we celebrated with the purchase of a colourful dress from Monsoon. She took a year out between school and university and started her first year at Newcastle in September 1987, a year before I moved to Durham. Throughout my years in Durham I was a frequent visitor to Newcastle – not only to see Lucinda, who continued to live there for a while after graduation, but also to participate in classical seminars.

In February 1986 I was invited by Nicholas Brett, Deputy Features Editor of *The Times*, to contribute pieces about recent classical research and discoveries to the paper's regular "Findings" column. The column ran for over two years and was thought to be very successful. My contributions certainly attracted a lot of interest and praise, and made me popular with those whose work I highlighted.

A very remarkable person with whom I started a warm friendship in 1987 was Beryl Bainbridge, novelist, artist, and eccentric. It arose out of her skilful and moving novel *Watson's Apology* (1984), based on the events of the life of the Revd John Selby Watson. I was working on an illustrated lecture about the editors and translators of Lucretius, and was including Watson, with whom I had some sympathy because we had three significant things in common: we were both graduates of Trinity College, Dublin; we both produced prose translations of Lucretius; and we both married Dublin women. To my credit, I did not do something else he went on to do. A man of varied scholarly interests and abilities, he had given sterling service as headmaster of the Proprietary Grammar School, Stockwell, in South London. But on 8 October 1871, when he was aged 66, he murdered his wife at home, fracturing her skull with a horse pistol. It was a Sunday, and the couple had attended church together in the morning. He was sentenced to death, but the sentence was commuted to penal servitude for life.

Beryl very kindly directed me to the house in St Martin's Road in which the Watsons had lived. This was important because the house, which I wanted to photograph, had changed its number. Later she invited me to her Victorian terraced house in Camden Town and introduced me to some of its occupants, including a wax model of Neville Chamberlain seated with an opened newspaper by a first-floor window, and Eric, a stuffed buffalo, the dominating presence in the hallway. She rescued Eric from a Liverpool cinema with the intention of sitting on his back while watching television, but the removers could not get him round the corner into the sitting room. Both Neville and Eric were efficient burglar-deterrents.

On 11 April 1989 I sent Beryl from Durham an article in *The Times* about the case of the Revd Shirley Freeman, aged 74, who, enraged because he had difficulty tuning in to *Desert Island Discs* on the radio, battered his wife to death and was put on probation. I wrote:

> Dear Beryl,
> No prize for guessing why I am sending you the enclosed item! The dreadful thought occurred to me that the reverend gentleman got the idea from your book, but a more likely explanation is perhaps that he is a reincarnation of "Wattie"!

Hope you are well.
Love and best wishes,
Martin

She replied:

Beryl Bainbridge,
42 Albert Street,
London NW1.
18.4.[19]89

Dear Martin,
Thank you very much for sending me the fascinating cutting, which I knew nothing about. How could he take two hours to batter her? It would be interesting to know who was on Desert Island Discs at the time. I shall certainly look into it when I have finished my new novel. I hope you are enjoying Durham – isn't there some row going on about them wanting to build a supermarket in the graveyard?

See you one day when we both get out from under.
Much love,
Beryl

For my last academic year in Bangor, 1987–1988, I was awarded a Leverhulme Research Fellowship to enable me to make progress towards the production of a major edition of all the known pieces of Diogenes' inscription with extensive introduction, Greek text, critical and explanatory notes, translation, and Greek index. I had not previously embarked on such a project, because the ongoing work at Oinoanda kept turning up new pieces of the inscription which would immediately have rendered a complete edition incomplete. But in the absence of any investigations since 1983 and with the death of Alan Hall in 1986, I judged that the time was ripe to make a start. At the same time I had not abandoned hope of seeing a renewal of activity at Oinoanda, and in 1987 I was elected to the Council of Management of BIAA and remained a member of it until 1994. The Leverhulme grant was paid to the University College to enable it to employ a full-time member of staff to do my teaching. Apart from the stressful "Romanian" matters described in Chapter 8, the year was happily devoted to research. As part of that research I visited Vienna in May 1988. The purpose was to examine the squeezes and notebooks of the Austrian epigraphists Rudolf Heberdey and Ernst Kalinka, who copied the pieces of Diogenes' inscription in 1895. The work I did in the rooms of the Asia Minor Commission of the Austrian Academy of Sciences was similar to what I did in the French School of Athens in 1975, and it was equally successful. An unexpected bonus was the discovery of a manuscript of the distinguished writer on Greek philosophy Theodor Gomperz, communicating to Heberdey and Kalinka his suggestions about Diogenes.

I gave twenty-five years of service to the University College of North Wales and, when I left, did not receive even a word of thanks from my employer. My memories of those years are mixed, but one thing I treasure are the friendships I made during my time there. Several of these survive to this day, for example those with Chris Collard, Professor of Classics in the sister college at Swansea, who retired to live in Oxford, with former students Jill Blurton (now Ayre) and Rosalind Lythgoe (now Smith), with former Classics secretary Nerys Hague, and with near neighbours of mine in the 1980s – Diane and Gordon Cockburn, Nancy and Tony Brown, and Sally Lovecy. Sally was kindly helping me sweep the floor of 2 Bryn Gwyn on my last evening, 30 August 1988, when something strange and disturbing happened. The flat was empty apart from my bed, which the removers were to collect early next morning. The weather was wild and windy. We had just about finished when the telephone rang, sounding rather eerie in the bare room. It was Conny Bullock-Davies to say that she had fallen and could not get up. So we hastened round to her flat, a few hundred yards away. She and I had developed an affectionate friendship in the last decade, and she much regretted that I was leaving. Whether her fall was in any way linked to my imminent departure I shall never know, but it was an unhappy end to my time in Bangor. She lived for another six months, and I did see her again in a care-home, but, after the ambulance came for her that stormy evening, she was never able to return home.

8

Communist Albania and Romania (1978–1988)

During my schooldays at The Downs, I developed, in addition to a passion for remote Scottish islands, an interest in remote territories. I remember, when I was twelve, stumping the master who was in charge of a current affairs class by putting a question about Tannu Tuva. The poor man had to admit that he had never heard of it. But the main focus of my remote-territorial interests at this stage was Tibet – hence my request for a book about it as a leaving present.

Sometime when I was in my teens Albania came to my attention, possibly when I heard or read it described as a "European Tibet". For years, I had no access to up-to-date information about the country, but, as I mentioned in Chapter 5, on my visit to Budapest in 1960 I bought a copy of the illustrated magazine *L'Albanie nouvelle*, produced and printed in Tiranë. I read reports of all sorts of events, political, social, cultural, and sporting, which were eye-openers, even allowing for significant elements of rose-tinted presentation. Readers were invited to enter a prize competition on the subject *Connaissez-vous la République Populaire d'Albanie?*. I answered the questions to the best of my ability, but I was at a disadvantage compared with those who were regular readers of the magazine and had easy access to other sources of information. The list of prize-winners was dominated by entrants from the USSR and other communist countries, but Martin Smith (Irlande) was placed fifth equal and won a free subscription to the magazine. I kept the letter of congratulation, which was later to prove useful.

My interest in Albania continued after university, its main attractions for me being its remoteness, its spectacular scenery, its remarkable history, its attraction for nineteenth-century travellers, and not least its important archaeological sites hardly ever visited by foreigners since before the Second

World War. Curiosity about the blend of communism and nationalism created by its leader, Enver Hoxha, was another consideration, as was the country's banning of religious practices and private car ownership. The absence of diplomatic relations with the United Kingdom added to the intrigue. Had my interest in Oinoanda not been greater, I would probably have visited Albania earlier than I did. Individual tourism by British citizens was not permitted, but one British travel agent, Regent Holidays of Bristol, offered guided tours, and I booked one for Betty, Lucinda, and myself for the last week in March 1978.

Our group of just over twenty was of varied composition. It included a Classics teacher at a London girls' school, a Canadian journalist disguised as a businessman, a Dutchman called Egbertus who seemed keen to be accepted by the Albanians as a political refugee and tried to hide in the hotel when it was to time to go to the airport for departure, and a man who made an anti-atheist scene in the Atheist Museum in Shkodër and was asked to go and sit in the coach. Lucinda, aged nine, was by far the youngest.

We flew to Albania from Belgrade with Pan-Adria, landing at Rinas Airport in heavy rain. An impressive thunderstorm with a gusty wind developed during the drive to the Hotel Adriatik near the coastal city of Durrës, wrecking the Party of Labour propaganda display in the hotel grounds. The weather was variable all week, but by no means a wash-out. Two places we visited early on were important in antiquity. Both were established as Greek colonies in the late seventh and early sixth centuries BC and came under Roman rule in the third and second centuries BC. One was Durrës, which the Greeks called Epidamnos and the Romans Dyrrhachium. It was a busy port and one of the two western starting-points of the Via Egnatia, the road which ran all the way to Byzantium or Constantinople. The city had an amphitheatre, which had disappeared under later structures and been only partly excavated. The other important place, and second starting-point of the Via Egnatia, was Apollonia, situated on a hill about five miles inland and called by Cicero "a great and impressive city" (*magnam urbem et gravem*) – great not only for commerce, but also for culture and learning.

Near the beginning of our stay, I gave our Albturist guide, Luljeta Zhara, the letter about the prize I had won back in 1960, information about my academic status, and a letter addressed to the President of the Albanian Academy of Sciences, Professor Aleks Buda. She told me that these items had been well received, but I was not prepared for the pleasant surprises that awaited me when our party arrived on a day trip to Tiranë on 29 March. I was detached from the group and taken to what was then the city's best hotel, the Dajti (rhyming with "mighty"). Awaiting me there was Frano Prendi, Director of the prehistory section of the Archaeological Museum. A friendly man with a good sense of humour, he spoke French and Italian, but not English. I was to see much of him on future visits. On this occasion he took me first to the National Library, where the Librarian, Marika Vogli, had kindly arranged in her office a display of Albanian translations of Greek and Latin Classics, most of them published under the Communist regime, i.e. since 1944. We then moved on first to the Archaeological Museum, telling the story of Albanian archaeology from the stone age to the medieval period, then the New Albania Exhibition and Ethnographic Museum. Finally, we drove to the Academy of Sciences, to which it was insisted Betty and Lucinda accompany us. There we met Aleks Buda, an extremely pleasant man, erudite and multilingual. He was born in Elbasan, but brought up mainly in Italy and Austria. As well as speaking all the principal European languages, he had a thorough knowledge of Latin, which I knew he had used to good effect when addressing participants in the First Congress of Illyrian Studies in Tiranë in 1972. On one occasion Latin came in handy during my conversation with him. He kindly presented me with four books and even had a book for Lucinda. I had already given two books to the National Library, and I promised to send more to the Academy and Frano Prendi. We had a wide-ranging conversation about Albania's archaeology and history and its relations (or lack of them) with the UK, punctuated with sips of coffee and toasts in Albanian cognac. We agreed on the importance of friendly relations between scholars of different countries, and this thinking was repeated on each of my later visits.

Rejoining the tourist group, Betty, Lucinda, and I visited in the afternoon Krujë, famous for its connections with Albania's national hero, Skanderbeg, who in 1443 deserted from the Turkish army and cunningly took possession of the fortress-town by presenting its Turkish governor with a forged decree, purporting to have been issued by the Sultan, that he should hand over the governorship to Skanderbeg, who for 25 years led a revolt against the Turks. About 350 years later, Ali Pasha of Tepelenë used the same forged-decree technique to get possession of Ioannina in northwest Greece.

Other places on our tour included Shkodër in the far north, Elbasan, Lake Ohrit (Ochrid), Korçë, and Berat. On a second visit to Tiranë we attended a lively performance by the State Song and Dance Ensemble. Along with more traditional pieces were songs like "The Congress Delegate", "The

New Constitution", "Long Live Our Party, Like Our Mountains", and "Hello, Enver Hoxha". No longer did the repertoire include, as it did in earlier years, songs in praise of Mao Tse-tung and the Chinese Communist Party. My first visit to Albania coincided with the rift with China, just as my first contact with it (to do with the magazine prize) nearly coincided with its rift with the USSR. I am not suggesting that I had anything to do with these momentous schisms! A remarkable undertaking in the late 1970s was the construction of many tens of thousands of bunkers all over Albania, for the defence of the country in the event of an invasion.

During the return flight to London Heathrow, some members of the party composed and circulated among themselves humorous comments on the trip. My offering named one of our hotel waitresses:

> A man in the Hotel Adriatik
> Had tendencies positively Bacchic:
> He took Aphrodite
> To lunch in the Dajti –
> A pleasure absolutely ecstatic!

The composition of a limerick, however uninspired, is an appropriate nod to the humourist and artist Edward Lear, who first travelled in Albania in the autumn of 1848. Sometimes he encountered hostility from Muslims when he was drawing. They called him "Shaitan" ("Devil") and even pelted him with stones.

My second visit to Albania was less satisfactory than the first. I had hoped that the warm reception I had received from Aleks Buda might signal a readiness to allow me to visit independently, but that did not yet happen, and once again I joined a Regent Holidays group – again for a week, but in mid-April and without my family. This time the flight was to Dubrovnik via Zagreb, with onward travel to Shkodër by coach. The outward overland journey was chaotic, but nothing compared with the journey back. We arrived in Shkodër in the early evening of Saturday, 14 April. It was disappointing to learn that the itinerary would be almost identical to that in 1978, and there would again be no visit to the south, where I particularly wanted to see the ruins of Butrint (Buthrotum).

Sunday, 15 April was Easter Day – no longer publicly celebrated in Shkodër, despite it having been a stronghold of the Roman Catholic Church.

Albania had recently declared itself an atheist state. Before breakfast in the hotel, I took a walk through part of the old city. Just before 7.20 I looked at my watch and reckoned I ought to retrace my steps. At that moment I heard a terrific noise, like that of a jet engine or a very heavy lorry passing nearby. Then came the violent shaking. I was close to old houses and moved quickly to avoid falling masonry and tiles. Big cracks opened up in walls, and there was frantic shouting. People ran out of houses, some clad in pyjamas or underwear. I was glad to have been out of doors when the earthquake occurred. My room was on the fourth floor of the hotel, and the tremors had been strong enough to throw people out of their beds as well as to damage walls, ceilings, and plumbing. The earthquake also severely affected parts of Montenegro, and the international media focused on the loss of life and damage there. The fatalities and destruction in Northern Albania were largely ignored, so that, when I returned home, my family had no idea that I had experienced an earthquake. In Albania at least 45 died, several hundred were injured, and several thousand buildings were destroyed or badly damaged. The Atheist Museum had to close its doors to visitors, and one wonders how many of Shkodër's Catholics regarded the Easter earthquake as a sign of divine displeasure at the banning of religious practices.

On the way through the city after breakfast, I noticed crowds at a hospital and many people congregated in parks and gardens. The damage was most apparent along the main road south to Lezhë. Some buildings were totally destroyed, and in places the road was strewn with boulders wrenched from the hillside above it. A few miles south of Shkodër we encountered a convoy of cars taking senior government ministers north to view and assess the disaster. One of them was the Prime Minister, Mehmet Shehu, still Hoxha's closest associate, but destined to fall out with him and die by suicide or assassination (18 December 1981). Later in the day of the earthquake it was promised that everything would be repaired or rebuilt at the expense of the State within six months, by 1 October 1979. The promise was fulfilled. After I returned home, I wrote an account of the earthquake and its aftermath for a meeting of the Albanian Society in London. For some reason I was not present to read it myself, but I had the honour of having it read for me by the Welsh actor Philip Madoc, who was much interested in Albania. By the way, I used to offer an illustrated lecture entitled "Albania, Wales of the Balkans". Amusingly, when I entered Albania in 1979, the copies of a Welsh dictionary and grammar which were among the books I had brought as gifts to the National Library were briefly confiscated by Customs. It had not occurred to me that either could be regarded as subversive.

The earthquake was followed, as earthquakes often are, by days of heavy rain. On the first day we visited the Naim Frashëri School in Elbasan. When we were invited into an English class, an eleven year old boy recited from memory a lengthy piece in praise of new Albania and in condemnation of imperialism and Khruschevite revisionism. It was a *tour de force*, although not a very entertaining one, and the teacher had difficulty getting the boy to stop. When she eventually succeeded, I walked round the classroom and found the children were reading *The Rooster and the Fox*. The journey back through Montenegro on 21 April was nightmarish. In places the main road was impassable on account of subsidence and landslips. Detours were mountainous, rough, narrow, and twisty – not at all suitable for our coach. The plan had been to reach Trebinje by early evening for dinner and an overnight stay, but this had to be abandoned. Instead, we were delivered to Dubrovnik Airport just before 2 a.m. and spent the night – the two or three hours that remained of it – in an unheated room on a bare floor.

Although I did not return to Albania for over two years, I did visit, in company with Betty and Lucinda, Albanian communities in Sicily and Southern Italy in the summer of 1979, as described in Chapter 7. I did not fancy another Regent Holidays package, with its limited and inflexible itinerary, and I was pleased when in 1981 I received an invitation from the Albanian Academy of Sciences to make a two-week visit. I flew to Tiranë with the Romanian airline Tarom on 23 September after picking up my visa at the Albanian Embassy in Rome. On arrival at Rinas Airport, I was greeted by Frano Prendi like an old friend. He was my companion and guide for the first week or so before handing me over to another delightful man, Seit Mansaku, a linguist who had studied Latin. The extensive tours which I made by car as a guest of the Academy or the (Albanian) Committee for Cultural Relations with Foreign Countries in 1981, 1983 (with Lucinda), and 1985, gave me rare access to archaeological and historical sites all round the country, not only touristic ones like Butrint (Plate 24), but also ones in "sensitive" locations, like the village of Lin, near Pogradec, which was in a frontier zone and required a special permit. I was able to make them better known through my lectures, and, above all, my acquaintance with them and relevant excavation reports on them in Albanian enabled me to revise and sometimes rewrite the first detailed account of recent archaeological work to appear anywhere outside Albania.

Above L: 24) Butrint, Albania: theatre
25) Ksamil, Albania: Lucinda swimming with Eduard Sulo in Corfu Channel, 2 September 1983

The delivery and publication of the account, by the Albanian archaeologist Zhaneta Andrea, was negotiated, with the epistolary support of Professor Eric Handley, Foreign Secretary of the British Academy, during my visit to Tiranë in 1983. The account was to be in English, but the version I received had been inaccurately translated from Albanian into French by someone who clearly knew nothing about archaeology and thought it a good idea even to translate titles of Albanian books and journals. Getting the piece into good order was a long and laborious task. Entitled "Archaeology in Albania, 1973–83", it appeared in *Archaeological Reports 1983–1984*, published in 1984 by the Society for the Promotion of Hellenic Studies and the British School at Athens. It was gratifying to hear afterwards that it had been hugely appreciated, not least by Greek archaeologists who previously knew little about recent developments inside a neighbouring country.

Another item that appeared in 1984 was my 30-page booklet *Classics in Albania*, published by the Albanian Society, a non-political organisation with the declared aims of disseminating factual information about Albania and promoting friendship between the British and Albanian peoples. It described the study of Ancient Greek and Latin in Albania, before providing a bibliography of classical publications for Albanian readers. I received much assistance from the National Library in Tiranë and several Albanian scholars. Most of the translations had been made in the post-war period, and sometimes one could detect or suspect that priority had been given to works of "progressive" content, such as Lucretius' *On the Nature of Things*, or local interest, such as Plautus's comedy *Menaechmi*, set in Epidamnos (Durrës).

In 1980 I had been elected Chairman of the newly-formed Campaign for Diplomatic Relations with Albania (CDRA). It attracted the support of several members of both Houses of Parliament and many others, ranging from members of the Revolutionary Communist Party of Britain (Marxist-Leninist) to the Glasgow-based pop and rock band that had chosen to call itself "Albania". The organisation was successful in obtaining publicity in the media and in making the British Government answer questions. The most memorable incident for me was a demonstration outside the Bank of England. The location was chosen because at the centre of Albania's quarrel with the UK was the refusal of the British to return with interest the quantity of Albanian gold held in the vaults of the Bank until such time as Albania should pay compensation for the so-called "Corfu Channel Incident" on 22 October 1946, when British warships entered Albanian territorial waters without permission or notification and two of the vessels struck mines. There was severe damage, and 44 lives were lost. On 2 September 1983 there was a completely peaceful British entry into the same coastal waters, when Lucinda swam out into the Channel with our Albanian companion (Plate 25). Among other unusual experiences she had during the trip was spending a morning as a pupil at the Secondary School for Foreign Languages in Tiranë.

A.L. ("Bert") Lloyd, the distinguished authority on folk music, who had made a collection of Albanian folk music in or about 1966, was President of the Albanian Society until his death on 29 September 1982. I was elected his successor. Although the position brought some duties, including attendance at meetings in London, the person who did almost all the work for the Society, whose Secretary he had been since 1960, was W.B. ("Bill") Bland. The Society's official address was that of his home in Ilford. On one occasion a local newspaper printed a photograph of the house and humorously suggested that it was the nearest thing to an Albanian Embassy in Britain. A day or two later Bill had a visit from an inspector from the local council, sternly warning him that, by allowing his home to be used for diplomatic purposes, he was in breach of planning regulations and liable to prosecution.

On one occasion, when Frano Prendi and I stopped for the night during a tour of sites in the east of the country in 1981, I had an attack of sickness and fever. When I was still unwell the next morning, a doctor was called. She arrived, accompanied by a nurse, within minutes and advised me to rest for another 24 hours. The next day, I was much improved, but Frano had an attack of arthritis. Instead of summoning the doctor again, he gratefully accepted my offer of paracetamol.

A few days later, I made my first visit to Tepelenë, where Ali Pasha was visited in 1809 by Byron and John Cam Hobhouse. There had been a bust of Byron in the town centre, but I was told that it had been removed for repairs. Undaunted, I stood in the street and, to the puzzlement of passers-by, declaimed lines from *Childe Harold's Pilgrimage*, including:

> And onwards did his further journey take
> To greet Albania's chief, whose dread command
> Is lawless law; for with a bloody hand
> He sways a nation, turbulent and bold.

In 1983 the bust was still missing, and I do not know if it was ever put back.

A more orthodox performance I gave was at the Academy of Sciences in October 1981 – an illustrated talk on "The Epicurean Inscription of Diogenes of Oinoanda". I started by recalling that Karl Marx was much interested in Epicureanism: in April 1841 he received the degree of Doctor of Philosophy from the University of Jena for a masterly dissertation on the differences between the philosophies of Democritus and Epicurus. No doubt he would have been interested in Diogenes too, but he died in 1883, the year before the first pieces of the inscription were found and nine years before any were published.

Another talk I gave was a brief one to the Second Congress of Illyrian Studies in Tiranë on 23 September 1985. It had not been scheduled and caused a bit of a stir, not least a few rows back in the auditorium, where Enver Hoxha's widow, Nexhmije, was seated. I am guessing she was asking her companions who on earth this speaker was who began in Albanian, continued in English, and made brief reference to her husband. He had died on 11 April. I did not directly eulogise him or even mention his death, but it was well known that he had taken a close interest in archaeology and history and made sure that excavations and research were properly funded. The bulk of my address was devoted to nineteenth- and early twentieth-century British travellers in Albania, including William Martin Leake, Byron and Hobhouse, Lear, and Edith Durham.

I remained President of the Albanian Society until 1991, but my visit to Albania in 1985 was my last.

***

Another Balkan country that appealed to me was Romania – another beautiful country, with a capital city often compared to Paris, a country inhabited by a people who were predominantly of the Orthodox faith but spoke a language derived from Latin. I first visited it for a week in the spring of 1985 (30 March–6 April). It had been arranged that I would give a lecture to the Society of Classical Studies (Societatea de Studii Clasice) in the Faculty of Letters in the University of Bucharest on 4 April. I also wanted to explore the state of relations between Nicolae Ceauşescu's Romania and Enver Hoxha's Albania, and to that end I had an appointment at the Albanian Embassy in Bucharest on 1 April for discussions over lunch with the ambassador, Zoi Toska, and the second secretary, Zoi Shahini. Just ten days later Hoxha was dead.

The only Romanian classicist whom I had previously met was Manuela Maria Tecuşan. The meeting had been a very brief one, on 1 September 1982, when she and I read short papers to the same session of the Eirene Conference in Prague. After her paper, we had a brief conversation and exchanged addresses, enabling us to send one another publications and Christmas cards. She spoke excellent English, and for that reason she was reckoned to be the most suitable person to take me sightseeing during my time in Bucharest. When she called at the Hotel Bucureşti on my first evening to introduce herself, I had no idea whether she was a supporter of the regime or not. While we were chatting over a beer in the hotel bar, I formed the impression that she was a strong supporter, but, when she collected me the next morning and we were out of doors, she hastened to tell me that all her remarks in the hotel had been made on the assumption that they would be picked up by informers. They were ubiquitous, and the main hotels were bugged.

Manuela was aged 28, nearly 29, at the time of our meeting in Bucharest. She was an only child, living with her parents, Constantin, a retired mathematics teacher, and Constanţa, a biochemist employed in a laboratory. Her father always spoke French to her, which meant that she was as fluent in that as in English. She herself was a peripatetic Classics teacher, working in seven schools. She also taught Greek in the University, mainly to philosophers, and this was what she found most satisfying. She was occupied with research, considering sympotic passages in Plato, including in his *Laws*. She had received encouragement and assistance from three British scholars – Oswyn Murray and Jonathan Barnes in Oxford, and Trevor Saunders in Newcastle.

During my visit she gave me her latest draft on the subject to pass to Oswyn for his comments. I did this of course. She had been invited to read a paper on symposia to a colloquium in Oxford in 1984, but, although the invitation was backed by the British Academy with a guarantee of funds, the Romanian authorities did not give permission until it was too late – a frequent tactic of theirs.

I was happy to have Manuela's company as we visited the magnificent Athenaeum – first to admire the architecture, later to hear a delightful baroque concert consisting of five sonatas for organ and violin – two by Bach, three by Handel, played by Nicolae Licareţ (organ) and Mihaela Martin (violin). We also visited museums and art galleries, and saw the vandalism being inflicted on Bucharest by Ceauşescu, who had ordered the demolition of a large area of the nineteenth-century city with its churches to make way for his megalomaniac and ugly developments, including the Victory of Socialism Boulevard. Manuela also took me to a supermarket with many empty shelves and nothing but bones for sale on the meat counters. She introduced me to academic friends, including the archaeologist and historian Alexandru Avram, and I was to meet more before and after the meeting I addressed. She also introduced me to her uncle Petru Creţia, a leading intellectual and dissident. Formerly Professor of Greek in the University, he was now a versatile researcher, editor-in-chief of the Romania Plato series and translator of, among others, Virginia Woolf and T.S. Eliot. On my last evening he entertained Manuela and me to dinner at the Writers' Union, where some of our fellow-diners were more than a little inebriated: one man fell off his chair, and another had a lively argument with a waitress, who, when he made a move towards her, grabbed his cap, swatted him with it, and pushed it down on his head so far that his eyes were covered. Her spirited response provoked much merriment and loud applause.

Before we parted, I used my sterling travellers' cheques to buy Manuela and her family a variety of superior items unavailable in ordinary shops but stocked by shops in the main hotels where payment had to be made in a convertible foreign currency – foodstuffs, including Sibiu salami, also Austrian coffee, Scotch whisky, perfume, and Benson & Hedges cigarettes. I also gave her, to be opened after my departure, a purse containing some Romanian currency to be used to buy flowers for her approaching birthday. She was a smoker, and I could understand why. With so little in the way of good food available, and above all with the restrictions imposed by the regime and the constant worries about informers and the secret police, cigarettes were a help to her. She and Petru kindly gave me some presents to take home.

Something I was surprised to hear from Manuela was that, despite her loathing of Ceauşescu and her contempt for his philistine and corrupt regime, she was a member of the Romanian Communist Party. Unlike in most so-called Communist countries, where membership of the Party meant you were part of a privileged élite, the Romanian Party had millions of members, and Manuela would not have been allowed to be a schoolteacher without being one. I had no idea whether I would ever see her again, but during the following twelve months we corresponded much more frequently than we had done before my visit, consolidating and deepening what I perceived to be an affectionate friendship. As the relationship developed, I received much encouragement from Judith Higgens (later Stancomb) – Cambridge graduate, expert on Thomas Lovell Beddoes, and Secretary in the Department of Classical Archaeology at University College, London. She had done archaeological work in Romania and gave much time to helping Romanian friends, including dissidents.

The next spring I returned to Bucharest (6–13 April 1986). This time I was booked into the Hotel Capitol. On 9 April I revisited the Albanian Embassy and had more interesting conversations with the Ambassador and Second Secretary. I should love to know what the Romanian authorities thought of my Albanian connections, if indeed they noticed them. But the main purpose of my visit was to see Manuela (Plate 26). The pattern of our days was similar to that on my first visit – viewing places of historical and cultural interest, seeing more areas being bulldozed on the orders of Ceauşescu, walking and sitting in parks, discussing Plato and Manuela's research, and on Wednesday, 9 April, returning to the Athenaeum, this time to hear piano pieces by Mozart, Beethoven, and Schumann. My last diary entry for the Wednesday reads:

> This evening, for the first time, we properly declared our love for one another.

Although our feelings for one another had warmed – at least mine for her had – we encountered more unpleasantness than in 1985. Informers in restaurants made us feel uncomfortable, and when on our last evening we sat down in a park after dinner, we were approached by two policemen with torches. They demanded our identity documents and wanted to take Manuela to a police

26) Bucharest: Manuela, April 1986

station without me. I refused to let them do that and asked what the problem was. The problem, they told her, was that being in the company of a foreigner is discouraged, and that she was behaving no better than the Romanian women who worked as prostitutes at the Hotel Bucureşti. To get rid of them, she paid them a bribe of 200 *lei*. They had demanded 500. On several other occasions, we had been followed, and once, as we sat on the grass in a park, we were photographed by a man who, as soon as I got up to challenge him, ran off.

A day or two earlier, Manuela gave me a special item, devised to enable us to communicate confidential information. All our letters would be opened and read, and any telephone conversations listened to. The "special item" was a sheet of paper – blank, except that in places there were empty rectangles. She had an identical sheet, and, when writing to her, I was to place mine under a thin sheet of paper of the same size and write the sensitive words inside the rectangles, incorporating them in a letter that would seem quite ordinary to the censor. Doing this was rather fun, with the added satisfaction of deceiving the rogues in the Romanian security service.

My relationship with Manuela was for me more than a romantic dream. A big part of it was our shared interest in Greek and Roman thought and in culture generally. But I went home to Bangor on 13 April very much aware that we were in a difficult position. It would be too dangerous for her to carry on meeting me in the way that she had done hitherto. One solution was for us to stop meeting, in which case she would retain her membership of the Communist Party and her employment as a teacher and be spared most of the harassment by the authorities. The other was for us to get married. As if I did not have enough to think about with regard to our future, I had two other problems immediately after my return. On 14 April I underwent an operation on my right eye, for recurrent corneal erosion, at Ysbyty Gwynedd (Gwynedd Hospital), and the same day I had the first of a series of severe nosebleeds – so severe that I was seen in hospital as an out-patient on 17 April and admitted as an in-patient for two days (18–20 April). On 16 April, after consulting Lucinda, I proposed marriage to Manuela by telephone, and my proposal was unhesitatingly accepted.

We knew that the process of getting permission for the marriage and for Manuela to leave Romania (the two events had to be in that order) would be long drawn out. We may not have realised how stressful it would be. I was buoyed up by the thought of *omnia vincit amor* ("love conquers everything"), and I flew to Bucharest for another week-long visit on 10 May 1986, staying, as in April, at the Hotel Capitol. Manuela met me at the airport and, on arrival at the hotel, told the reception staff that we were engaged, whereupon she was allowed for the first time to accompany me to my room for a few minutes. There I re-proposed to her and placed on her finger the engagement ring which I had bought in Wartski's the jewellers in Llandudno a few days before. The firm had been founded by a member of the family from whom I had bought Derwen Deg in 1966. Because my eyesight was still troublesome, and because I knew her good taste, I asked Jean Lindsay, the wife of an academic colleague, to accompany me to the shop and help me choose. The day after my arrival in Bucharest was a Sunday, and a very happy day it was for me and, I hoped, Manuela. The remaining days were predominantly happy too, but much occupied with business matters and sometimes anxious. On the Monday morning I went to the British Embassy about my intention to marry a Romanian citizen. The Vice-Consul, Steve Seaman, was exceptionally helpful. I returned there in the afternoon and twice on the Friday. Meanwhile Manuela's mother made progress in her dealings with the Notary Public. On the Tuesday, she, Manuela, and I negotiated business at the State Notary's office in the Ministry of Justice. It was a long and tiring business, and the day began and ended unhappily for me because Manuela twice expressed disapproval of my interest in Albanian affairs. This was the first time either of us had made any significant criticism of the other, and, although she became more friendly before we parted at the end of the day, I returned to my hotel feeling deeply upset. In the following days I tried to convince myself that it was a minor glitch, caused by a misunderstanding and perhaps aggravated by her tiredness and anxiety, but, in retrospect, it was probably the beginning of difficulties between us.

On the Wednesday afternoon we visited the office of the State Council, where we presented various documents and Manuela filled up, for both of us, two sets of forms, the second, the longer one, being an appeal to "Comrade President". It was a relief when we heard from the lady on duty that all was well and received the all-important receipt of our marriage application. The news lifted our spirits, and we enjoyed a celebratory dinner, after which I escorted Manuela to the area in which she now had a room of her own – a room I never actually saw.

The cloud cast by Manuela's disapproval of my interest in Albania – an interest about which she had known for over a year – was not the only worry during my post-engagement visit. On 26 April 1986, my birthday, three days after her birthday, and ten days after she and I became engaged, there was a major accident – an explosion and fire – at the Chernobyl nuclear power station in Ukraine, at that time part of the USSR. Shortly afterwards the radioactive fall-out affected parts of Europe. One of those parts was North Wales, some mountainous areas of which were to remain contaminated for over twenty years. Unknown to me, because there had been no warnings from the British meteorologists or government, the radioactivity was overhead when, walking on the sands at Anglesey's Red Wharf Bay, I got caught in a torrential downpour and was soaked to the skin. I rather enjoyed the experience at the time, but later regretted that I had not been advised to have a shower or bath as soon as I got home. Bucharest is only a few hundred miles from Chernobyl, and its inhabitants were taking precautions. The streets were being watered; the advice was to wash one's hair every day, and the markets were, unusually, full of leaf vegetables, which few wanted to buy. In the restaurants we refrained from eating green salads.

My fourth visit lasted over a fortnight (10–27 August 1986), more than twice as long as each of the previous three, and Lucinda came out for a week (17–24 August) to meet her future stepmother and see a bit of Romania. She had been under stress, partly because of the natural conflict of loyalties to her mother and father, partly because she had taken her Advanced Level Examinations in Greek, Latin, and Ancient History and had been awaiting the results. These, received just before she left home, were outstanding, despite her being only seventeen – a year younger than average.

I arrived laden, as usual, with an array of gifts, including foodstuffs, alcohol, cigarettes, books in French for Manuela's parents, stockings, flowers, and chocolates for Manuela, and a box, tied up with beautiful yellow ribbon, from Judith containing lace and other items that might be useful to her for the wedding. Among the foodstuffs, as on my second and third visits, were bananas, a favourite fruit of Manuela's virtually unobtainable in Bucharest. I must say that I was surprised to be criticised later for bringing such small ones (they had to be small to be squeezed in at the top of my rucksack) and for the unsatisfactory flavour of the ground coffee!

Manuela met me at the airport, looking very attractive. I had again booked Hotel Capitol. We had a light evening meal and a drink with Petru. Both of them were extremely tired, since they had been up much of the previous night discussing philosophy. A few days previously, Manuela had been summoned to interview about her application to marry and leave the country. The official had been courteous. In two days' time she would complete the "little fills". The second stage, the "big fills", would be more tiresome and costly, but the process of getting a passport and being able to leave would be nearly complete.

On Monday 11 August I went, accompanied (after an argument with the Romanian guards) by Manuela, to the British Embassy to see the new Vice-Consul, John Jeffrey, to put him in the picture about Manuela's progress and to keep up the pressure on the British side. He was as helpful as his predecessor. Earlier I had had a pleasant exchange of letters with Tim Renton MP, Minister of State in the Foreign Office, who was expected to make an official visit to Romania soon. Tuesday the 12th was Manuela's "big fills" day – a long and stressful obligation. Saturday the 16th must have been unhappy for me, because my diary entry for the 17th begins:

> Up 7.50 after sleepless night full of worry and misery. I cannot endure any disharmony with M[anuela] – I love her so much.

The next morning Manuela confessed that she had had a bad night too for the same reason and said that she was not feeling very well. We sat by a lake, trying to sort out our problems, and my diary reads:

> The difficulties, and they are small, stem from the highly unnatural and frustrating situation in which we find ourselves, unable to have any privacy and having to separate in the evenings and being subject to various pressures and forms of stress.

That evening (Sunday, 17th) Manuela and I were at the airport to meet Lucinda, who took an hour to get through security and customs, during most of which interval we could see one another and exchanged many waves. On arrival in the city centre, we were joined by Petru, who generously presented Lucinda not only with a bunch of pink roses and a book, but also, having heard that she did not eat meat or fish, with a box of vegetarian food. The four of us had a cheerful dinner together. On Monday, Lucinda was introduced to some of the architectural glories and eyesores of the city, and on Tuesday to the unpleasantness of some of its citizens. Manuela took her and me to the scenic Herăstrău Park, where we hired two hydrocycles. After a tranquil start, we were approached on the water by an aggressive man, who claimed to be "quite desperate". I warned him to leave us alone, and eventually he left. But worse was to come. Several young men swam out to Lucinda and Manuela's craft, took hold of it, and tried to capsize it. Manuela heard them say "let's drown them", although they also said: "We had better not, because the girls' father is on the scene"! I pedalled towards them, yelling like mad. For one thing, Manuela was carrying my camera, and I did not want *that* drowned! The men let go of the craft and retreated, so we came through unscathed, but the trip was much less relaxing than we had hoped.

For Wednesday, Petru had arranged a day-trip by train to the town and mountain resort of Sinaia. He also brought food for a picnic. He and Manuela arrived late at our hotel for the taxi ride to the Gara de Nord. Petru had nearly been crushed by a bus, the driver of which, he was sure, had seen him. A robust and prolonged argument had followed. There was more unpleasantness when we returned to the city in the late evening. An inebriated *Miliţia* man interrogated Petru for several minutes and wanted to take him to a police station for an undisclosed reason. In between these incidents we enjoyed Sinaia – both the town, the views of its castles, and its mountain scenery. We ascended, partly on foot, partly by cable car, to about 2,000 metres. Near the upper cable-car station we attempted to get lunch in the rather grubby restaurant, but Petru was told that there was no vegetarian food, and that Lucinda could not eat the picnic food on the premises: "If she is vegetarian, she should have stayed in London". After this display of bad manners and inhospitality, we descended to a pleasant hotel at a lower level. From there we walked to the railway station. At one point, when Lucinda walked on ahead, Manuela and Petru asked me what, if any, political changes I thought were possible in Romania. I replied that I thought Ceauşescu and his regime so corrupt and rotten that they would not last very much longer. My opinion was sharply dismissed as being wholly naive ("You don't understand"). But just over three years later (December 1989), Nicolae Ceauşescu was overthrown and he and his wife, Elena, were executed by the army.

Before Lucinda returned to Britain, Manuela and Petru generously bought her a mandolin. She obtained enjoyment from it and achieved a good level of proficiency. Sometimes she did some busking, including in Durham when she was living in nearby Newcastle. I am not sure how lucrative her efforts were. I remember hearing that on one occasion she was offered payment to stop playing, but the story may have been a joke. Before entering Otopeni (Bucharest Airport) to catch her flight home, she bandaged her right hand – a cunning ploy to maximise the chances of someone offering to carry her heavy luggage! Her visit had, it seemed to me, been successful. Manuela and Petru had been very welcoming, and she had got on well with them, particularly with Petru.

But the state of my relationship with Manuela continued to be a worry for me, and she and I had several discussions between Lucinda's departure and mine three days later. I had to make allowance for her not feeling very well in addition to the circumstances quoted above from my diary. But, hard though

I tried, I struggled to find these explanations entirely convincing. When we had talked about her arrival in Britain, she had told me that she would prefer to come slowly, by train, rather than fly, and I fully understood and accepted that, but I was troubled to hear that her first priority was not to come with me to Bangor and settle into the home we were to share, and not to meet Barbara and Henry, both of whom had written nice letters to her after our engagement, but to go first to Oxford to see Oswyn Murray about her research. I was troubled too that, when for a rare moment, we were alone outside a washroom, and I wanted to kiss her, she rejected the advance. When I left her at Otopeni on 27 August, I still wanted and expected to marry her, but had significant doubts as to whether my feelings and wishes were reciprocated.

Over the next four months (September-December 1986) we kept in touch by letter and telephone, but no word was received about the progress of our application to marry, let alone an acceptance. I had not intended to go to Bucharest again in advance of the permission and the marriage, but Manuela urged me to make a short visit early in the New Year. I flew out on Saturday 3 January 1987 and back on Wednesday 7 January, so was in Romania for just three full days. I stayed at Hotel Modern. I hoped that the visit would benefit Manuela's and my relationship. We greeted one another affectionately, and there were exchanges of presents, but we had little time to ourselves. The weather did not help. Bucharest was under snow, and the streets and pavements, totally untreated, were like ice-rinks. I had brought multiple pairs of tights for Manuela and thick stockings for Petru, but I had not brought footwear suitable for the conditions and had three falls – one on my left side, one on my right side, and one on my backside. My room was hot – far too hot – but only the major hotels and their restaurants were heated, and the temperature in the Academy Library, for example, was freezing cold. The reason for the lack of heating, like that for the lack of snow- and ice-clearing, was to make financial savings on the orders of the Government. One night, the heating failed even in my hotel, but I was lucky still to have hot water.

Sometimes, Manuela had things to do without me, and I went twice to the British Embassy. On the first occasion the Ambassador was just leaving for a meeting with the Head of the Consular Section in the Ministry of Foreign Affairs. Ours was one of several cases he intended to raise, so I returned to the Embassy to ask if there had been any progress. The answer, in a word, was "no". Although there was no significant disharmonious incident during my visit, I sensed a lack of real warmth on her side, and the icy weather that persisted from the moment I arrived to the moment I departed seemed not inappropriate to her attitude.

I returned home still wishing and intending to get married, but in the early months of 1987 I developed increasingly strong doubts about the genuineness of Manuela's feelings. I shared these with Judith, who understood the reasons for my unhappiness, but also the stresses and strains of Manuela's predicament. My agitation increased when Manuela, just over a year after completing her application for permission to marry, heard that it had been successful. My reaction to the news was a breakdown, and I could not bring myself to make a scheduled telephone call to her. I should like to have put the engagement on hold until after she had left Romania, but this was not an option: she could only leave the country if married, and she had already lost her job and been expelled from the Communist Party. Judith's advice, which I accepted, was to go to Bucharest, talk things over with Manuela, and, if she affirmed that her feelings were genuine, go through with the wedding and hope that, once she was in Britain, all would be well.

On 20 June Manuela's father wrote a letter not to me, but to Henry, about the importance of the marriage going ahead. It included the remarkable claim that my attempt to kiss his daughter outside the washroom had been sordid and repellent. Henry did not reply, and I am not sure that I saw the letter before leaving for Romania. I flew out on Saturday 27 June, carrying, in addition to various items of food and drink, not only my wedding clothes, but also Manuela's – a wedding dress designed and made by Calvin Klein, a sash, tights, white satin shoes, satin handbag, and three-piece lingerie set, all obtained with Judith's help. It seemed very odd to have the wedding clothes in my suitcase, not knowing whether there was going to be a wedding. I had not booked my return flight, in case I wanted to fly straight home.

I stayed, as in January, in Hotel Modern. Manuela did not meet me at the airport, and I saw her only very briefly at the hotel. The next morning we took a taxi to Herăstrău Park and sat on the grass under three big trees. There I told her that I loved her and asked her if she loved me and wanted me as a husband. She assured me that she did. "In that case", I said, "let's get married", whereupon she gave a great sigh of relief and lit a celebratory cigarette. The next days were busy. We were both required to undergo medical checks, including blood tests, in separate clinics, and there was a bit of excitement when the nurse taking my blood brought on such a flood of it that not just a plaster but a tourniquet was needed. The swift completion of the tests and also the securing of an early date for the marriage ceremony were achieved through the payment of bribes.

The marriage was fixed for 12.45 on Thursday 2 July. After breakfast I went with Petru to a flower-market to buy a posy for Manuela to carry at the ceremony. I chose one of pink roses, with some mauve and white blooms and a bit of orange. I also bought some fine roses to display at the reception. After I had changed into my wedding attire, we went by taxi to Stradă Caporal Ruică, the tree-lined road where Manuela's parents lived, to collect them and her. Manuela looked lovely, her appearance being the more delightful for her dress not being at all elaborate (Plate 27). Petru and I drove ahead in one taxi, while the others followed in a second one. Soon after we reached the Registry Office in Municipality District 3, guests started arriving. There were about thirty, all carrying flowers, many of them gladioli. As good classicists, Manuela and I entered the building, for good luck, *pede dextro* ("right foot [first]"). In the marriage room, she stood on the right, I on the left, facing the lady Registrar, who, wearing a sash in the colours of the Republic, sat on the platform behind a long table. The ceremony was very brief. After each of us had affirmed the wish to marry the other, the Registrar read a declaration about the way in which the State protects marriage and the family, how marriage is

27) Bucharest: Martin, Manuela, and Petru Creţia, 2 July 1987

to be an equal partnership, how the interests of the children are paramount, etc. She then said (in Romanian):

> In the name of the Executive Committee of the Romanian Communist Party, and in my own name, I wish you both to be happy, and I invite you to kiss.

We kissed twice. After that, we signed the register, and the guests came up to congratulate and kiss us. They then exited before us and, standing on either side of the steps, formed a guard of honour, holding their gladioli aloft.

The reception was in Constanţia and Constantin's flat, where wine and lovely food prepared by Constanţia were offered. It should have been a happy occasion, but throughout the party Manuela practically ignored me. At one stage, three of her friends tactfully left her and me alone on a balcony. It was the first time that we had been by ourselves all day. She refused an embrace on the grounds that one of the guests might see us or think our absence strange. I knew then that the assurance she had given me the morning after I arrived was false, and that she had only married me to escape the country. There was no possibility of a further test when bedtime came, for we had agreed long before to consummate our marriage when she had escaped from Romania rather than in a bugged hotel bedroom in Bucharest.

During my last two days I saw virtually nothing of her on her own. Despite the knowledge that I had been deceived, I bought the usual "luxury" items for her in the dollar shops and gave her a significant sum of money for her travel expenses and other costs. I had no expectation that she would change her mind about me – I just thought it was the decent thing to do. She arrived in London on 5 December 1987. Judith met her and had kindly arranged for her to rent a flatlet in the same building in which she lived. I paid the rent with generous help from Barbara.

A few days after Manuela's arrival, I wrote to invite her to come to live with me. When she refused, I sought an annulment of the marriage on the ground that she had wilfully refused to consummate it. The uncontested decree was issued at Chester County Court on 25 April 1988 and made absolute on 9 June. Apart from a chance meeting (described below) in 1993, I have had no contact with her.

9

Durham (1988–1995)

In 1988 the property market in England was very much a seller's one, and there were many cases of gazumping. Although I had the potential disadvantage of not yet living in the area where I wanted to buy, I had the great good fortune to acquire, at a fair price, a desirable house in pretty Shincliffe Village, just outside Durham, before it was advertised on the market. I had received a tip-off that the widowed owner was wanting to sell. She had lived at 2 Wood View for a very long time, and her main concern was that it would be bought by someone who would appreciate it.

The property was part of a terrace of seven houses, six of them, including no. 2, built between 1895 and 1897. It had two reception rooms, a living kitchen, a nice staircase, four bedrooms, and two bathrooms. At the front were a lawn, flower beds, and a productive Bramley apple tree (Plate 28). At the back was a yard, with a lockable door leading to the access lane for vehicles, on the far side of which was the garage and another piece of garden with rose bushes, a greenhouse containing an exceptionally *un*productive vine, and space for growing vegetables. There was lovely countryside on all sides. My favourite walk was through woodland with alternating bands of bluebells and wild garlic. All one could see of Durham was the top of the Cathedral tower from the upstairs windows, and then only when the trees had shed their leaves.

In preparation for the move from Bangor, I made several visits to Durham and Shincliffe – to inspect progress on alterations to and decoration of the house, to transport in the Dormobile books which the two institutions had agreed should accompany the transferring members of staff, and to discuss courses. The minor works in the house included quite a lot of paint-stripping, since the previous owners had painted almost everything, including

28) Shincliffe Village, Durham: 2 Wood View, August 1993

the cupboards and attractive original fireplaces, white. Some of the stripping was done by Lucinda and her boyfriend at the time, but most by a delightful young couple, Bill and Beth, who ran a business called The Strip Joint in Langley Moor. Beth spent a couple of days tackling the fireplace in my bedroom cum study, enabling me to boast that I had an attractive blonde stripper performing there. I was to be blessed with good neighbours, especially Shirley and Malcolm Fodden in no. 1.

Most of my discussions about courses were with the Professor of Greek, Michael Stokes, whose speciality was Greek Philosophy. Michael was an amiable and clever man, but had a reputation for being a bit absentminded. In fact, when I arrived at the beginning of term, there was a rumour circulating among departmental staff that he had recently failed to identify the Ann who had phoned him in his room as his wife, telling the caller "I don't know anyone called Ann". The rumour was thought to be too far-fetched to be credible, but, since I had been in Michael's room when he took the call, I was able to confirm it.

Early in my first term he and I were involved in discussions about a freshman who wanted to change his College. At lunchtime one day I bumped into him (Michael) in the street and thought I heard him say "I have just seen General Hamilcar". "Have you really, Michael?", I said. "Are you sure? General Hamilcar has been dead for over two thousand years". Michael laughed and said "I mean Anil Janorkar", the name of our student. No absentmindedness on his part there of course, just my deafness and playfulness.

I was to spend seven years in Durham, and very happy years they were. The old part of the city, built on the Peninsula, the near island created by the River Wear, is a visual treat and of exceptional historical interest. The view of the Cathedral and Castle from the railway line near Durham Station is one of the great architectural sights of Europe. Coming in to work from Shincliffe Village, I would usually leave the Dormobile in a small car park on the east side of the river close to the wall of the prison and then walk across the pedestrian Kingsgate Bridge with a fine view of the river and its wooded banks, and, straight ahead, the east end of the Cathedral. It would be hard to imagine a more inspiring walk to work.

The Department of Classics and Ancient History occupies two attached historic houses at 38 North Bailey, close to the Cathedral and opposite the entrance to Hatfield College. I occupied and used for some of my teaching a large room on the second floor, beautifully quiet except when beautifully noisy with the sound of the Cathedral bells. I kept most of my books and did most of my research at home, where I was rarely disturbed and my valuable library was more secure and fully insured. The wisdom of this was confirmed one morning, 24 February 1994, when I arrived at the Department to find that there had been a break-in during the night and much vandalism perpetrated.

There were two medium-sized rooms for teaching in the building. Teaching of large classes usually took place either on nearby Palace Green or across the river, at Elvet Riverside.

Durham, England's third-oldest university, founded in 1832, was one of the few institutions in the UK still able to attract good numbers of what one might call full classicists – students, mainly from public (i.e. private) schools, who had passed, if not A-Level Greek and Latin, at least Latin. If just Latin, they were likely to start Greek at University. For me, who had taught so few full classicists in Bangor, it was a stimulating change to be teaching good-sized classes in both languages in Durham. Also stimulating was the interaction with departmental staff colleagues. Three of those colleagues were professors – Michael Stokes (Greek), Tony Woodman (Latin), and Peter Rhodes (Ancient History). My own position was Professor of Classics, as at Bangor, and I believe that I was the first in Durham University's long history to have been so titled. All three of my professorial colleagues were very helpful and congenial, with great expertise in their specialist fields, Michael's being Greek Philosophy, Tony's Latin Historiography and Late Republican and Augustan Poetry, and Peter's Greek History, especially Politics and Political Institutions. I had first met Peter in the early 1970s when we were often first in the queue to be admitted to the Bodleian Library, Oxford, during the summer vacation. He was always a source of good advice. When I took over as Head of Department, I could not make sense of the financial statements I received from the Treasurer's office until Peter told me that a minus sign meant a plus. Tony too I had known for many years, since at least 1975. It was not easy to see him in his room because he was usually hidden in a thick fog of tobacco smoke. Having scarred lungs, I had tried at Bangor to get smoking stopped in the Council Chamber during meetings. I scored only a partial victory: it was agreed to ban smoking during the first hour. On arrival in Durham, with the support of another staff-member, I asked the Head of Department, Oliver Dickinson, to request no smoking in the Ritson Room at 38 North Bailey during meetings. Tony did not like this at all and said so. I could understand that, because at that time attitudes to smoking were very different from what they are now. A little later, I was very grateful to him for assisting me in a crisis. It blew up – literally as well as figuratively – when, attempting to bleed the radiator in my room during the lunch hour, I was horrified to find that I had released a powerful jet of scalding water which threatened to flood not only my room but also Michael Stokes' room immediately below. I rushed out on the landing and bellowed for help. Tony promptly responded, and, while we awaited the University's emergency services, we took it in turns to fill metal wastepaper baskets and empty them out of the window, fortunately without injury to any passers-by.

Of my other departmental colleagues, I knew best the two who had moved from Bangor, Gordon Cockburn and John Moles, and Senior Lecturer David Hunt, with whom I first became acquainted years earlier when he was on the staff of University of Wales, Swansea. An erudite but modest man, with a good sense of humour, his specialities were Later Roman History and Early Church History. My contacts were by no means confined to the Department of Classics, but involved colleagues in several other departments, including Archaeology, English, Geography, History, Philosophy, and Theology. In the Philosophy Department was Paddy Fitzpatrick, who for many years was a competitor in the fiendishly-brainy BBC radio programme "Round Britain Quiz". He was also a Roman Catholic priest, whose views were sometimes unorthodox. When, as a labour of love, my aunt Ro was completing for publication in *The Downside Review* an article on Cardinal Newman by my late aunt Jean, I asked her if she would like me to seek Paddy's opinion of Newman. She said that she would be most interested to hear it. But when I approached Paddy just before a Board of Studies meeting, I was startled to receive an assessment which I felt unable to pass on: "Personally, I think he was a wicked old bugger".

Much more fruitful was an approach I made to the German Department about the same time. I needed someone to decipher the Gomperz manuscript which I discovered in Vienna in 1988. There were thirty-seven pages of late nineteenth-century German handwriting (*Kurrentschrift*), often cramped and untidy. I was offering a payment and asked a young German member of the Department if he could help. He apologetically declined on the reasonable ground that he had never learned to write or read *Kurrentschrift*. Then somebody suggested Hilde Thomas, the German widow of Peter Thomas of New College, Durham. She was born in 1920 and brought up to use the old script. When I showed her Gomperz's notes, she confirmed that she could read them. She made a wonderful job of the decipherment. I only had to help with things like Greek philosophical terms and the names of ancient writers and modern scholars. When she had finished, the Classics Department's brilliant secretary, Sylvia Stoddart, produced a transcript which follows the pagination and, where possible, the lay-out of the manuscript. On completion,

I deposited two copies in the Asia Minor Commission (Kleinasiatische Kommission) in Vienna – one annotated by me, the other unannotated. That was very satisfying, but for me the most precious result of Hilde's work was a warm friendship between us that lasted until her death, aged 97, in 2018, and continues with her daughters, Barbara and Nickie. Cheerful, generous, cultured, interesting, interested, and courageous in her battle against a serious illness, she was the best of company (Plate 29). The most remarkable of her experiences in wartime Germany was being saved in 1942 from enrolment in the Nazi Party by an air-raid siren which sounded off while she was in the presence of the interviewing committee. As for Sylvia, she remains a valued friend, over 35 years on from her joining the Department of Classics.

During my first two years in Durham University, its Vice-Chancellor and Warden was Fred (later Sir Fred) Holliday. I liked him. Soon after my arrival he showed me the council chamber used for Senate meetings in Old Shire Hall, remarking that the acoustics were poor. "Oh dear", I said, "that must make things difficult". "On the contrary", he replied, "it is a great advantage: it speeds up the business enormously". When he retired from the University in 1990, he was replaced by Evelyn Ebsworth, whom I found a less sympathetic and congenial character. During my time as Head of Classics (1 August 1991–

29) Durham: Hilde Thomas, Martin, and Martini Rosso, 22 Orchard House, March 1994

31 July 1993) and therefore its representative on the Senate, I clashed with him so frequently and vigorously (making myself heard despite the poor acoustics!) that he invited me to visit him at home on a Saturday morning in the obvious hope of thereby reducing my hostility. My main objections, shared with those of the Theology representative and, I suspect, many others who feared to put their heads above the parapet, were to the introduction of a growing number of measures and policies which I saw as damaging to the University's academic staff members' teaching and research, while landing them with an increased burden of administration. After Ebsworth's mini-equivalent of "beer and sandwiches at no. 10", I may have barked less loudly, but I continued to voice my unhappiness. He remained in post until after I left Durham, then retired to Cambridge, where a friend of mine happened to encounter him at a private dinner party at which they were both guests. She did not take to him and was amused when, distracted in conversation, he coated his strawberries with mayonnaise instead of with cream.

When I arrived in Durham, the Chancellor was Dame Margot Fonteyn. She fulfilled the role, to which she had been elected in 1981, wonderfully. At degree congregations she stood, which was not easy for her since she had become quite crippled, and addressed wise words to the graduates in a firm voice, speaking without notes. One afternoon in 1989, I had the pleasure of meeting her. A paperback update of her autobiography had just been published, and she was signing copies in the SPCK bookshop on Saddler Street. Because of my teaching schedule I arrived rather late, after everyone else had been and gone, and we had a pleasant, unhurried conversation. Her successor as Chancellor, after her death in 1991, was Peter Ustinov, another very special person.

The main research I did while in Durham was concerned with Diogenes. The first aim was to complete the edition which I began as a Leverhulme Fellow during my last year in Bangor. I finished it in 1991, but the printing and proof-checking of it took a very long time, so that it was not actually published until early 1993, appearing in Naples just in time for the opening of the Epicurean Congress described below. After that I produced two articles on non-philosophical discoveries at Oinoanda, and before it I went twice more to Vienna, to read papers at an international conference on Ancient Lycia (6–12 May 1990) and at the centenary symposium of the Asia Minor Commission (23–25 October 1990), both of the papers explaining and discussing the Austrian contribution to work at Oinoanda. On the way back from Vienna in

May 1990, I gave a lecture and directed a seminar in Fribourg, Switzerland, at the invitation of Professor Dominic O'Meara, son of John J. O'Meara, whom I remembered as Professor of Latin at University College, Dublin when I was a student at Trinity College. Also, I engaged in polite but robust exchanges with Luciano Canfora of Bari about the date of Diogenes' inscription, which improbably, indeed impossibly, he wanted to place in the first century BC, making Diogenes a contemporary of Lucretius.

As well as working on Oinoanda matters at my desk, I persevered with attempts to get work on the site restarted. There was much correspondence, including with Jim Coulton, now working at Oinoanda's neighbour Balboura, David French, and others in BIAA, and in 1990 I was in Turkey (25 July-4 August), partly to see Oinoanda again before completing my book, partly to discuss the possibility of an excavation with staff of the Fethiye Museum, with Jim Coulton on the site, and with the Directorate-General of Antiquities and Museums in Ankara. The situation in Fethiye was tricky. The previous director had been relocated, contrary to his wish, to Amasra on the Black Sea coast and was trying to get his old job back. Among other considerations, he and his wife owned three gift-shops in Fethiye. At the time of my visit he was back in Fethiye on holiday. He had a low opinion of the acting director of the Museum, and the acting director had a similar opinion of him. So I had to proceed with great tact and caution. On 27 July I spent several hours at Oinoanda with Jim and the government representative assigned to the Balboura project. The acting director of the Museum came with us until the hill became too steep for him. The next day I visited Balboura with the ex-director. Jim and his team were pleased to receive from me gifts of superior cherry jam, a bottle of whisky, and (some of them) a recent copy of *The Times* which they avidly read for the cricket scores.

In the following days I spent time visiting Turkish friends in Seki and İncealiler. They were social calls, but also information-gathering. For example, I got one knowledgeable local to write down for me all the place-names he could think of in Oinoanda's territory, for comparison with the list of settlements given in the Demostheneia Inscription. One day, I made an expedition to Lake Girdev (Girdev Gölü) with my İncealiler friend Sami Işık, the one-legged player of pan-pipes. The lake, situated south of Oinoanda, is formed of melted snow and is almost dry in the summer months, when it becomes a fertile place for growing wheat and other crops. The earth road from the north was rough and bendy and took us over the top of a pass about 6,000 feet (1,830 m.)

above sea-level. On arrival, we were guided to antiquities and other things of interest by a young local man, Ali Yanatma. I inspected Greek inscriptions and Sami reclined on a lion-tomb. Afterwards we met the whole Yanatma family, who only lived at Girdev from early spring to late autumn. I gave them presents, and had to decline generous gifts from them of a live hen and a sack of potatoes. I was to return to Girdev several times and always found it and its climate delightful. I went on to Ankara to fulfil my appointments there, but, as usual, felt much less at home in the city than in Lycia.

A friend who provided much support during the years of Alan Hall's hostility to me was Martin Harrison, Professor of Archaeology at Newcastle University (1972–1985) and Professor of the Archaeology of the Roman Empire at Oxford University from 1985 until his death in 1992. Like Terence Mitford, he was outraged by Alan's behaviour, as were others at home and abroad, including (I was told) Professor Glen Bowersock of Harvard University. On Martin's initiative, the Northern Society for Anatolian Archaeology (NSAA) was launched at a meeting in Newcastle University on 29 October 1976, with him as Chairman and Sir Steven Runciman as President. The society was a welcome supplement to BIAA, with a pleasanter atmosphere. I was a founder-member and, like Sir Steven, was an overnight guest of Martin and his wife, Elizabeth, after the inaugural meeting. As a raconteur, I was outshone by both Sir Steven and Martin, although, when the conversation turned to the Inner Hebridean island of Eigg, previously (until 1966) owned by Sir Steven, I was able to hold my own in conversation. Between 1977 and 1984 five issues of NSAA's journal, *Yayla* [*Upland Pastures*], were published. But, when Martin moved to Oxford in 1985, he was no longer "northern", and a stroke he suffered in 1986 was a further problem. So the society's short life came to an end, but soon a new one, called Phoenix, arose from its ashes. The inaugural meeting was held in Durham on 31 October 1990. Again Sir Steven was President, and the Committee included John Ruffle (Keeper of Durham's Oriental Museum), John Norton (expert on modern Turkey and Turkish), and myself. Martin Harrison died on 9 September 1992, aged 57; Sir Steven Runciman on 1 November 2000, aged 97.

It was not compulsory for a new staff-member to join one of the University's Colleges, and I did not want to be closely involved in the life of any of them, but I heard good reports of Van Mildert College, including of its cuisine. Occasionally I took guests to dinner there, but I usually preferred to take them to a restaurant or to entertain them at home. My own cuisine often received praise, although some of the credit was often owed to Marks & Spencer. My most frequent guests were Diane and Gordon Cockburn, Jane and Richard Abram, and Hilde Thomas. On one occasion when I entertained the Cockburns and another couple, Diane kindly brought a huge bunch of flowers, which I placed in the middle of the table. A fifth guest, Judith ("Judy") Turner, Principal of Van Mildert College, was seated at the far end of the table from me, and whenever the two of us were conversing, we had to lean to one side or the other. It was a bit comic, and, if one got a bit tipsy, even a bit hazardous. Judy, a biologist, was a delightful colleague and a big part of the attraction of Van Mildert for me and, I am sure, for many others.

I rarely had staying visitors. They can make a lot of work and may want to talk at breakfast. I heartily agree with Oscar Wilde's dictum "only dull people are brilliant at breakfast". The people I most happily remember staying at Wood View are Sally and Ian Lovecy and their two young daughters, all delightful, and Sally always in full control and always brilliant except at breakfast, ensuring minimal disturbance and maximum assistance. My reunion with my Bangor student Jane Abram came about near Durham's Magdalene Steps one day in the autumn of 1989. It came as a complete surprise to me, because I had no idea that she lived in the area. As I walked down the street towards Elvet Bridge, I saw an attractive lady coming uphill. To my surprise, she came across to me and said: "You are Professor Smith, aren't you?" We had not seen one another for nearly twenty years, and it was lovely to meet up again. During my years in Durham, as well as often dining with her and Richard both as a guest and as a host, I shared with them enjoyment of concerts and other cultural events. The very first event we attended together, with their elder daughter, was an excellent performance of Handel's pastoral *Acis and Galatea*. If I remember rightly, the venue was Durham School, and I was tipped off about the forthcoming event by my dentist, Tony Borthwick, in Newcastle, who was in the orchestra, playing first violin.

Like Jane and her family, Tony was a great find. On arrival in Durham, I had difficulty in identifying a good dentist. Peter Rhodes told me that he went to one on Old Elvet who was "quick", but I wanted one who was expert and thorough. When I mentioned my difficulty to neighbours in Shincliffe, they immediately recommended Tony. I have been with him for over 35 years and can say that he is not only a brilliant dentist, but also one of the nicest people I know. Lucinda, who was his patient during her time in Newcastle, and my granddaughter, Ciara, previously terrified of dental treatment, are also fans of his. His wife obtained her doctorate in Music from Durham University, and the whole family is musical.

My friendship with John Moles and his wife, Ronnie, continued after the move from Bangor. Shortly before they left Wales, Ronnie gave birth to a daughter, Rachel. When Rachel was just a few months old, I invited her parents to dinner in my flat. I said that it was fine to bring the baby. While we were having preprandial drinks in the sitting room, Rachel started wailing and shrieking and, despite the best efforts of Mum and Dad, would not stop. Eventually I said: "Shall I have a go?" My offer was received with scepticism, but not rejected. As soon as I took Rachel into my arms and made soothing movements and noises, she stopped crying and remained fast asleep all evening. I sensed that the parents' reaction was one of relief combined with disappointment about their failure to quieten the baby themselves. In Durham I behaved irresponsibly with Rachel when she was about five. Her father had brought her into the Department of Classics after school, and I showed her how to make paper darts (a skill I had mastered at preparatory school), which she then launched from the landing outside my room at the shiny moving target in the hallway two floors below – Michael Stokes' bald head.

Lucinda proved the wisdom of her choice of university by obtaining a first class Honours degree in Classics at Newcastle University in 1990. She was beautifully dressed for the degree congregation (Plate 30), except for her casual footwear. Since her father had got married in shoes with holes in them, he was in no position to make any adverse comment – not that he minded anyhow. Betty attended the ceremony and was as proud of our daughter as I was. Lucinda has many amusing stories about the teaching staff in the Newcastle Classics Department, but these must be reserved for her memoirs!

Barbara and Henry were interested in my move to Durham, but Barbara was too weak and unwell to visit me there, and she died, aged 86, in Kidderminster General Hospital on 4 April 1991. She had had heart problems for many years, and, after she suffered a stroke, hospital was the only option. Henry accompanied her there, and, on arrival, while still in the ambulance, she gave him an urgent instruction: "Don't forget to feed the cats". A day or two later I saw her for the last time. She was tossing and turning in a sort of cot, often revealing what was under her nightclothes in a way that would have been immodest if she had not been delirious. When I held her hand, she kept repeating "Let's go home now, Mart, let's go". It was a heart-rending plea, and I could only squeeze her hand and say "Yes, Mother, when you are well

30) Newcastle University: Lucinda after graduation as BA (1st class), 29 June 1990

enough". I knew there was no hope, and she died two days after I returned to Durham. Later, her sister Lou remarked to Colin: "Barbara was no angel". Maybe not, but for all my life she seemed to me to be like one. The funeral took place in the chapel of Stourbridge Crematorium on 12 April. I gave one of the readings. Her ashes were scattered at Silligrove in the Side Dingle, close to where her pets were buried. After the funeral, there was a buffet lunch at Silligrove. I picked and arranged the flowers and greenery, all from the garden she loved so much, and was rather touched when somebody asked which florist had supplied them. But she never much cared for bought flowers any more than she cared for bought cakes.

Henry visited Durham once in my time there. That was after Barbara died. He was able to view not only my new house, but also, more importantly, Lucinda's new baby, Ciara, born in Newcastle on 17 September 1991. Soon after that, his health declined and he died in Malvern on 17 May 1992, aged 90. My last visit to him is described in Chapter 1. His funeral also took place at Stourbridge Crematorium. The previous night was the last I spent at Silligrove. I was alone in the ancient creaky house, and I did not sleep well. That was partly because of the memories and thoughts flooding into my mind, partly because the security lighting installed after a break-in a few weeks earlier kept flashing on and off. On this occasion the intruders turned out to be hedgehogs on the lawn.

Soon afterwards, Colin, Carol, and I had the melancholy task of selling Silligrove and dividing between us the furniture and other possessions that were not to be sold. Eventually the house and land were bought by good people who still own and occupy them after well over 30 years, but earlier a crank who lived in a council house in London and had virtually no money amused himself by posing as a wealthy buyer. In his pretended role, he made several unreasonable demands which aroused the suspicions of Carol and myself, but were initially brushed aside by Colin, who feared that the keen buyer would withdraw if we resisted. The man's behaviour had its comic aspects, but his time-wasting was not amusing at the time.

On 1 August 1991 I took over the rotating headship of the Classics Department, and for two years I was too busy with administrative work and other things to take much in the way of a break. "Other things" included finishing off my edition of Diogenes and seeing it through the press, and making a second revision of my Loeb edition of Lucretius. But from 19 to 27 May 1993 I was in Italy to participate in the International Congress on Greek and Roman Epicureanism (*Epicureismo greco e romano*) in Naples and Capri. When I went to Gatwick Airport to catch my flight, I met up with Don Fowler of Jesus College, Oxford. He and his wife, Peta, were both Lucretian scholars of a high calibre and good friends of mine. In 1988 Don very kindly invited me to be his "distinguished guest" at the Domus dinner in his College on 18 March. I did not often wear evening dress, and the only dress shirts

I had were green and pink. I decided to wear the green one. When I showed it to Lucinda, she commented: "You can't wear that, Daddy". "Of course I can", I replied. "Lots of other men will be wearing coloured shirts". "I bet they won't be", she said. She was right of course. Every other male guest was wearing a white shirt, and, when Don led me into the room where pre-dinner drinks were being offered, I received a disapproving glare from former Prime Minister Harold Wilson, one of the few who was already there. I expect I was breaking the Domus-dinner dress-code. I also sinned by forgetting to bring my cufflinks.

To return to Gatwick, Don and I were chatting, when David Sedley arrived unexpectedly with Manuela Tecuşan, the two having come from Cambridge by taxi. David courteously introduced me to Manuela. She looked very uncomfortable, and I could have said all sorts of things, but I just remarked that we had met before. All four of us then engaged in ordinary conversation, and I spoke to Manuela again on the plane and after arrival at the hotel in Naples, but there was no mention of the past. Except that some of the early papers long overran the allotted time, the conference was very good, although, as is often the case at conferences, many of the most important exchanges took place outside the lecture-hall. Our hosts gave each participant a copy of my 660-page edition of Diogenes, which was welcome publicity for me and Oinoanda, but a rather heavy item for folk to carry home.

The Hotel Mediterraneo, in which I stayed, was not far from the Galleria Umberto I. Late my first evening, I noticed many prostitutes accosting male drivers near the steps of the arcade. Many of the prostitutes were mini-skirted, and I assumed they were female. But, as I learned the next morning, they were actually male, mainly from Brazil, and plied their trade in several other Mediterranean ports, including Marseilles.

Almost everyone of significance in the world of Epicurean studies was present at the conference. In the morning of 23 May we were transported by hydrofoil to Capri for the second part of the conference. It was my first visit to the island, and May was a delightful time to be there, before the heat became too great and the tourists too numerous. We were taken in small buses from the Marina Grande to the Hotel Europa Palace in Anacapri. The luggage came up separately. I was to visit Capri again in 2002, and I was to write about it, and especially about Anacapri, in telling the remarkable story of Richard Williams Reynolds and his family (see Chapter 13). I enjoyed exploring the island, visiting the Villa San Michele, the home of the Reynolds family's

Swedish friend Axel Munthe, and walking to the Villa Jovis, the Emperor Tiberius's main residence on Capri at its northeast corner. I remember having many pleasant and interesting conversations, including with Jonathan and Jennifer Barnes. Jonathan, elder brother of the novelist Julian Barnes, was born in Much Wenlock, Shropshire, a few miles from Silligrove, and Jennifer in Malvern, where her father was headmaster of Malvern Link (Preparatory) School, attended much earlier by Henry, and just across the Malvern Hills from Colwall, which played such a big part in my childhood. I also had a memorable meeting and private conversation with Marcello Gigante. As President of the Organising Committee, he was very much occupied throughout the conference, but by chance we found ourselves, for a few minutes on the last evening, the only occupants of the hotel's terrace. Our conversation was about the Herculaneum papyri and Diogenes' inscription, and so was a fitting prelude to my illustrated lecture the following morning on "A 'Herculaneum' in the Mountains of Turkey: Oinoanda as a Source of Epicurean Texts". The session, the last of the conference, was chaired by Marcello, who began with a copy of my edition in his hands. Francesca Longo Auricchio told me that my presentation was the best of the conference. When I queried that, she said: "Well, you heard the length and volume of the applause". I like to think that the applause was for Oinoanda and Diogenes.

While in Anacapri, I learned that the University of Dublin was to confer the degree of LittD (Doctor in Letters) on me in recognition of my published work on Lucretius and Diogenes (Plate 31). I flew Newcastle–Dublin the day before the Commencements on 9 July and had lunch with John Dillon, Regius Professor of Greek, and tea with my old friend and fellow-scholar Robin Miller. I treated myself to accommodation in the Shelbourne Hotel. Sally Lovecy kindly came over from Bangor to attend the ceremony, during the latter part of which a violent thunderstorm developed. Torrential rain was still falling when we processed out of the Public Theatre, and, by the time we had run across Front Square to the reception in the Buttery, we were both soaked. Fortunately for me, my polyester gown dried quickly, and we were soon warmed not only by the wine but also by the delightful company of John Luce and Seamus Heaney. During the conversation I recalled my undergraduate contacts with Michael Longley and Derek Mahon. Both, like Seamus, were Belfast poets, and Michael had been taught by John. At the time of our meeting, Seamus had a Chair at Harvard University and was Professor

31) Dublin (TCD): Martin before receiving degree of LittD, 9 July 1993

of Poetry at Oxford. Two years later, in 1995, he was awarded the Nobel Prize for Literature.

My tenure as Head of Department came to an end on 31 July, and, just before the start of the new term, I treated myself to a week's holiday in the

Scilly Isles, staying in the comfortable Island Hotel on Tresco and making trips by boat to the other islands – Bryher, uninhabited Samson, St Martin's, St Mary's, and St Agnes. Each one was enchanting. The only jarring incident occurred just after my arrival on Tresco when, out for a walk, I surprised two men engaged in vigorous homosexual activity behind a rock. Although I had often been in Cornwall, I had not visited the Scillies before. Nor had I previously flown in a helicopter (Penzance–Tresco–Penzance). The long (nearly nine-hour) train journeys (Durham–Penzance–Durham) were part of the holiday: I travelled first class with a good supply of smoked salmon sandwiches and, when not looking out of the window, did some reading and writing. I sometimes did more reading and writing in the hotel's dining room, but was often distracted by the sight of, or even conversation with, other guests. The head waiter's practice was to place new arrivals well away from the big windows and move them nearer to them later in their stay. But, when it was my turn to be promoted, I asked to stay put, so that I had a view of the whole dining room as well as the scenery outside the windows. In some ways the dining room and its occupants reminded me of those in Jacques Tati's *Les vacances de Monsieur Hulot*.

In 1993 I first made the acquaintance of three visiting scholars who quickly became friends. Two were the classicist and historian of ancient philosophy Jackson ("Jack") Hershbell, of the University of Minnesota, who came to Durham with a Research Fellowship at Hatfield College, and his psychologist wife, Anne Snyder Hershbell, who accompanied him. The third was Kathleen ("Kathy") M. Coleman, of the University of Cape Town, born and brought up in Zimbabwe, an expert on Latin Literature, the institutions and culture of the Early Roman Empire, and Roman arena spectacles. She was soon to be Professor of Latin at Trinity College, Dublin, and later at Harvard. She had produced an admired edition of Book 4 of Statius' *Silvae*, which inspired me to propose a solution to a textual crux: "Ducks' Eggs in Statius, *Silvae* 4.9.30?" (*Classical Quarterly*, 1994). In the same year I acquired another valued friend, and one who remains that after over thirty years, even though I have never met him, and that is the classical philologist and philosopher Alexander Verlinsky of the State University of St Petersburg. Through him I sent the Bibliotheca Classica (Classical Library) in St Petersburg various publications, including classical periodicals, and I was kindly invited to submit articles for publication in the St Petersburg classical journal, *Hyperboreus*.

Another treasured friend, whom I got to know nearly a decade earlier (1984), is Angiola Maria Volpi, a classical and English scholar, of Italian nationality, but resident in Paris. We met in the Bodleian Library, Oxford, when a reader caused a disturbance by dragging down the reading room a tall and heavy step-ladder. Angiola happened to be sitting next to me, and we exchanged smiles before going off to chat in a café. She loved to visit Oxford each year to stay in Somerville College and work in the Bodleian, and we coincided there on a number of later occasions. She is the author of *Dryden traducteur de Juvénal* (1989), and her State Doctoral Thesis is titled *Sources et influences classiques dans la poésie de Dryden* (2004). She is the kindest possible person, and fittingly this angel (*angiola*) inhabits a Parisian street called "House of God" (*rue Maison Dieu*). Sometimes fact is more incredible than fiction.

The summer of 1994 at last saw some activity at Oinoanda (11–21 July). The team consisted of Stephen Mitchell (director), Nicholas P. Milner (epigraphist), Jeremy Rossiter (archaeologist), and myself, accompanied by a Turkish Government representative, İlhan Güceren. Stephen, at that time a Professor at University College, Swansea, was a fine historian and epigraphist, with much experience of archaeological work, especially in Turkey. He was well qualified to direct work at Oinoanda, but was reluctant to commit himself to a lengthy project there. Jeremy, from the University of Alberta, was also well qualified, but he too had other commitments, including in Tunisia. For both of them, it was a first visit to Oinoanda, and the main purposes were to enable them to familiarise themselves with the site and assess the feasibility of an excavation. Neither of them was ever to excavate at Oinoanda, but Stephen's involvement was very important on account of his influential position in BIAA, of which he was soon to become Honorary Secretary (1996–1999, 2009–2014).

Jeremy arrived late and departed early, but the rest of us spent five days at Oinoanda itself, then another five in its territory. The second part of the exploration was particularly interesting. We went to Lake Girdev, on the way to which we were attacked by bees near the top of the 6,000-foot pass. İlhan was badly stung and was grateful for the antihistamine tablets I had with me. I drove the Land Rover to Girdev, but Stephen was at the wheel for the return journey, for which, after some heavy rain, the earth road had become dangerously slippery. I insisted on walking down one steep downhill stretch, not fancying the idea of falling several hundred feet in the Land Rover. Most of the other places we visited were previously unknown to me. Our most extraordinary find was made near the village of Çukurceylan. Beside the road, we noticed a very large stone (2.54 m. wide), which must have been the door lintel of a church (Plate 32). On one side were a large Maltese cross, carved inside a circle, in the centre and on either side two figures on horseback blowing trumpets. The figures were much damaged. On the other side were a cross in the centre and two discs on either side. Underneath was another cross. Stephen was surely right in thinking that the piece belonged to a very early church, perhaps early fourth century or late third century. One may be almost sure that the church was previously a temple of the Dioscuri (Castor and Pollux), for the horsemen, if one removes the trumpets that mark them out as Evangelists, are very similar to portrayals of the Dioscuri in local iconography. The lintel is a fascinating indication of the transition from pagan religion to Christianity, and of the way Christians exploited pagan images in their presentation of the new religion. Three years later (19 April 1997) I identified the site of the church at nearby Karagaç and saw two more large lintel-blocks, both with Maltese crosses. During the investigations of Oinoanda in 2007–2012 I recommended my colleagues to view the site. They did so very briefly and with what I thought was a surprising lack of interest. Admittedly by that time the main lintel was in the garden of the Fethiye Museum. One "Oinoandan" who was and is very interested is Nicholas Milner.

32) Çukurceylan, near Oinoanda: door-lintel of early church, W 2.54 m, 20 July 1994

As in 1993, I took a few days' holiday (20–28 September 1994) just before the start of the new academic year. This time my destination was the Shetland Islands – as far from the Scilly Isles as one can get in the United Kingdom. The visit was to have momentous consequences for me, as will soon be revealed.

Sometime in the mid-1990s, on a visit to Oxford, I first heard a wonderful baroque music ensemble with the intriguing name Charivari Agréable ("Pleasant Tumult") performing by candlelight under its Malaysian-born director, Kah-Ming Ng, in the chapel of Lincoln College. I was entranced, and for several years, before the group became nationally and internationally famous, gave modest support as a "friend". It specialises in the use of period instruments.

The eyesight problems which erupted in the weeks before my degree examinations in 1962 had recurred at intervals during my teaching career and necessitated frequent visits to eye-consultants, one of whom bought Derwen Deg in Bangor after it ceased to be the Roman Catholic hostel. It was a strange experience having my eyes examined in my former home. In 1986 the same consultant operated on one of my eyes in the new Ysbyty Gwynedd, but no complete cure resulted, and in 1994 I was certified as being unfit to continue in my employment, which, involving as it did a combination of teaching and examining, administration, and research, put excessive strain on my deficient eyesight. So I gave notice of early retirement, to start at the end of the 1994–1995 session. The notice was accepted, and the way was clear for me soon to leave Durham, which I did on 29 June 1995, with the title "Professor Emeritus of Classics". It is as well that I retired when I did, for further problems with my eyesight were to develop.

In 1994 I had been at work on my next book, and, helped by a grant of research leave during my last term at Durham, I was able to submit it on 24 May 1995 to the Asia Minor Commission in Vienna – the section of the Austrian Academy of Sciences to which I had been elected in 1990. I describe the book in its Preface

> as intended to supplement and complement the content of my edition of Diogenes of Oinoanda published by Bibliopolis in 1993.

The volume, *The Philosophical Inscription of Diogenes of Oinoanda* (1996), contains scale-drawings and descriptions of the stones, numerous photographs

(217 figures on 64 plates), and precise details of find-places. Its presentation was helped by two Durham University friends of mine – Yvonne Beadnell (Archaeology), who produced the final versions of my drawings, and Michele Johnson, now Allan (Geography), who photographed the epigraphic squeezes.

I am thankful for my years in Durham, and in many ways I was sad to leave it and my nice house in Shincliffe Village. I sold the house several months before I moved and rented a convenient modern flat in nearby Bishop's Court. I recall only one brief excitement there. Soon after I had returned late one evening, the doorbell rang. The caller was an attractive lady who with her young son occupied the flat above mine. She was in her dressing gown, and her opening words were: "Martin, I'm desperate". I felt a bit deflated when she explained that her problem was the recurrent reverberation of an airlock in my flat's plumbing.

My departmental colleagues very generously gave me a leaving present of cash to spend on baroque music CDs, and treated me to a leaving party in Castle (University College), and several of them also entertained me in their homes or Colleges. They and other friends included Tony and Dorothy Woodman, Clemence Schultze, Jocelyne Nelis-Clément and Damien Nelis, Hilde Thomas, and Jane and Richard Abram. I was very touched by everyone's kindness. Mention of Clemence reminds me that, a year or two earlier, she and I had found ourselves in a crowd of southbound passengers at Durham Railway Station. No trains were coming through because of damage to the line north of Newcastle. Clemence consulted her husband on her mobile phone. He advised her to take a Virgin train, prompting her to exclaim in the hearing of scores of other would-be passengers: "But there aren't any Virgins".

I was equally touched by the reactions and gestures of my students, both as individuals and as classes. Early in 1995 the University had agreed the wording of a teaching-evaluation questionnaire to be distributed to the students in each class. There were eleven questions about the lecturer's performance, and each was to be marked out of five. There was also a space for "any comments (criticisms or compliments)". The forms were to be completed and returned anonymously. The marks for the four courses taught by me and me alone were very high. I blush to quote some of the comments on the forms, especially those that confer divine status on the teacher!

2H Roman Philosophy

Your lectures are the highlight of my week – without them my life would be a meaningless void. Through them I have achieved true *ataraxia* [tranquillity of mind].

I see that camper van appearing and I know that life has meaning again.

1H Introduction to Ancient Philosophy

A wonderful course – fantastic lectures – a truly fabulous lecturer.

I thoroughly enjoyed this course [which] was about as good an introduction to philosophy as it is humanly possible – *floreat deus Smith* – to give! SPLENDID!!

Prof. Smith is a god. (Plate 33)

TEACHING EVALUATION QUESTIONNAIRE

Lecturer : M.F. Smith

Introduction to Philosophy

Please circle the answer which you consider most appropriate to each question. Where the figures 1-5 are given, 1 is the most negative response and 5 the most positive: e.g. in answer to the first question, 1 would indicate that the lectures are completely inaudible, 5 that they are clearly audible. Please be honest in your replies: if they are unfavourable, they will not be held against you; in any case anonymity should be preserved and you should not put your name on the form or give it to me in person.

Thank you very much for your help.

Are the lectures audible?	1 2 3 4 (5)
Does the lecturer speak to the audience (rather than to the blackboard, ceiling, etc.)?	1 2 3 4 (5)
Are the lectures intelligible?	1 2 3 4 (5)
Are the lectures well organised?	1 2 3 4 (5)
Is the amount of material in the lectures too much / (about right) / too little?	
Is the treatment of the material in the lectures too advanced / (about right) / too elementary?	
Are the lectures interesting?	1 2 3 4 (5)
Do you get useful notes from the lectures?	1 2 3 4 (5)
Are you stimulated to think by the lectures?	1 2 3 4 (5)
Is the use of the blackboard helpful?	1 2 3 4 (5)
Is the course bibliography helpful?	1 2 3 4 (5)

Please write any comments (criticisms or compliments) below. Continue on the back if necessary.

Prof. Smith is a god.

33) Durham University student's evaluation of Martin's teaching, April 1995

10

Foula, Shetland (1994–)

I mentioned in the last chapter that the short holiday I took in Shetland in September 1994 had "momentous consequences" for me. I had not visited the islands before, but I had long been interested in them, especially those that were small and/or remote. I had pored over maps and done a lot of reading – of books and the weekly newspaper *The Shetland Times* to which I subscribed. When the privately-owned Shetland island of Grunay in Out Skerries was offered for sale in 1993, I put in a bid for it. Fortunately it was unsuccessful.

The island which fascinated me most was Foula, home to Britain's most isolated island-community with a population then of about 40. Situated 14 miles west of Watsness, the nearest point on the Shetland mainland, 20 miles west of Walls, and 24 miles west of Scalloway, and separated from all these places by open Atlantic, it measures about 3½ miles north to south and about 2½ miles west to east and occupies an area of about 4¾ square miles. Despite its small size, it has five hills, including the Sneug (1373 feet) and the Kame (1234 feet) (Plate 34). The latter, an almost sheer cliff, is often called Britain's second highest sea-cliff, after St Kilda's Conachair, but the claim that Conachair is higher may be questionable because, although the uppermost parts of it are steep, they are not sheer.

Shetland is further north than many Britons realise, being situated about 100 miles north of the Scottish mainland, about 200 miles from Aberdeen, and about 240 miles west of Bergen in Norway. Foula is just north of 60 degrees of latitude, about the same as the southern tip of Greenland among other places. Shetland and Orkney belonged to Scandinavia until 1469, when Margaret, daughter of the King of Denmark, married Prince James of Scotland, and both groups of islands were pledged to Scotland as part of her dowry. Hitherto Shetlanders spoke Norn, their version of Norse. Well, that was the language that arrived with the Vikings around AD 800. But the islands had been inhabited since at least 4,000 BC. Whether Foula was inhabited quite so early cannot be proved, but it is not unlikely. The island is bare now, but in earlier times it was wooded. There was also plenty of peat for burning, and an excellent supply of fresh water. Not least of its attractions were its countless seabirds and their eggs. The history of the house-site that was soon to be mine can be traced back to the late eighteenth century, but it is likely that the immediately-surrounding area was first occupied many centuries, perhaps several thousand years, earlier. One of its main attractions will have been its abundant spring-water, and the nearby stream. Less appealing may have been the violent winds to which the area is prone: Shetland is the windiest part of Britain; Foula is the windiest island in Shetland; and the place I was about to acquire is, when westerly winds are gusting off the hills, at least as windy as any other in Foula. Wind-speeds in excess of 100 mph are not infrequent, and I recall several hurricanes that did significant damage to buildings and dry-stone dykes and caused my ears to pop with the sudden changes of pressure. The island's notorious gusts are known locally as "flans".

Many early arrivals in Shetland from the south will have made landfall at or near Jarlshof at the southern tip of the Shetland Mainland. Jarlshof is an

34) Foula from Hamnavoe

archaeological site whose rich remains span a huge period of time extending back to the Neolithic Age. Appropriately, it is close by the place where many of today's travellers to Shetland arrive – Sumburgh Airport. It was there that I arrived at lunchtime on Tuesday, 20 September 1994. I spent my first night in Lerwick's Shetland Hotel – expensive, with its view of the docks obscured by dirty windows, and serving an inedible kipper for breakfast. The hotel's poor value was no doubt explained, but not excused, by the roaring trade it did in accommodating and feeding visiting oil workers. It was not a great start to my holiday. Things could only get better, and they did.

Early on the Wednesday morning I took a taxi to Tingwall Airport, about five miles north of Lerwick, and flew in a Britten-Norman BN-2 "Islander" plane to Foula. The aircraft normally carries up to seven adult passengers, but it can depend on their weight and the amount of freight. It is a bit like a minibus with wings. On this occasion there were three of us, the other passengers being a male surveyor and a woman who, unknown to me at this stage, was my landlady. We landed on Foula's airstrip from the north, which meant that we had the slightly alarming sensation of heading downhill into the sea. The landing was a bit rough too, the surface being gravel. Travelling to Foula, whether by air or sea, is not for the faint-hearted. Although neither the plane flies nor the boat sails in the most extreme conditions, the former is small and light, and the latter – the *New Advance* since late 1996 – small (overall length 15 m., width 4 m.) for open-Atlantic travel (Plate 35). Embarking and disembarking at Foula Pier is not done by any sort of gangway, but often (depending on the state of the tide) by means of a vertical ladder attached to the quay or, as a luxury, by way of some slimy and slippery steps. A big difference between sea and air travel is the duration of the journey – two hours by boat from Walls, fifteen minutes by plane from Tingwall. Both methods of transport have a good safety record, but on 19 May 1996 an "Islander" plane, not making a scheduled flight, but returning at night from an ambulance flight to Inverness, crashed on its approach to Tingwall Airport, killing the pilot and seriously injuring the doctor on board. Like other residents, I have endured rough sea-crossings and uncomfortable flights. One of the worst sea-crossings was made after dark from Scalloway in exceptionally rough conditions in the reserve boat, the *Koada*. On arrival at the departure-quay, I learned not only that I was (unsurprisingly!) the only passenger, but also that there was only one crewman. Enquiring what my status was, I was told "first mate". The crossing to Foula from Scalloway usually takes three hours. During the voyage the skipper, an Orcadian, put his head round the cabin door three times. First, after an hour, he said that we would have to turn back, to which I replied: "You can't, when we have already got so far", adding "of course I am only the first mate". An hour later, he estimated that we were still only about half way. Fortunately this was an under-estimate, and at last he communicated the glad tidings that he could see Foula's harbour-light. Rough sea-crossings are not pleasant, although I have a 100% record of not being sick, and the same is the case with turbulent flights. More troublesome are the frequent long delays, often of many days' duration, to one's travel to and from the Shetland Mainland. At the same time they enhance one's pleasure at making it out or back home and one's gratitude to the boat crew and pilots who make it possible. On two occasions I have been taken out by air ambulance. The first was on Sunday 19 March 2006 when I had fallen and damaged my nose. There was no nurse on the island, and the wound needed stitching. I had to wait many hours, because the plane had had to go to Aberdeen with another patient. To add to the excitement, it was long after dark when my turn came, the pilot had never landed on Foula in darkness before, and the lighting on the airstrip was dim. My other emergency flight was on 27 February 2025, with heart failure. A Coastguard helicopter was summoned to convey me to hospital, and took only about

35) Foula: New Advance approaching harbour, March 2025

twenty minutes to arrive. It turned out that the chief paramedic, responding to his very first call-out with Shetland Coastguard, was from North Wales and Welsh-speaking. He was a bit surprised when his first Shetland casualty addressed him in Welsh.

I had booked three nights at one of Foula's two guest houses, offering bed, breakfast, and an evening meal. It was called Broadfoot, and its proprietors were a Northern Irish couple, Penny and Frank Millsopp. They had been in residence for thirteen years and had converted a very small and unmodernised crofthouse into a spacious and comfortable dwelling. Frank was a skilful builder and joiner and added three extensions, the first one including a large workshop in which Penny gave spinning, weaving, and dyeing courses. The second was a wing containing three bedrooms and a bathroom for the family. The third was a dining room, reached through the original house's sitting room. There were two guest-bedrooms on the ground floor, and two attic rooms upstairs, with two box-beds in one of them and a third box-bed on the landing. There was not much in the way of a front garden, and the kaleyard had not been recently cultivated. There were several stone outbuildings, the most substantial of them ruinous. The property was at the south end of the island, in the settlement called the Hametoun.

Frank drove me the short distance from the airstrip to Broadfoot, where I met Penny. I handed over a bottle of sherry I had brought as a gift. I thought it would be sufficient for my whole visit, but it was all consumed the first evening, despite my hosts also producing Jameson whiskey and a bottle of champagne – not their usual tipples, they explained, but to celebrate Penny's success in having just obtained her licence after taking a month-long driving course in Northern Ireland.

I spent the first day (Wednesday) exploring the island, making an almost complete anticlockwise circuit of it – an indication of how fit and energetic I was at the age of 54, and also of how I was hurrying to "do" Foula as thoroughly as possible before the weather changed from grey and somewhat misty to something worse, which it did for the next two days, both of which brought persistent rain. That did not prevent me from walking, but I did not walk so far and kept to the low ground. On the Friday, my last full day, I first visited Jock Ratter at North Biggins, to buy metal paperknives he had made in his workshop. He was definitely a "character". He had served in the Merchant Navy and been a prisoner of the Japanese during the Second World War. I was warned never to mention the Japanese to him in any context! What I did mention was the weather, thinking that as a local man and retired seaman he would probably have a good idea of what it would do. He replied: "It may get better, it may get worse, or it may stay the same". His father had built Broadfoot around 1912, and, when the Millsopps added the extensions, he had growled to Frank: "You're turning it into a bloody village".

From Jock's place at the south end Frank drove me to Isobel and John Holbourn's house, Freyers, at the north end. It commands a view of the spectacular natural arch known as Gaada Stack. Isobel Margaret Holbourn, *née* Boyd, had lived on Foula almost all her life since 1956, when she was in her mid-teens and her father was appointed the island's schoolteacher and missionary. She was knowledgeable about its history and way of life, and she had kindly agreed to speak to me about them. During the conversation I put to her a question which I had put to Penny and Frank the previous evening: "Supposing one wished to live here, how easy would it be to buy a property?" Their answer had been something to the effect that it might be possible, but that it would be more difficult if one wanted land. Isobel's first response was much the same, but, just as I was leaving, she said: "Between you and me, I think that you may find the house in which you are staying will be available shortly". "That is very interesting", I replied. "Thank you for telling me".

Walking back to Broadfoot, I passed the old school, where Frank had an office from which he ran the Shetland Energy Advice Centre, informing folk in the islands about how to use energy most economically. Given that Foula was not connected to the mains electricity enjoyed by most Shetlanders, but was supplied inefficiently and expensively by a poorly-maintained combination of wind turbine, diesel generator, and water turbine, the location of the service on the island seemed a little surprising. Frank was sitting in the window and, when I waved, he not only waved back, but also beckoned. From his opening words it was obvious that Isobel had telephoned him after I left her house, and that she had said something on the lines that your visitor is seriously interested in coming to live here. Anyhow, Frank confirmed that he and Penny would soon be moving off the island, explaining that, when their two girls went to secondary school, they wanted them to live at home rather than be boarders at the Anderson High School in Lerwick. He also told me that Penny had been offered a post as an occupational therapist on the Shetland Mainland on condition that she had a full driving licence. Now she was free to accept the offer and would be starting in just ten days' time. The coincidence of her return with her licence and my arrival as a visitor was remarkable. Another coincidence is that Professor Ian Holbourn, who bought Foula at the very beginning of the twentieth-century, was, like me, a scholar with a strong interest in Classics. It may be mentioned too that my birthday, 26 April, coincides with Simmermill, reckoned by Foula folk to be the first day of summer – even when the weather is far from summery. I had the feeling that Fate had led me to the island.

When we reached the house, it was too wet and dark to view the outside, but I was shown all over the inside. I was leaving on Saturday morning, when for the first time I saw the island under blue skies and in bright sunshine. By the time I departed, the Millsopps were telling me that, if I wanted the house and made a satisfactory offer, it was mine, and I was telling them that I was very interested, but needed to sober up, think, consult, and arrange a survey. Before I went home, I had ample time for reflection, staying three nights in the comfortable Busta House Hotel near Brae and having long walks on the islands of Muckle Roe and Unst. As for consultation, I no longer had a wife or partner or parent. Naturally I consulted Lucinda, who, like me, thought the idea an adventure. I also needed to consult Durham University about the early retirement necessitated by my poor eyesight, but that went smoothly. By the end of January 1995, the property was mine – no longer known by the corrupt name Broadfoot, but as Braidfit – "broad meadow by a stream". It had been settled that, although Penny Millsopp and the couple's daughters had already moved to the Shetland Mainland, Frank would stay on in Foula to carry out agreed alterations to the property, including putting a new roof on the south end of it, converting the workshop into a drawing room, enlarging one of the guest bedrooms by adding part of the workshop to create a study, and, at the other end of the house making one large bedroom out of two small ones; he would also restore the two main outbuildings, converting one (an earlier crofthouse) into a large garage and the other (formerly a byre) into a storage shed with a washhouse (WC and sink) partitioned off at one end. The conversion of the workshop included blocking up several of the windows, removing a bank of louvred cupboards and two sinks, building a chimney, and installing a fireplace and gas fire which I bought in the Durham area. Central heating, previously very limited, was now to be extended by the installation of many new radiators and by the conversion of the Rayburn cooker's fuel from peat to kerosene.

Before moving into Braidfit, I made two short visits to Foula. The first was on 13–16 March 1995, when I was accompanied not only by Frank, but also by two nice and knowledgeable ladies from the Lerwick interior design and decoration firm of Frank Williamson, Alison Sinclair and Judy O'Neill. With their help I chose curtains, carpets, paint, and new kitchen units. The second visit was on 1–4 May, to coincide with the delivery of my furniture and other possessions, packed and transported to Shetland by Pickfords. All were in specially-made wooden containers, with the main contents of each marked on the outside. This sounds very sensible and orderly, but the Shetland firm to which Pickfords sub-contracted the delivery to Foula and Braidfit was neither sensible nor orderly. The containers were brought across on a vessel, chartered from the Shetland Islands Council, called the *Spes Clara*, which made two runs on successive days from West Burrafirth. The Latin name and its meaning, "Bright Hope", seemed happy auguries, and the crew did their job splendidly. But the three removers paid little or no attention to the descriptions on the containers, which they delivered in any order. With the exception of one bookcase, all the big items arrived after the small ones – the opposite to what was desirable. As for the transport of containers from the pier to the house, they rented a lorry without properly functioning brakes and a tractor trailer from which pieces kept dropping off. The first day was dry, but the second brought some rain. The brakeless lorry skidded at Braidfit, shunting a car into a link fence and nearly sending it crashing down a bank into the house, and the men muddied the new carpets, despite the contract with Pickfords stipulating that protective covers would be used. Virtually no time was left for the unpacking which they were supposed to do. That was probably just as well, because one of the men almost immediately broke an item of glassware.

On one of its runs the *Spes Clara* also brought in a vehicle I had bought from a garage in Bixter (Plate 36). I had considered bringing the Dormobile with me, but decided that that would not be sensible, given the ferocity of Foula's winds. Like the Dormobile, which had served me so well for 24 years, the replacement vehicle was quite a character. It was a long-wheel-base Land Rover "Defender", previously owned, until it was involved in a bad accident, by the Electricity Board. Under my ownership, it was soon to be much in demand for pulling vehicles out of ditches. On several occasions it was also commandeered (with its driver) for ambulance duty, and on two occasions, despite being bright red, as a hearse. For the funerals I covered the floor at the back with a piece of ribbed rubber carpet-underlay, which had the double advantage of being charcoal-coloured and non-slip – the latter consideration being particularly important because the coffin had to jut out of the back, and the approach to the burial ground is uphill. One of the ambulance call-outs occurred when a visiting workman fell off the roof of the water house and appeared to be concussed. An air ambulance was called, and on the way to the airstrip Maggie the nurse knelt on the passenger seat of the Land Rover and reached into the back to slap the patient's face. I think she suspected that he was faking the concussion, and, on arrival at the airstrip, I looked in through the back window and saw one of his mates stick a fag in his mouth. It seems that he just wanted to get back to "civilisation".

I took up residence at Braidfit on Friday, 30 June 1995, arriving by plane in the late afternoon. The house was full of unpacked boxes, and the baths and kitchen sink were full of dead flies. All of my cleaning materials were packed, and I had no idea where. One of my first actions was to arrange for a kind and efficient resident, Allison Gutcher, to come round in the morning and do some essential cleaning. She came with her six year old daughter, who entertained me with her fluent chatter while helping me unpack books. Making the cleaning arrangement that first evening cheered me up a bit, but my morale was still quite low when, just before going to bed, I went outside at the front of the house and looked across the fields. Although it was 11.30 p.m., it was still daylight, and the air was full of the cries of tirricks (arctic terns) as

36) Foula: Martin's Land Rover being offloaded from the Spes Clara, 3 May 1995

they hovered and picked up insects. It confirmed to me that I had come to a very special place.

But I did not know whether I would find happiness in Foula. My decision to come to live on a small island without a shop, without any place of entertainment, and without a reliable supply of electricity – none at all for most of the night – was a bold one, perhaps even rash: Hilde's friend Waltraud Coles had predicted that I would not last more than a fortnight without access to a Marks and Spencer food hall. She was mistaken: I have managed not only without Marks and Spencer, but without any shop, for more than thirty years. When people are asked how they would cope with life on Foula, a frequent answer is: "I would go mad". That did not happen to me, probably because I was mad already. At any rate my wish for living in isolation developed at an early age, in my preparatory school days, and my temperament and attitude of mind have not changed fundamentally since then. Moreover, in my more mature years I have come to realise the wisdom of living a simple life, growing my own vegetables and being satisfied with telephoning my weekly order for provisions to a family-run country shop which does not have a big stock of groceries, but can usually supply the basics, including bread and fresh fruit. Quite often the list returned in my boxes has "SORRY NONE" written against some of the items, and sometimes other items arrive in less than perfect condition, but I reflect that none of these items is essential, that I am much better off than most folk in the world, and that it is morally good for one to go without from time to time. Visitors to the island, too, have to manage without shopping, although I sometimes tell them that, while Foula has no duty-free shop, they might be able to get a duty-free sheep. At Braidfit I keep good stocks of most things likely to be needed, including medicines, also pasta, rice, and other staples, batteries, and a spare pump and fan for the Rayburn. I have an emergency generator for long power cuts and a battery-powered back-up system which keeps the lights on in the event of shorter cuts. I always have at least one spare cylinder of gas, and ensure that there is plenty of kerosene in the outdoor tank. Getting kerosene delivered can be quite difficult and is always expensive: the fuel is delivered from Lerwick to Walls Pier, where it is pumped into a bowser for conveyance to Foula. On arrival at Foula Pier, the bowser is attached to a tractor and towed up to Braidfit, where the fuel is transferred to the tank by means of a small electric pump. Only about 900 litres can be brought in each time. This is the present system. For 28 years my fuel was transported in 200-litre (45-gallon) barrels. This was somewhat cheaper, but the barrels were too heavy to be handled comfortably and safely.

On the catering front, I faced an early challenge. In the second half of August 1995 I was to have three staying visitors for three days – Colin, our aunt Ro, and Hilde. It was his suggestion, approved by me. Before accepting the invitation, Ro, aged 83, checked with me that she would have access to an indoor loo. Although I was able to allay her concern about that, I was troubled about my ability to provide good meals. So I contacted Bo Simmons, a professional cook with an excellent reputation in Shetland, who with her husband, Henry Anderton, owned and ran the Burrastow House Hotel on the west side of the Shetland Mainland. She was very happy to help, we agreed the menu for every meal, and everything was sent over just before the guests arrived. It was the start not only of a nice business arrangement, but also of an enduring friendship. Every year Bo has fulfilled at least one order for me.

The food Bo provided for my guests – fresh tomato soup, lobster mayonnaise, new potatoes and salad, and lemon tart the first evening – could not be faulted, but the visit was not a complete success. The two ladies were perfectly charming and highly appreciative, but Colin less so. I had been expecting to accompany my guests to the Busta House Hotel, which was to be the base for the rest of their holiday in Shetland, but I pulled out of that arrangement, instead flying out one day to meet the three of them for lunch in Lerwick.

From the resident population I received a mixed reception. Most folk were very welcoming and helpful, a small minority hostile. Early on, I had a clash with my nearest neighbours, Dal and Maggie Prytherch, whose house, the Breckans, was close to the point where my track joins the public road. One evening, when Frank was staying with me, the two of us were eating in the kitchen, when Dal called uninvited and, sitting down, made to light up his pipe. Seeing the look of horror on my face, he stopped and said "Oh, do you mind my smoking?". It was Frank who answered: "Yes, Martin does not allow smoking in his house". "OK", said Dal before walking out. I thought that was the end of the matter, but a day or two later, when I was walking by the Breckans, he shouted at me to come in, on the pretext that he wanted a lettuce. He and Maggie, but especially he, then berated me for my inhospitality in not allowing smoking in my house. They did not do so for long, because, after wishing them a very good afternoon, I rapidly departed.

Peace with the Prytherchs was soon established. I invited them both to a party I gave for all residents in September – with a request that there be no smoking indoors! Dal did not come, but Maggie conveyed an apology for his absence and was as pleasant and appreciative as everyone else. Until the end of 1995, when she retired after 25 years' service, she was Foula's community nurse. She also had a small craft shop, selling knitwear among other things, and I soon became a frequent customer. With Dal I never felt quite comfortable. He had a reputation for being a Walter Mitty, and I heard some amusing stories about some of his claimed exploits. Consistent with them in a small way was an incident at Braidfit in March 1996, when I had two workmen doing various maintenance jobs, including rebuilding the doorway and wall of the generator shed. The younger man was working on the doorway, while his senior colleague was doing another job, when Dal appeared, clearly after having had a drink or two – his favourite was Glenmorangie Malt Whisky with a chaser of Carlsberg Special Brew. I went out, just in time to hear him say: "This work is absolute crap. I was a civil engineer, so I know. What you need is a bloody big lintel." The young man, a shy and sensitive soul, was visibly shaken. Before apologising to him, I addressed the intruder: "Dal, these men are experts. They know exactly what needs to be done, thank you."

The only serious hostility I encountered came from a reclusive resident of the Hametoun. I have a great admiration for her scientific knowledge, her energy and skill as a crofter and horticulturalist, and her simple way of life, and I deeply regret that she soon declared war on me. Her hostility pained me, and I am very sorry if I quite unwittingly caused her pain. I like to think that, somewhere along the line, there may have been a misunderstanding on her part. The problem, as *I* understand it (she has never explained how she sees it) is that, while the Millsopps were doing voluntary work in Kenya for two years before my arrival, they allowed her, informally, to put sheep on Braidfit and cut hay. She also worked an uninhabited croft which she normally accessed on foot or on a quad-bike via Braidfit, passing through its yard and very close to the house. When I bought Braidfit, what I got was the house, yard, outbuildings, and a very small area round the house. All these were decrofted. I did not want or expect to acquire the three fields, the tenancy of which the Millsopps had retained. I just wanted to have a slightly larger area around the house, to create a medium-sized front garden, and to cultivate the kaleyard. I did not want anyone tramping or driving through my yard, least of all someone who sometimes carried a gun and did not even say "good morning", but I was prepared to pay for the provision of an alternative route. But all the offers were rejected, and eventually the Millsopps bought the fields from the landlord and sold them on to me. The arrangement cost me an arm and a leg, but it assured my independence and privacy.

I made several attempts to improve relations. On 7 January 1998, she and I were the only passengers on the plane from Tingwall to Foula. Before the pilot arrived, I was asked to sit at the front, and she at the back because she had a young dog with her. I turned round and wished her "Happy New Year". No reply. I repeated my greeting, then added: "How is your new dog settling down?" This time there was a response: "Look, you've ruined my life. We'll meet in Hell". I might have commented that this was an unusually harsh reply to a sincere New Year greeting and friendly enquiry, but all I said, truthfully, was: "I don't know what you are talking about". The next time I saw her and wished her a good morning, she snapped back: "Drop dead!" I have never said anything unpleasant to her, and I continue to wish her well.

As soon as I became the owner of the fields, I needed to put stock on them. Otherwise the Crofting Commission could have objected, and, at least in theory, compelled me to let the land to a tenant. I first considered llamas or alpacas and, to keep my options open, erected an unusually-tall (llama-proof) fence along part of the boundary of my croft. I bought literature on the care of llamas and corresponded with the British Camelids Society. The advice was that Foula's wet and windy climate was far from ideal for llamas, but what finally decided me against them was a visit to the Paris Zoo, where I watched the llamas chasing ostriches around their shared enclosure and bunting them up their backsides. I did not fancy receiving similar treatment. After further thought and discussion, including with my near neighbour the late Eric Isbister, I decided on Highland kye (cattle). I joined the Highland Cattle Society, and my experience with kye at Silligrove helped, although we never kept Highlanders. In 1998 I bought two yearling heifers from the Strathmore Farming Company at Glamis Castle – Frangag II of Glamis Castle, granddaughter of Macbeth, usually known as "Fran" (Plate 37), and Ailsa, another coo of noble birth, whose genealogy I have mislaid. Ailsa was the better-looking beast, but, as the vendors must have known, had a bad temperament. This was noticed by a drover at Aberdeen when he was putting her aboard the ship for Lerwick. He rang up to tell me that she had given him much trouble. When she arrived at Foula Pier on 30 July, she glared at me menacingly from her pen on the deck. I never felt comfortable with her, and, the larger she got, the more dangerous she became, so I sold her. My last sight of her was putting a horn through a Foula crewman's jersey as he passed her pen on the deck. I replaced her with a Highlander of much humbler birth, acquired from the owners of the island of Vaila, near Walls. Not wishing her to feel inferior to Frangag, I called her (the Empress) Plotina, after the Epicurean widow of the Emperor Trajan and adoptive mother of Hadrian. She and Fran gained fans around the world and are the heroines (although not portrayed as Highlanders) of Ana Vicente's delightful and instructive children's book in Portuguese, illustrated by Madalena Matoso, *Quanto Pesa um Quilograma?* [*How Much Does a Kilogram Weigh?*] (2009).

37) Braidfit: Frangag taking breakfast in -10C

At Braidfit, the kye kept away twitchers and other potential intruders. They were wonderful grazers, eating coarse stuff which neither sheep nor ponies would touch, including reed canary-grass, in Foula called "ruir", which used to be cut for thatching. In this and all sorts of other ways they helped to create an environment which encouraged insects, birds, and wild flowers. Traditionally, Foula folk kept kye, and it is a great loss that they have rarely done that in recent times. A notable exception was Eric Isbister. For winter feed, I cut a small amount of hay myself with a scythe, but bought most of it as well as cobs. But another significant item, and a home-grown one, was Shetland kale, which flourished in my kaleyard, where I would sometimes set out as many as 360 plants in April for use through the following winter, the plants having spent the previous eight months (August-March) in my plantiecrub – a circular drystone structure out on the scattald (common pasture ground) designed to protect them from the worst of the weather and from rabbits. Braidfit was classed as an ESA (Environmentally Sensitive Area), and I received a modest grant to compensate me for some of the work I did and the restrictions I observed. One year, I received also a grant from the Royal

Society for the Protection of Birds under its Cattle for Conservation Scheme. The downsides of my hospitality to Frangag and Plotina included: the need to feed and water them in all weathers; the likelihood that handling their hay in the small outbuilding in which I stored it did more damage to my already-scarred lungs; and the damage they did to fences, especially when they were attempting to get at grass on the far sides of them. Veterinary visits could be quite challenging: the kye needed to be penned in the cattle crush, but one did not want to get them in there unless and until confirmation of the flight happening was received. On one occasion I had a lady visitor who, as well as gallantly participating in Foula's contribution to Shetland's famous Spring Clean-up (Da Voar Redd Up) by collecting rubbish from ditches and verges, helped me gather bovine droppings to send away for laboratory analysis. When I reported these activities to Lucinda, she commented: "Gosh, Dad, you sure know how to give a girl a good time".

Despite the success of my September 1995 party, I never gave another one on that scale. Indeed I made it increasingly clear that I am not a sociable animal. So I issued few invitations and received few. But I socialised more in the earliest years of my residence than at any later time. Isobel, as well as being helpful with information and advice, kindly invited me to have dinner with her and her two staying guests – John (later Sir John) Scott, Lord Lieutenant of Shetland, and his wife, Wendy. John had been a senior boy at The Downs School when I entered it in 1948. We had not seen one another since then, and we exchanged reminiscences. Wendy was and is one of Shetland's most expert gardeners, and, within days of our meeting at Isobel's, she and John came up with good suggestions for the lay-out of the front garden I wanted to create at Braidfit. At that time they lived at Gardie House on Bressay, five minutes by ferry from Lerwick.

Another friendly person, who invited me to her house to have lunch with her and her family, was Edwina Cook. She has an English degree from Manchester University and was married to the skipper of Foula's ferry – yes, to Captain Cook! They had two children in Foula Primary School. Their chalet home, Skerrig, was towards the north end of Foula, and I decided to go on my Hercules bicycle, bought new from Halford's in Kidderminster in 1950 for fifteen guineas. It served me well before I became a car driver, but had spent most of its later life rusting away in garages and sheds. The ride to the Cooks' house was the first and last I had on Foula. Because the brakes were defective, I did not dare ride downhill; because the gears did not work properly, I could not ride uphill. According to Lowell Thomas Jr. (*Out of This World*, 61), there is an old Tibetan saying:

> If he doesn't carry you uphill, he is no horse; and if you don't walk down, you are no man.

I could not help recalling this the day I visited the Cooks, with the thought that my bicycle was of less use to me than a horse to a Tibetan. Oh, yes, and on the outward journey there was a strong headwind.

Alan Cook's position was far from satisfactory. Foula had been awaiting a new ferry, based on the island, since 1989. The *Westering Homewards II*, an unsuitable vessel that cost £430,000, had been a dismal failure in sea trials. The replacement for the intended replacement was not to be ready until late in 1996. So Alan, appointed to serve from 1 June 1995, had no Foula boat to skipper, only the less than perfect *Koada*, shared with the island of Papa Stour. Moreover, when the new boat was delivered, he was no longer in post. In August 1996 he had resigned, and he and his family had departed to Orkney. He was replaced by Andrew ("Andy") Hurley, an experienced and efficient seaman. His wife, Denise, was a nurse, and they had two young children.

An interesting early invitation I received was from Penelope and Phil Holbourn to visit them at Mucklegrind. Phil was the youngest and only surviving son of John ("Ian") Bernard Stoughton Holbourn (1872–1935), who, having first sighted Foula on his way to Iceland in 1899, had bought it two years later. If you think "Phil" is here short for "Philip", you are underestimating the eccentricity of his father. Each of his three sons had at least four forenames, including a Greek one, indicated below with an underlining. The eldest was Athelston <u>Hylas</u> Major Lauchlan Stoughton Holbourn, the second Laurence Alasdair <u>Menander</u> Stoughton Holbourn, and the youngest <u>Philistos</u> Rognvald Howard Stoughton Holbourn. Mucklegrind, which was soon to become dilapidated, is situated a little before Freyers. It was built with materials left over from the making of Michael Powell's iconic film *The Edge of the World* (1936), inspired by the evacuation of St Kilda in 1930 and shot in Foula with the co-operation and, in some cases, participation of its inhabitants. Phil was struck by the similarity of some of my interests to those of his father, who was knowledgeable about the ancient Greeks and Greek civilisation. I was interested in what he had to say about his family and the island, but regretted that, almost every time Penelope started to say something interesting, he interrupted her. They lived in Brecon, Powys, and only came up to Foula on holiday in the summer. They insisted on coming and going by sea, as in the old days, until they had a literally-bruising crossing in the *Koada* and were forbidden to do it again. The Holbourn family remains an important presence in Foula, all members of it being children, grandchildren, and great grandchildren of Hylas and his wife, Joyce. I shall introduce the children shortly.

The short early-evening drive to Mucklegrind gave me an early introduction to the variability of Foula's weather. Braidfit and the whole south end of the island were enveloped in thick mist, and the last item I expected to need was my dark glasses. But, on the way, the mist first thinned, then cleared to bright sunshine, with the mist south of the high hills looking like a waterfall as it rolled over their north-facing sides. Two hours later, when I drove home, the mist there was as dense as when I left.

In the autumn of 1995, probably with Edwina's encouragement, I attended a Hallowe'en fancy-dress party in the Hall, wearing a placard advertising:

Foula Spiritual Services Unlimited

–

The Revd Abel Dewitcher

offers a complete spiritual service to meet your requirements

–

Specialities include

Exorcisms – Hallowe'en offer: two for the price of one
Blessing boats (sadly, no recent commissions)
Prayers for:
diverting flans from your property
the success of your crü [round-up of sheep]
uninterrupted electricity
– and other miracles!

–

No success, no fee

Hylas Holbourn was a university teacher and researcher first in Oxford, then in Aberdeen. He was a well-regarded physicist, who died in 1962, when in his mid-fifties. He had married Joyce Helen Brown in 1938. When I moved to Foula, W.S. ("Bill") Watt, who had been Regius Professor of Humanity at Aberdeen University (1952–1979), was interested because he and his wife had been near neighbours of the Holbourn family.

All four of Joyce and Hylas' children, who had got to know Foula on family holidays, took up residence on the island. The eldest, John, was Isobel's second husband until they separated two days after my arrival. After that, he lived just below Freyers, at Ristie, reached by a rough track, which he spent much time trying to improve with only moderate success. He was in charge of the electricity scheme – again, but through no fault of his own, with only moderate success! He had a rather mischievous sense of humour. He contracted multiple sclerosis, and spent his last years in sheltered housing in Wiltshire, dying in November 2012. It was with his encouragement that in 2007 the Bath and Comerton Archaeological Society investigated and excavated an ancient stone circle on Da Heights at the north end of Foula.

The second son and youngest child of Joyce and Hylas, Robert ("Rob") Alexander, also had the misfortune to contract a horrible disease, leukaemia, from which he died in April 2000 aged 51. Living in the Haa or laird's house right by the pier, he was a seaman and naval architect, who skippered the boat for many years before being told that his colour blindness disqualified him. He then served briefly as the boat's engineer. Other roles he performed included those of Foula's Peat Marshal and Grazings Clerk – both concerned with the division and exploitation of the "scattald". He married Anne Holden, a French scientist who had come to Foula as part of an international group that volunteered to help create the airstrip. They had three children – Euan (deceased), Magnus ("Magnie"), and Vaila. Magnie is the present skipper of the boat and much involved with the power scheme, which is now a mix of solar and wind power with diesel back-up. He is the Grazings Clerk and a part-time Foula Ranger. Also, he and his Polish-born wife, Justyna, who have three children, have established Foula Wool, which in recent years has attracted grants totalling £146,000 from the Scottish Government's Island Communities Fund to open a spinning mill on the island. The business has gained an international clientele for its high-quality knitting yarn produced from the naturally-coloured fleeces of Foula's sheep.

Sheila Catharine, Joyce and Hylas' second child and elder daughter, is an outstanding naturalist, who took a degree in zoology at Aberdeen University and has never ceased to take a keen interest in Foula's geology, plants, and birds. In 1964 she married Foula crofter James ("Jim") Ross Gear. In recognition of her many years of service as an adviser, local assistant, and field adviser to PhD candidates from Glasgow University during their seabird studies directed by Dr (later Professor) Bob Furness, she was awarded an honorary fellowship of the University in 2003. For many years she was the island's postmistress. The post office was open for two hours (9–11 a.m.) three days a week (Monday, Wednesday, Friday). She was paid a pittance, but did the job for the sake of the community and visitors. The first time I visited, I thought that she said that she had just been attending to the llamas. A near-neighbour of mine in Shincliffe Village had kept llamas, so I was not hugely surprised that she kept them too. She laughed and said she had been in the lamb-house (in Foula-speak "laamus", pronounced as in "alarm us"). A few days later I brought her some flowers from my garden. They were "Bishop of Llandaff" dahlias, with deep-red flowers and dark leaves. They were favourites of Barbara, and the tubers I had brought to Foula were originally hers. Unexpectedly and touchingly, my gift to Sheila was received with something like rapture. Unknown to me, it was her and Jim's wedding anniversary, and red dahlias had been part of her wedding bouquet. The post office closed on 25 October 2018, but is often shown as still open – in tourist information and the Wikipedia article on Foula, for example, and even on the Foula Ranger website. A skilled crofter and breeder of ponies, Sheila is a part-time Foula Ranger and the author of two fine books: *Foula: Island West of the Sun* (1983) and *Flora of Foula* (2008).

When I arrived, Sheila's husband, Jim, was not only the island's community councillor, but also one of the representatives of the West Side on the Shetland Islands Council, so often the official voice of Foula, although Isobel was often vocal too until her death on 19 December 2010. A tall, strong man, he played many roles, including as crofter, pony-breeder, fisherman, crewman and skipper of the boat, building contractor, and musician. He died on 19 January 2024. Sheila and he had three children. The eldest, Ross, married an American citizen and lives in the United States. Kevin, of Veedal, was skipper of the boat and is the island's efficient part-time postie. Since he ceased to be skipper, the speed of his delivery service has much improved! Previously he could not be expected even to begin sorting the mail until he had had a meal after a full day on the boat. Penny Gear, the youngest of the three, lives at North Harrier. She is a fine sheep-rearer and a brilliant pony-breeder who has won many prizes. She does fire-duty at the airstrip, teaches art in the school, and participates in the counting (for scientific purposes) of seabirds. Since the outbreak of Covid 19, she has cut my hair, and recently done me all sorts of other kindnesses, including gardening. Her sons, Robert, Paul, and Jack Smith, are often on the island, and they have helped me too.

Joyce and Hylas' third child, Frances ("Francie") Moira Ratter, is, like her elder sister, a fine naturalist. She has a degree in botany from Durham University. She is the ex-wife of John Andrew Ratter, son of Jock, and mother of Moira (deceased) and Amy. Amy is a resident and an active crofter who, as well as caring for her sheep, grows all sorts of fruit and vegetables in her "polycrub" or Shetland greenhouse, assisted now by her daughter. Like many other residents, she has also taken on a variety of jobs in the service of the community, including Water Board employee, refuse collector, and firefighter.

The Gear family has long been important in Foula and continues to be so. Jim's elder brother, Kenneth ("Ken") Robert William (1937–2006), was a fine seaman and former skipper of the boat. He also fished, especially for lobsters. He was a man of great intelligence, but had the misfortune to suffer from a disruptive illness, alcoholism. In connection with one incident, when he had been the worse for wear when out in his boat, I heard someone remark that he would feel safer at sea with an inebriated Ken than with many others who were sober. He was Isobel Holbourn's first husband and had three sons with her, one of whom, also Kenneth, after working abroad for many years and marrying a Myanmar-born woman, now spends most of his time on Foula, where I am lucky to have him, Mai, and their two children as my nearest neighbours. His distinguished career in industrial instrumentation has taken him to many parts of the world, including to offshore energy platforms west of Shetland, to Australia, and to Laos. He now works for an electrical consulting firm based in Rotterdam involved with projects in China, Thailand, the Middle East, and Western Europe. Another son of Ken and Isobel, Bobby, is also on the island at times, living in what was his mother's house, Freyers. Ken senior also had a son, Magnus, by his second marriage, to Barbara Gear, who was a resident in my early years. Magnus follows his father in being a fine seaman and in fishing, including for lobster. He has his own fishing boat, the 8-metre *Utilise*, and is a member of the island's boat crew. He is the Keeper of Foula's unmanned lighthouse, chairs the Foula Airstrip Trust, and is a member of the fire crew. He and his partner, Fran Dyson-Sutton, have four young children. Like many mothers, she is an energetic multi-tasker, not only domestically but also in the community, working among other things as Early Years Practitioner and IT instructor in the school, Water Board employee, Airstrip Trustee and Treasurer, and Foula Heritage Ranger/Guide. Before making Foula her home, she obtained a BA degree in Geography at Oxford University and an MSc in Conservation and Land Management at Bangor University (formerly UCNW).

Magnus and Fran live at Dykes, in the Hametoun. Its previous occupant was Edith Gray, a much-loved single woman, who until weakened by old age was a very active and skilful crofter, attending to her sheep, cutting hay, and cultivating her kaleyard. She was also a brilliant knitter. Born on 27 January 1918, she well remembered the time when Foula had a much larger population, and how girls from the north and south ends of the island would often meet half-way to talk and laugh together. It was also a time when there was growing of corn and tatties, and when there were kye to be tended and milked. Like everyone else, I loved visiting her and hearing her interesting and amusing stories, and every summer she came to Braidfit to see the gardens and have tea. Although the distance from Dykes is only about 300 yards as the crow flies, she used to announce that she was "going west to Braidfit". She died, aged 97, on 9 August 2015.

An equally-delightful lady was Edith's elder sister, Aggie Jean Isbister, widow of Robert ("Bobby") Isbister. Born on 3 February 1910, she was aged 85 when I came to Foula, and its oldest resident. Until recently she had been an active crofter, and she retained her mental capacity and keen sense of humour to the end. She was aged 92 when she died on 30 March 2002 on the same day as another great lady – Queen Elizabeth the Queen Mother. When I started growing Shetland kale, she gave me some firm and wise instructions as to what to do. The seed was to be sown in the plantiecrub not later than 31 July, and in the spring the plants were to be set out fourteen inches apart. I first thought that surprisingly close, but soon understood the reason for it, which is that the grown plants support one another even in quite violent winds. One of my ambulance missions was to take her, as a stretcher case, to the airstrip on her way to hospital. I did not expect her to come back, but come back she did very soon, walking and laughing. The problem had been undiagnosed type 2 diabetes, aggravated by her love of Lucozade.

Aggie Jean lived in the island's southernmost house, South Biggins, with her bachelor son, Eric. By choice they lived without mains water and electricity, as did Francie Ratter for many years. I did not meet Eric until early 1996, when I discovered mice at Braidfit and needed someone to stop up holes in the airing cupboard and elsewhere to prevent them from getting access to the living quarters from the loft. I soon discovered that he was good at joinery, and later he erected a picket fence round my new front garden. He often looked after Braidfit in my absence. He was a suitable person to do that because he never went away, and he was used to handling kye. I say "he never went away". That is not quite true because, as he used to say, he went away to be born in 1943, and he accompanied his parents to the Shetland Mainland for a week in 1975. Only much later, towards the end of his life, did he go out another time, when his health declined and he and his house needed attention. On one occasion, when I was going away in mid-winter and he had kindly agreed to check on Braidfit and feed the kye, I said: "You will go across every day, won't you, even if it is snowy?" His reply was: "I will if I can get over on the quad", to which I sternly retorted: "Eric, you must go on foot, if necessary. Animals cannot be left unfed, least of all in snow". He took my point, but it is a fact that he rarely walked anywhere if he could use his quad, even when crossing his big field, and the consequent lack of exercise did his health no good at all. Although I have done quite a lot of travelling, I sympathise with his aversion to it, and in recent years I have travelled very little, even on Foula. I have always preferred to walk from home rather than drive the car to walk somewhere else. I have very rarely driven the three miles to the north end of the island, and I have only done it three times in the last seven years. But Eric, for all his preference for staying at home, was far more sociable than I am, and, despite having no internet connection or any other advanced means of communication, he was remarkably well informed about ships and shipping and world affairs in general. He was also a brilliant storyteller and fine musician, who composed as well as played. One of his passions was skiffle and that rock 'n' roll skiffle-influencer Buddy Holly, and I remember his astonishment at discovering that Foula's professorial newcomer was able to sing along with him from memory not only "Peggy Sue", but also Tommy Dee's song "The Three Stars", composed after the death of Buddy, Ritchie Valens, and "The Big Bopper" in a plane crash on 3 February 1959:

> Buddy's singing for God now and His chorus in the sky.
> Buddy Holly, we'll always remember you
> With tears in our eyes.

Gee, we're gonna miss you;
Everybody sends their love.

Eric died on 5 December 2021. Whether he is playing and singing for God now, I rather doubt, but, gee, he is missed.

Bryan Taylor of Leraback too was mildly surprised when he initiated the singing of the Dubliners' song "The Seven Drunken Nights" at a leaving party for our Dubliner nurse, Marybeth Casey, in or about 1997 and it turned out that I was the only other person who knew the words. He was a brother of Maggie Prytherch, and it was after she was appointed community nurse that he and his wife, Marion, moved from Edinburgh to Foula and built a new house and later three chalets for letting. Marion ran a dinner, bed, and breakfast establishment. Bryan has served as a boat crewman and skipper, but his greatest passions, along with watching Scotland's rugby team in action, are motor vehicles and engines. He has been of great help to me over the years, repairing and servicing my vehicles, as well as laying tar and chips on my drive and track. The approach to Leraback is, in most folk's eyes, not beautified by numerous vehicles that would not look out of place in a scrapyard, but I imagine that Bryan sees them differently – as a rich source of spare parts. A favourite poem of his is Ted Hughes's "Tractor", which might easily have been written about him and one of his machines. He is by no means the only resident to have owned vehicles that have seen better days. Being an island without a bridge or car ferry, Foula is exempt from the normal requirement for a vehicle to pass an annual Ministry of Transport test, and it is a common practice for residents to buy cheaply vehicles that have failed the test. Such vehicles do not usually last long.

Bryan is kind, but sometimes a bit unrefined in his language, as when he welcomed a lady visitor of mine at the airstrip with the words: "And he told me you were an *ugly* bitch". Fortunately, she took the words as the big compliment they were intended to be.

One afternoon in December 2008 the Leraback chalets went on fire, and were lost because the island's fire crew, who had arrived at the scene, were disgracefully instructed by fire chiefs off the island not to attempt to extinguish the blaze. Bryan survived, but his dog perished. Thankfully, he still lives on, but Marion died on 21 March 2015. She was a lively and cheerful person, who led a busy life but also knew how to enjoy herself. She was always kind to me. From Leraback there is a good view of the approach to the Voe

(Foula's harbour), and she would often telephone, in those far-off days before one could get the information from a computer, to tell me that the boat was approaching. She also mended my jerseys, but the most memorable kindness she did me was on the day I had my fall and required a "medivac" by plane. She came to Braidfit and sat with me for several hours, until the plane arrived.

Marion and Bryan's son, Stuart, has always been a great help to me. If there is some emergency – for example to do with the heating or plumbing or a leaking roof, a telephone call usually brings him round in minutes. He is extraordinarily quick at diagnosing any problem and fixing it and, if need be, improvising a solution – by making a new part, if necessary. He is an excellent joiner, and walks about a roof nonchalantly in all conditions. There used to be a repair workshop in Lerwick called Last Ditchology. It was a useful service, and Stuart would be well qualified to carry on a similar business.

A valuable member of Foula's community since she joined it in 2005 is Lynn Robertson, who lives at Skerrig. She came when she needed a farm placement as part of her Livestock Production course at Orkney College. She has a natural way with animals, including the Foula sheep and Shetland ponies which she breeds. Her pony stud, named Charliemay, has played a leading role in encouraging genetic testing for skeletal atavism, the type of dwarfism found in Shetland ponies. This is just one of several research projects in which she is involved. Another interest is the breeding of Shetland ducks. Her YouTube videos, account name "Awoowa pup", make entertaining viewing. She is a member of both the boat crew and the fire crew.

Foula means "Bird Island", and the choice of name is no surprise. Its bird population is massive and diverse. It is an ornithologist's paradise. A friend's teenage daughter, pretending to misunderstand my meaning, expressed amusement and amazement when I mentioned the ubiquity of shags along its coast. When I holidayed in Foula in late September 1994, the breeding season for birds was over, but, when I took up residence in summer 1995, it was in full swing, and I immediately encountered the three species most likely to attack those who enter their territories – bonxies (great skuas), allans (arctic skuas), and tirricks (arctic terns). In 1995 Foula was pretty well the bonxie capital of the world, or at least of the western hemisphere. There were thousands of pairs, more than anywhere else, and at first I found them quite intimidating and used to advance with a stick above my head. A bonxie is about the size of a farmyard hen with a wing-span of 24 inches. When it is attacking, it usually has the decency to give a warning cry, to come from the front, to approach at moderate speed, and to aim to go just over the top of one's head. An allan, on the other hand, although a bit smaller (wing-span 22 inches), can be more dangerous, often coming at high speed with little or no warning from the side or back, and may scratch or scrape the top of one's head or an ear. When Lucinda first visited Foula in August 1996, Ciara, then not quite five, found the bonxies hilarious, especially when they were threatening her mother, and was completely fearless, as befits one who in adulthood has worked among the big seabird colonies on islands off the coast of Northumbria. The area around the airstrip is one of the allans' main breeding grounds: making the short walk there from Braidfit, I would often take a path along the border between allan-territory and bonxie-territory. With luck, the two species would be so busy attacking one another that I could slip through unmolested. Tirricks too used to breed in the area around the airstrip, but their numbers, like those of bonxies, are now much reduced, by avian influenza among other causes. In my early years on the island, I was likely to get attacked by them while I was walking along my track.

Braidfit is a haven for native and migratory birds, especially since I have planted extensive hedges of *rosa rugosa* around both the front garden and the cultivated area of the kaleyard, with additional shelter provided by a variety of trees, mainly willows, but also birch, hornbeam, and sycamore. I am not an ornithologist, but I am happy that my croft is a special place for birds. Rarities noticed in my time include Bobolink, Bonelli's Warbler, Sykes's Warbler, Isabelline Shrike, and Siberian Redthroat. Among the chief guardians of the kaleyard are wrens, which promptly remove any caterpillars from my kale. The hedges and trees also afford good protection against Foula's fierce salt-laden winds. They even managed this on what I call "Black Tuesday" – 11 June 2000 when an exceptionally savage summer storm not only swept tens of thousands of seabirds' chicks and eggs into the ocean, but also blew down or defoliated plants, bushes, and saplings. Heartbreakingly, the storm decimated a new plantation of willows which, to the acclaim of *The Shetland Times* (17 September 1999), I had set out in the early spring of 1999. The kale and other vegetables inside the kaleyard survived. The varieties of wild flowers (see cover image) and plants are as rich as those of birds and include rarities such as bog bean.

Foula's aggressive birds were far less of a worry to me than its mid-winter celebrations, which with careful planning and ruthless unsociability I have managed to avoid. Some residents celebrate Christmas and New Year on 25 December and 1 January respectively, but most hold their celebrations of Yule and Newerday in accordance with the Julian Calendar on 6 and 13 January, when there is all-night (or very late-night) partying. I have always been happy to exchange gifts with other residents, but that has been the extent of my involvement. Often I arranged to be away on both dates, which also suited my programme of research: libraries re-opened in early January after the holiday and hotel rates were often low at that time. Looking in my diary for January 1996, I see that I was away 3–23 January, visiting Durham, Birmingham, Bangor, London, and Oxford. This was typical timing and a typical programme.

But I was lucky to escape on 3 January 1996. During the night of 23–24 December (1995) Shetland experienced one of its most severe blizzards in living memory. When I awoke early on the 24th, I was aware that there had been snow during the night, but I had no idea how much. I made the mistake of going into the porch in my pyjamas and opening the house door to have a look. The snow was drifted up over the whole door, and a wall of it fell into the porch. I had great difficulty in getting the door closed, and only managed it after some frantic shovelling, with more snow blowing in all the time. I awaited daylight before doing anything more. What daylight revealed was beautiful but challenging – deep and long drifts up against the north side of the house, all around the yard, up the drive and over the big gate at the top of it. The telephone was still working, and I used it to ask Hilde to tell my nearest and dearest that I might not be able to wish them happy Christmas tomorrow. I was right in suspecting that it might go off soon. The greatest miracle was that the electricity and water kept going. The credit for this was due not to the beneficent intervention of the Revd Abel Dewitcher, but to Penny Gear's partner at that time, Steven Smith at North Harrier. Steven was keen on gadgets and unusual machines, and he had surprised folk by buying a snowcat, a tracked vehicle. I cannot swear that anyone said he was crazy, but it was remarked that he would probably find little use for it. However, after the blizzard it was a godsend, above all because he could collect John Holbourn and enable water-pumping and generator maintenance to continue. He could also carry fodder for animals. The result was that Foula managed better than most other parts of Shetland, where many folk lost their electricity supply and had no back-up. Few had emergency generators and some had no supply of calor gas for cooking or fires. At one stage there was talk of getting the army in to help. The Sumburgh Hotel, close to Sumburgh Airport, had planned to close for a short Christmas holiday, but reopened to accommodate and feed stranded travellers. With the road up to Lerwick, 26 miles to the north, impassable, the only way to get there was by sea. With Foula's essential services uninterrupted, I rather enjoyed being totally cut off, including from my nearest neighbours, but I soon began the long job of clearing the approach to my garage and the whole length of my drive up to and beyond the gate. One problem was that, even when it was not snowing, there was a lot of snow blowing around and drifting. The work took me several days, but was completed in time for my scheduled departure. By the way, in those days the "Islander" pilots in Shetland were not averse to using snow-covered runways and airstrips (Plate 38), which is sadly no longer the case. On 19 November 1996 I was collected from Foula in several inches of snow, which would be unthinkable now: the pilot had flown in Antarctica and revelled in the conditions. Someone who did not share his delight and mine was the Foula firefighter on duty who had to trudge through the snow and had quite reasonably reported that the airstrip was not in a suitable state. Foula's celebration of New Year's Day on 13 January is not, as is often claimed, unique in Britain. The same tradition is observed by the isolated community of Cwm Gwaun (Gwaun Valley) in Pembrokeshire. The old New Year is called in Welsh *Hen Galan.*

38) Foula: Britten-Norman "Islander" on the airstrip, February 2001

Sometimes travel to and from Foula is represented as being unbelievably rapid. On 19 July 1996 *The Shetland Times* printed a letter in which I described a remarkable offer I had received:

> When I took up residence at Braidfit, Foula, a year ago, I did not expect to enjoy all the services available to me when I lived on the British mainland. It seems I was mistaken. ... I have just received from *Time* magazine an unsolicited communication which includes an itinerary thoughtfully prepared for "Martin F. Smith and partner" on the generous assumption that I shall be the grand prizewinner in a sweepstake. The prize is a three-day trip to New York as a guest of the magazine, and I am much looking forward to winning it, for every provision is made for my comfort and convenience. The timetable reveals that on the first day, prior to departure from London at 10.15 a.m. by British Airways first class, a "chauffeur-driven Rolls Royce calls at Braidfit, for transportation to Heathrow", and that, when I return to Heathrow, I shall be "met by Rolls Royce for the journey home to Braidfit". Disappointingly, but significantly, the details of the journey from Braidfit to Heathrow and back are omitted.

Braidfit to Foula Pier is just over a mile, and the sailing Foula–Walls takes two hours, but there is no roll-on, roll-off ferry. Starting in Walls, the chauffeur would have needed to drive 30 miles to Lerwick, make a fourteen-hour voyage to Aberdeen, then drive about 550 miles to London.

For many years, until the arrival of the pandemic, I was flattered to receive invitations to be Father Christmas at the party in the school. As well as handing out presents, I might describe my journey from Lapland to Foula and offer jokes and riddles, never with any smutty content. Sometimes I confessed that I had been given the sack. I enjoyed the events, and, much more importantly, the bairns seemed to do so too. The only drawback for me was the quite dreadful, ill-fitting costume provided by the school. When Christine Else, Foula's wonderful teacher 2006–2011, first saw me in it, minutes before I was scheduled to perform, she threw an uncontrollable fit of giggles, which I found quite unnerving. A later teacher did something worse, wanting me to participate in the partying with the bairns before and after my performance. I declined to shatter the dramatic illusion and any belief in Santa.

In many areas of activity I have been much less useful than most of my fellow-residents, but an exception is the postal service. When I came to live in Foula, the mail arrived by sea, which meant a maximum of three deliveries a week in summer and two in winter. In late September 1996, a parcel of books was sent to me by express airmail from Vienna. It arrived in Shetland in early October, but was not delivered until 31 October, the boat having sailed only on the first and last days of the month. During the same period there were several Loganair flights to the island. I complained to Royal Mail and wanted to know why they were not using the plane. I also complained that the staff in the Lerwick Delivery Office were recording Special Delivery items for Foula as having been delivered, not when they had reached addresses in Foula, but when they were still in Lerwick. My campaign to persuade Royal Mail to send in the mail by plane as well as by boat was at first not popular with some residents, their fear being that, if it were successful, it might undermine the argument for Foula having its own boat. I did not agree and received strong support from Alistair Carmichael, MP for Orkney and Shetland, and Tavish Scott, Shetland's first Member of the Scottish Parliament. Royal Mail said that the island had been classed as exempt from the provisions of Section 4 of the Postal Services Act 2000 relating to a universal postal service. Success came in January 2003, when Postcomm (The Postal Services Commission), the regulator of the mail industry, issued "a decision document and regulation" about exceptions to the Universal Service Obligation. This removed Foula from the exceptions list, so enabling it to receive mail up to six days a week instead of up to three – an arrangement that persists to the present day.

11

Turkey 3 (1997–2006)

In my early years on Foula, I travelled outside Shetland quite frequently. In 1996, for example, as well as visiting England and Wales, I went to Orkney, the Netherlands, Norway, and France (twice). The trips to Orkney and Norway were recreational, but the others were work-related or partly so, as I continued with my scholarly research and writing. My second book on Diogenes, published that year, had been completed just before leaving Durham, and the first product of my research on Foula was an article on "An Epicurean Priest from Apamea in Syria" (*Zeitschrift für Papyrologie und Epigraphik*, 1996). The priest, celebrated in a Greek inscription, was remarkable for also being head of the local Epicurean School, despite Epicurus' teaching that the gods have no desire or power to intervene in human affairs. One of those who read the piece prior to publication was Dirk Obbink, an American at Oxford University. That was in January 1996, when he was highly regarded for his fine scholarship, and rightly so, and years before the emergence of scandalous allegations that he had sold papyrus fragments which were not his property. The allegations can be read on the internet.

In the Netherlands I lectured on Diogenes in Groningen and on Lucretius and Diogenes at the Royal Dutch Academy in Amsterdam. I also went to Leiden and Utrecht. In Groningen I enjoyed the hospitality of Simone Mooij-Valk, author of an annotated translation of Diogenes into Dutch, and her mathematician husband J.J.A. Mooij, while in Amsterdam I joined other participants in an international colloquium. The visit to Groningen did not start well. On its approach to the city, my train came to a stop and did not move for what seemed like an age. It emerged that an inmate of a nearby mental institution had committed suicide on the track. That was bad and sad enough, but a bit later, when I met up with Groningen University's Professor of Greek, I found her in a badly shaken state. She lived near the mental institution and railway line, and on her walk to her local station, she had come across a second tragedy, although I did not hear whether there had been a second death. The weather in Amsterdam was extraordinarily cold for late June: the hotel put on its central heating, and my Shetland thermal clothing was much envied, especially on a canal trip. The day after the colloquium ended, a Sunday, I visited Utrecht. Sitting in an outdoor café to have a beer, I watched in amazement as a procession of young women and men went by, all with flowers in their hair, and then as a man sat down next to me with a parrot perched on each shoulder. He did not have a drink, but the parrots tore up two beer-mats.

During the colloquium I met for the first time José Kany-Turpin, then a university teacher in Reims. She is the author of an acclaimed French translation of Lucretius, an expert on Epicurean philosophy, and a fine Latinist. In Paris she introduced me to many academic friends and colleagues of hers and enabled me to broaden my knowledge and appreciation of French culture. It was at this time that I developed a love affair with French baroque composers, notably Jean-Baptiste Lully and Jean-Philippe Rameau – both, especially Rameau, far too rarely heard in the UK.

In April 1997 there was at last some promising activity involving Oinoanda. With the welcome support of Stephen Mitchell, it had been agreed that, subject to the approval of the Turkish Government, an excavation would commence as a joint project of the British Institute of Archaeology at Ankara and the Fethiye Museum, with the direction shared between the Museum Director, İbrahim Malkoç, and myself. I was designated Scientific Director. This was a significant development, because no scientific excavation had ever been conducted at Oinoanda before. Previous work had involved searching the surface. At the discretion of Turkish Government representatives, the exposure of likely-looking stones had been permitted, even encouraged, and during the whole period of my involvement with the site, local treasure-hunters had been active, sometimes with metal detectors, in search of coins and artefacts. They were not interested in inscriptions, but turned up quite a lot of them in their search for treasure. The addition of any new pieces to the text of Diogenes' work is welcome, but the investigations are best conducted by experts. This point is well illustrated by finds at Oinoanda in 1997. One block (NF 129) was turned up by illegal excavators and in such a way that its architectural context is unclear, whereas the find-place and architectural context of every piece found by the archaeological team was precisely recorded.

On 15 April I made a preparatory visit to Oinoanda with Jean Öztürk and Julian Bennett, both from Bilkent University, Ankara, José Kany-Turpin, and Cengiz Aslantaş of the Fethiye Museum. Jean is British, and her family name, Öztürk, sometimes caused mild amusement in her adopted homeland, since it means "Real Turk" or "Pure Turk". She is a delightful person and capable archaeologist, and it was a great pity that she was unable to work at Oinoanda in 1997. Unfortunately she was not the only one in that position. We had planned to start work on 23 June with a team of eight or nine, but the Government permit was inexplicably delayed so long that, by the time it was issued, most members were not available. During the summer, as the waiting dragged on, a shocking piece of news came to me from Turkey: my friend Mehmet Atçı, who had served as Oinoanda's watchman for about 25 years, had died in the most distressing of circumstances, killed by one of his own sons during an argument. He was as generous and kind as he was energetic and loyal. When at last I got to İncealiler, the nearest village to Oinoanda, the first thing I did was to visit his widow and take her flowers. After that, every time I climbed the hill to the ruins, I could hear her wailing in the most pitiful way. The only consolation was that Mehmet's successor was another son, Sedat.

I flew to Dalaman on 25 October and spent several hectic days in Fethiye and Muğla, seeing officials, dealing with all sorts of bureaucratic procedures involving residence permits, spending time in the Museum to discuss the excavation and payments to workmen, and buying equipment, including wheelbarrows, spades, picks, shovels, a crowbar, cutlery, crockery, a gas "bomb" for boiling water for hot drinks, and foodstuffs. Until the late evening of the 30th I was still awaiting the arrival of the only other full-time team member, Andrew L. Goldman of the University of North Carolina at Chapel Hill, an archaeological student preparing to write his doctoral dissertation and therefore of limited experience. Julian Bennett was to make two short visits, and we usually had just two workmen. A member of the Museum staff was present each day, but, after the illness and hospitalisation of the Museum's first choice, Hüseyin Köktürk, its best archaeologist and someone keenly interested in Diogenes, it was not often the same person. The small size of the team was one problem. The short duration of the season was another – just ten days on the site (31 October–9 November). Another potential problem was the weather: Oinoanda is about 1,400 m. above sea-level, and in normal circumstances one would try to avoid working so late in the year at that altitude. In the event, conditions remained dry, although chilly, throughout. That was lucky. Less lucky were the frequent power cuts and telephone outages in Seki, where we were staying, my frequent eye trouble, and ongoing bureaucratic difficulties to do with residents' permits. But, for me, by far the worst moment was when a member of the Fethiye Museum staff gave me the very sad news that Betty had died on 3 November. I was working in a trench at the time, and, after receiving the condolences of the watchman and workmen, I sat alone for a while and wrote a letter to Lucinda to be faxed from Fethiye to North Wales via Durham. The news was not unexpected: when I last saw Betty a few days before I went to Turkey, it was obvious that she had lost her brave battle against cancer. She was too weak to say much, but the occasion was a moving one for both of us, I think – certainly for me when she whispered: "I loved you all along, you know". Lucinda and I had agreed that, if her mother were to die during the work at Oinoanda, I should not return for the funeral, because it would have involved the abandonment of the project, and I am sure that Betty would have approved, given her unselfishness and her interest in Oinoanda.

Those ten days at Oinoanda brought some good finds. Three trenches were opened on the so-called Esplanade, now known to have been the city's earlier agora (market-place). One (Trench 3), opened at the insistence of the Museum Director, produced nothing of significance. Another (Trench 2) revealed a limestone bench, an honorific inscription, and a water pipe – interesting, but not sensational. Only Trench 1, opened roughly in the middle of the Esplanade's south side, was fruitful for Diogenes, and it was very fruitful indeed, containing seven new blocks of the inscription – four in a stylobate-course, three in a step-course (Plate 39). Parts of the blocks in the step-course were hidden under blocks edging the stylobate. Otherwise the texts were well preserved. These discoveries were made on 1–2 November. Afterwards, Andy Goldman spent what I considered an inordinate amount of time in Trench 2. In the afternoon of 6 November he grudgingly agreed to return to Trench 1. There, or rather just east of the trench, we almost immediately uncovered the largest fragment of Diogenes yet known (NF 126): it is 1.65 m. wide and the only block that carries all or part of six columns (Plate 40). It is part of a discussion, in the *Physics*, of theology and religion. Moreover, its text links up with that of a 4-column block in Trench 1 (NF 127 I-IV),

39) Oinoanda: Trench 1 from N, November 1997.
Numbers are those of Diogenes fragments, NF series

40) Oinoanda: Diogenes NF 126, the largest known fragment,
49 x 165 x 30+ cm, November 1997

which in turn immediately preceded a passage recorded in 1974 (fr. 20). The whole section, destined to be further extended in 2009 by the columns (NF 167) that immediately preceded NF 126, and in 2010 by the columns (NF 182) that immediately followed fragment 20, is now called *The Continuous Theological Physics-Sequence*. It is of exceptional interest. Not least interesting is this pronouncement in NF 126:

> A clear indication of the complete inability of the gods to prevent wrongdoings is provided by the nations of the Jews and Egyptians, who, as well as being the most superstitious of all peoples, are the most abominable of all peoples. (III 7 – IV 2)

Unfavourable treatment of Egyptian and Jewish religious beliefs is common in Greek and Latin literature, but Diogenes' statement is unparalleled in Epicurean sources.

Andy Goldman, far from being delighted at the discovery of NF 126, accused me of "treasure-hunting" and refused to continue the investigation of the Trench 1 area, saying that Julian Bennett would not approve. I replied that major additions to the text of Diogenes are certainly "treasure", that I (not the absent Julian) was Scientific Director of the work, that I was supported by the Museum's representative on the site that day (Ali Dervişağaoğlu), and that I had a responsibility, in accordance with BIAA's conditions and those of our other sponsors, to give high priority to the philosophical inscription. Andy then left the area containing world-class material and returned to the third-class contents of Trench 2.

The total haul for 1997 was ten new Diogenes fragments, increasing the known text of his inscription by about 500 words. The additions included three short *Monolithic Maxims*, probably composed by Diogenes himself:

> Life becomes pleasurable when fear of death is absent. For [the fable about Tartarus is vain]. Death is to be laughed at, being like a mask that frightens small children; for indeed they believe that that will bite, but it does not bite. (NF 130, full text exposed 2011)

> Vain desires, like those for fame and suchlike, are not only vain, but, as well as being vain, also difficult to fulfil. It is not unlike drinking much, yet always being thirsty. To be master of Pella [Alexander the Great], but

> [to have troubles for company, is vain]. (NF 131)

> Seldom does the fortuitous, which we term chance, interfere with life, and usually it is we who are in control. (NF 132)

In the early morning of the last day of the excavation, I climbed the hill of Oinoanda on my own, well ahead of Andy and Julian, who were to drive from Seki to İncealiler in another car. I was carrying a lot of money – sufficient to pay the workmen, two watchmen, and the expenses incurred by the Museum. I was about two thirds of the way to the site, when a single gunshot rang out from a position higher up the wooded hillside. I stopped briefly, wondering whether I should await the arrival of my colleagues, but decided to proceed. Since I lived to tell the story, the gun was probably fired by a hunter.

The intention had been to continue excavation in the summer of 1998, but I felt obliged to withdraw as director for two reasons: first, because I thought it preferable to have an experienced archaeologist in charge; secondly, because my eye problems were so significant that they might interrupt my work at any moment, and I was advised that, if the director were unable to continue, the excavation might have to be abandoned. The day I returned to London from Turkey, I went straight to Moorfields Eye Hospital to see a consultant, and in the following years I was quite a frequent visitor there, including, on one occasion in 1999, for an operation. I also visited an eye hospital in Paris and, in May 2002, the clinic of an Iranian-born eye-doctor in Fethiye. He insisted that I wore an eye-pad for several days, prompting frequent jokes about Captain Hook. But what was to happen the following year was no laughing matter.

The obvious person to take over in 1998 was Julian Bennett, an archaeologist who now had some familiarity with the site and had the advantage of living and working in Ankara, where he should easily have been able to consult and liaise with both BIAA and the relevant Turkish authorities. But it never happened. Julian and BIAA's Acting Director were unable to do what was necessary in time. A permit was issued in September, but by then it was far too late for Julian to be able to use it because of his teaching commitments. The following years were also ones of hopes raised and dashed. Funds were not usually the problem. I had been generously supported not only by my friend John Fraser, an ardent fan of Diogenes employed by the United Nations in Geneva as a translator, but also by the British Academy and the Seven Pillars of Wisdom Trust. The full story is too complicated and painful to relate in detail here, but it is probably fair to say that most blame was attributable, not necessarily in equal measure, to poor handling by BIAA and problems with the Turkish authorities. Applications to work at Oinoanda were submitted and rejected in 1999, 2000, and 2001. In May-June 2002 I made a private visit to Turkey, to have discussions in Fethiye and inspect Oinoanda. During this visit I made, in the company of a friend, a seven-hour walk from İncealiler to Bayırköy, following, at least part of the time, the road Diogenes is likely to have followed when he was heading for neighbouring Tlos and the coast of Lycia – for example, on his way to Rhodes, where he had Epicurean friends and liked to spend the winter months. Our armed guide had never made the walk before and gave much-exaggerated forecasts of the distance, which, having a map, I was able to disregard.

In June 2003 I returned to Oinoanda for three days with Hugh Elton (Director of BIAA, 2001–2005), Angela Kalinowski (University of Saskatchewan), and Jeremy Rossiter (University of Alberta). Jeremy had been to Oinoanda in 1994, to help assess the feasibility of an excavation. This time the intention was to prepare the way for an excavation, to be directed by him and to start in 2005. The omens looked favourable, not least with respect to the attitude of the Turkish authorities, but Jeremy's attempt to obtain a grant from just one source in Canada failed and he withdrew his application for a permit. It was a bitter disappointment, and incomprehensible to me that he did not cast his fund-raising net more widely.

A few weeks after my return from the 2003 visit to Oinoanda, I went to Aberdeen to spend a weekend with a friend who was coming up from England. I arrived two or three days before she did and took the opportunity to work in Aberdeen University Library. On Friday 8 August, just after a sandwich lunch in the sunshine, I boarded a bus to take me to the airport. Minutes later, the vision in my right eye went completely blurred with a sort of waterfall effect. I did not think much of it at the time, supposing that it was just a bit of eye-strain, but when, by the following morning, there was no improvement, I headed for Aberdeen Royal Infirmary, where, after a long wait, I was seen by a Syrian eye-doctor and a registrar, who gave me the bad news that the loss of vision was permanent. What I had suffered is known in the trade as CRVO – central retinal vein occlusion. Although I was not completely blind in the eye, I had lost about 80% of the vision, which meant that I could dimly distinguish major pieces of furniture in a room, but not read anything.

It was not the ideal start to what was expected to be a relaxing weekend, but we made the best of it, and the following morning we got a special wave from HM Queen Elizabeth II after we attended Matins at Crathie Kirk near Balmoral. I did not experience any pain and I was still allowed to drive, but my vision was impaired: for example, when I was pruning shrubs, I could no longer see exactly where the stems were. As for driving, I could no longer use a right wing-mirror, and joining a main road from a side road could be tricky. When Lucinda, Ciara, and I made a day-trip by sea to Shetland's Out Skerries and took a car, which I had to reverse onto the small ferry, Lucinda helpfully explained to the crew that I was doing it so slowly because I had no sight in my right eye. The men then gaped open-mouthed in astonishment that I was able to do it at all without ending up in the water. In the weeks and months after the CRVO, I was seen several times by a retina specialist in London, who gave the eye laser treatment to prevent neovascularisation, which occurs when the retina produces abnormal blood cells in a misguided attempt to heal itself.

Although I should prefer to have usable vision in both my eyes, my overwhelming feeling is one of huge gratitude that I still have usable sight in one of them and have been able to continue with my research, writing, and normal life in general for over twenty years since the Aberdeen episode. I rejoice to continue to see not only beautiful things, but also less attractive ones like my face in a mirror and weeds in my gardens.

During the years 1998–2004, when seemingly-endless applications for more work at Oinoanda were made and rejected, I was not exactly twiddling my thumbs. I published two books and about twenty articles. The first book was the "American" version of my translation of Lucretius. I worked on the revision and expansion of the 1969 version in the winter of 2000–2001. Frequent failures of Foula's electricity meant that I often had to work by the light of a "Tilley" (kerosene fuelled) lamp or candles, but on 19 February 2001 I got everything away to my wonderful editor at Hackett in Cambridge, Massachusetts, Deborah Wilkes. On 2 March I left Foula in deep snow by sea on my way to Glasgow to catch a plane to Iceland and then another to New York, arriving 6 March. It was my first visit to the USA. In New York I felt like a fish out of water, and I was glad to move on by train to Boston, also under deep snow, where I was hospitably entertained by Deborah, her husband, Peter Buck, her daughter, Scarlett Hoffman, an employee of my other American publisher, Harvard University Press, and the family's two cats – a Maine coon who loved to be in the shower and the Piffkin, who spent much time contemplating a blank wall. There was mild amusement when one morning I accompanied Scarlett to her office at HUP, but for the most part I was in Deborah's offices, where we finalised various matters to do with the book. My hosts took me down to their holiday home on Cape Cod. When we went out for the day from there, they left the house unlocked. I was pleasantly surprised that a practice common in Shetland and almost universal in Foula was found anywhere in the USA. But I still insisted on having my briefcase locked in the boot (trunk) of the car.

The second book, published in Naples ten years after my 1993 edition of Diogenes, was *Supplement to Diogenes of Oinoanda, The Epicurean Inscription*, 2003. Dedicated to Francesca Longo Auricchio, it includes the new texts discovered since 1993 and summarises all the work done during that period. I only started to use a computer in 2001 and had the extra challenge of learning to word-process Greek. I was lucky to receive some patient instruction from a friend, and I was able to complete work on the *Supplement* on my own. The book was awarded the "Theodor Mommsen" International Prize for Herculaneum Papyrology (Premio Internazionale di Papirologia Ercolanese) for 2004. I received the prize at a ceremony in Pozzuoli on 12 January 2005, and the following day the book was presented at a meeting in Naples by Alberto Grilli and Nicola Pace from Milan. As I remarked in my acceptance speech, the award of a papyrology prize for a work not concerned with papyri was at first sight rather strange, but in the case of Diogenes was justified because of the way his inscription is modelled on unrolled papyri. In Pozzuoli I had the thrill of being accommodated in the Hotel Solfatara, right on the edge of a volcano, with a strong smell of sulphur pervading the air.

Some of my twenty or so articles in 1998–2004 were about Diogenes and/or Oinoanda, others about other matters. I mention two about Diogenes. One, "The Introduction to Diogenes of Oinoanda's *Physics*" (*Classical Quarterly*, 2000), concerns two of the best-known passages of the inscription in which Diogenes describes his philanthropic mission and the purpose of his work. Because the *Physics* treatise was carved above the second main treatise, the *Ethics*, and meant to be read first, its introduction serves also as an introduction to the whole inscription. In the article I argue that twentieth-century scholars (myself included) placed the two passages (fragments 2 and 3) in the wrong order, pointing out that Diogenes' own words show that fragment 3 preceded fragment 2. It is amazing how blind scholars can be when they follow one another like sheep. The other article presents a new fragment (136) discovered in the theatre at Oinoanda in 2003. Part of Diogenes' writing *Old Age*, it begins with mention of "an elaborate house with fretted and gold-spangled ceilings", evidently as something to be avoided, and goes on to recommend simple clothing and food, specifically cabbage. It pleases me to think that Diogenes would have approved of Shetland kale.

I had lecturing engagements in London, Paris, Würzburg, Geneva, and Naples. One of those who came to hear me in Paris (13 February 1999) was the poet, novelist, and mathematician Jacques Roubaud, who had recently (1997) included Diogenes in his idiosyncratic book of biographical essays *L'abominable tisonnier* [= *The Abominable Poker*] *de John McTaggart Ellis McTaggart et autres vies plus ou moins brèves*. My Geneva talks were given at the invitation of Professors André Hurst and Jonathan Barnes, and I had the pleasure of staying in nearby Versoix with John Fraser and his charming Finnish wife, Petra. Jonathan brought me an unusual gift from his wife, Jennifer – some roots, dug up in their garden in France, of *echinops bannaticus* (blue globe thistle) to take back to Foula. She was right in thinking rabbits would not touch the plant, but unfortunately the cool climate has prevented it from ever blooming satisfactorily. I had not been back from Geneva very long when something very strange happened. At Foula's airstrip I fell into conversation with a departing Swiss tourist from Geneva, who, when he heard I am a classicist, declared his passion for ancient Greek poetry and lamented the lack of opportunity to hear it and read it. Well, I was aware, from what John Fraser had told me, that André Hurst organised readings of Homer and other authors and welcomed the participation of anyone interested. It was remarkable that the gentleman from Geneva had to come all the way to Foula to learn this.

The lectures in Würzburg (October 1998) and Naples (September 2002) were delivered at international colloquia – the former on Epicureanism in the Late Roman Republic and Empire, the latter marking the 250th anniversary of the discovery of the papyri at Herculaneum. My Naples paper was entitled "Herculaneum and Oinoanda, Philodemus and Diogenes: Comparison of Two Epicurean Discoveries and Two Epicurean Teachers". The colloquium was an opportunity to meet up with many scholarly friends from Italy and elsewhere, but sadly not with Marcello Gigante, who had died on 23 November 2001, or Don Fowler, who had died on 15 October 1999. Both were greatly missed. After the colloquium I made a second visit to Capri and found it as delightful in the early autumn as it had been in the spring, especially once the day-trippers had departed.

Recreationally, there were also visits to Scotland, including Skye, Lewis and Harris, and Sutherland; to Iceland; and to France, including Alsace, Provence, Normandy, and Brittany. In Brittany José and I stayed in Le Conquet, where there is an abbey founded by the sixth-century Breton monk Saint Tanguy, to whose statue I made obeisance in honour of my Cornish Tangye mother. Because of stormy weather we did not venture to Ouessant – wisely to judge by the demeanour of ferry-passengers disembarking at Le Conquet, but we visited the islands of Belle Île, Groix, and Chausey. In Belle Île we stayed in the hotel favoured by President Mitterand when he developed prostate cancer. Groix, famous for the tuna wind-vane on its church tower, is smaller and nicer, and we explored on bicycles. At dinner in the hotel we overheard a male guest referring to us, rudely and inaccurately, as *les rosbifs*, whereupon we proceeded to speak loudly in French for his benefit. Chausey, the group of little-known (to Brits) French Channel Islands, is remarkable for, among other things, its huge tidal range – the greatest in Europe. At high tide there are 52 isles and islets, at low tide 365. In Paris for Christmas 1999, I experienced the hurricane that struck the city very early in the morning of 26 December. It did great damage in northern and central France. Friends joked that it was my Shetland gift. The following day we took a train to Provence and saw the arrival of the year 2000 in Nîmes (Nemausus), home-city of the Empress Plotina. Just before Easter 2000, I was staying in the Inverlochy Castle Hotel near Fort William. Descending the staircase before dinner, I immediately recognised a man standing in the lounge area as the British Conservative Party leader William Hague, despite his having his back to me and my never having met him before. I went over and introduced myself. He explained that he had stayed in the hotel with his stag party and had climbed Ben Nevis on that occasion. He was now doing the same with his Welsh wife, Ffion. I bumped into her on the same staircase after breakfast the next morning, when she was descending, all togged up for the climb, and had a friendly word with her – *yn Gymraeg wrth gwrs* ("in Welsh of course").

On a brief visit to Sutherland in early October 2000 I stayed in the comfortable Inver Lodge Hotel above the village of Lochinver. I had some good walks, enjoyed excellent food, and, with the hotel nearly empty and about to close for the winter, benefited from an end-of-season discount. One evening I noticed, among the few diners, two men chatting over their meal, and I could not help overhearing that one was a resident, the other not. After dinner, diners moved to a bar area for coffee and mints, and there I overheard the following exchange between the two:

> *Visitor.* Your wife was murdered, wasn't she?
> *Resident.* Yes, she was.
> *Visitor.* And you were suspected of being the murderer, weren't you?
> *Resident.* Yes, I was.
> *Visitor.* And they didn't find out who murdered her, did they?
> *Resident.* No, they didn't.

What I shall never know is whether this was a serious conversation, or a spoof. I am inclined to think that it was serious. I was not sitting very close to the pair, and I pretended to be absorbed in my book. Their expressions, from what I could see out of the corner of my eye, did not give any hint that they were acting. When they parted company, I followed the resident at a respectful distance. He unlocked the door of the bedroom next to mine.

I had another strange experience in a Scottish hotel five years later. In the evening of Friday 7 October 2005 I flew from Glasgow to Stornoway, arriving in heavy rain. It was my first visit to Lewis and Harris in the Outer Hebrides, and I was looking forward to seeing them not only on account of their scenic beauty, but also because they were where my Macaulay ancestors came from. I also hoped to enjoy the hospitality for which the islands are noted. But Stornoway is a town to which I have no wish to return. For one thing, the car I rented was in poor condition. Among its deficiencies, the headlights were maladjusted, the horn did not work, and the tyres were so worn that I took the vehicle to the police station to ask if they complied with the law. The officer on duty declined to assist because, he alleged, he was not allowed to step outside to have a look. I suspected that the real reason was that he did not wish to get involved in a dispute with the local firm. But his behaviour was nothing compared with that of my hotel's staff at breakfast on the Saturday morning. I had been told, when I checked in the previous evening, that breakfast was served from 7.30 a.m. Arriving in the dining room just after that time, I found it unlit and unstaffed, and when, after twenty minutes, two waitresses appeared, they savaged me for entering the room before 8 a.m. and for sitting at a table set with pink paper-napkins, which (I was supposed to divine) were the places reserved for members of a coach party. On arrival at the friendly and comfortable Harris Hotel at Tarbert in the evening, I went into the bar and was asked if I had had a good day. When I related my experience, two other guests told me that they had been similarly abused a day or two earlier.

One afternoon I climbed a hill at the south end of Harris and was rewarded with a distant view of St Kilda. My ancestor the Revd Kenneth Macaulay, Minister of Ardnamurchan in Argyll from 1761, went to St Kilda in 1758 as missionary from the Society for Propagating Christian Knowledge and wrote *The History of St Kilda* (1764). Dr Samuel Johnson met him in Cawdor on 27 August 1773 on his journey to the western isles of Scotland with James Boswell. Johnson, who never set foot on St Kilda, had read Macaulay's book and thought most of it rather good, until, on meeting him, he decided that Macaulay was too stupid to have written it himself. A big part of the problem was that the Anglican Johnson and Presbyterian Macaulay had predictably disagreed about bishops. One of the things Johnson later (2 October) pooh-poohed was Macaulay's statement that from the third day after visitors arrive, the whole population of St Kilda goes down with a cold. There are similarities between St Kilda and Foula, notably remoteness and precipitous cliffs, but also big differences: in St Kilda Gaelic was spoken, in Foula, until the eighteenth century, Norn; in St Kilda folk lived on a street, in Foula scattered all round the eastern side of the island. Today Foula remains a community of individuals, which is not to say that they do not act together on important issues, such as in the campaign for an island-based boat, and in emergencies such as when a hurricane removed a corner of Maggie and Dal's house. It is because of the independent mindedness and lifestyle of Foula's people that I have been so content living on the island, knowing that I will always be helped if I ask, but not disturbed if I do not. It probably helps sometimes that I am an incomer, unrelated to any other resident and not in any sort of close relationship with one, but on friendly terms with almost everyone.

Descending the hill on Harris, I found the only gateway in a long, tall fence blocked by a stationary herd of about twenty Highland cattle. Being experienced with the breed, I nudged my way through them, wondering how many other visitors would have done the same.

A few days earlier I had the pleasure of staying, and not for the first time, in a Catholic convent in Oxford. When researching my Catholic aunt Jean Smith, I was generously helped by Sister Helen Forshaw, archivist of the Society of the Holy Child Jesus, with which Jean had been closely associated. In 1937 she had spent two months in the Society's Oxford premises at Cherwell Edge. In 1970 the Society moved to 14 and 16 Norham Gardens, and it was there that I stayed at Helen's invitation while I was working in the Bodleian Library. Lancashire-born, she was a very special person, totally unprejudiced, and great fun to be with. On one occasion she had bicycled from Oxford to London to raise funds for Nicaragua and been embraced by President Ortega in the Albert Hall. She was a regular bell-ringer at a nearby Anglican church, and she had a passion for gardening, which she indulged on her allotment in north Oxford. She showed me the allotment when I arrived on a Sunday evening, and I took her out to dinner. She then showed me my room, and we said goodnight. We did not see one another on the Monday. She had an engagement in Birmingham and was away until the Tuesday. On the Monday it must have been about 10.30 p.m. when I returned to the convent and unlocked the front door. To my consternation, in the semi-darkness I could not find my room. The building was two large houses knocked together, and there were two staircases. I ascended one of them, but without success, so I tried the other, but again everything looked unfamiliar. I was standing on a landing wearing a raincoat and carrying a briefcase and wondering what on earth to do next, when a door opened, and one of the sisters emerged from a bathroom in her nightdress. I quickly introduced myself and apologised profusely for getting lost. She apologised (quite unnecessarily) for not wearing a dressing gown and showed me which way to go. I must have been forgiven, because an invitation to have dinner with the sisters, including Helen, on the Tuesday evening was not withdrawn. No reference to my nocturnal wanderings was made.

In March 2006 there was a welcome development to do with Oinoanda. Since November 1997 BIAA had been paying the salary of a site watchman – a separate post from that of the watchman employed by the Fethiye Museum. It was now agreed with the Turkish authorities that BIAA's commitment should end. I welcomed this decision because it opened the door for another body to apply for a permit to work at Oinoanda. No time was wasted in exploiting this opportunity. In late May Jürgen Hammerstaedt, Professor of Classical Philology and Papyrology at the University of Cologne, and I discussed the possibility of a collaborative project at Oinoanda. Jürgen, who had already developed an interest in Diogenes and prepared for publication a lengthy article on the text of the inscription, took vigorous steps to identify a suitable person to direct a new survey and was rewarded with success, when in

December Martin Bachmann, Deputy Director of the German Archaeological Institute (Deutsches Archäologisches Institut), Istanbul, an expert on ancient architecture, agreed to take on the role of director and submit an application to start work in 2007.

41) London: Martin, with Lucinda (L) and Ciara (R), at Buckingham Palace after his investiture as OBE, 18 October 2007

12

Turkey 4 (2007–)

On 14 May 2007 I received a letter from the Secretary for Appointments at 10 Downing Street:

> 11th May 2007
>
> Dear Sir,
>
> The Prime Minister has asked me to inform you, in strict confidence, that, having taken the advice of the Cabinet Secretary and the expert Honours Committees, he has it in mind, on the occasion of the forthcoming list of Birthday Honours, to submit your name to The Queen with a recommendation that Her Majesty may be graciously pleased to approve that you be appointed an Officer of the Order of the British Empire.

My appointment as OBE was, it was later revealed, "for services to scholarship", and it can be assumed that the Honours Committee(s) had in mind especially my contributions to knowledge of Diogenes. This was confirmed at the investiture when The Queen mentioned to me my work in Turkey.

Although somewhat dubious about the British Empire, of which so much was inglorious and so little remained, I warmly welcomed the national recognition of Diogenes' importance. Hitherto there had been little recognition of it in the UK. Neither the British Academy nor its Scottish equivalent, the Royal Society of Edinburgh, thought it worthy of notice. The Queen's official birthday was on 16 June (Barbara's real birthday), so complete secrecy had to be maintained for just over a month. Then another four months passed before the investiture at Buckingham Palace on 18 October (Plate 41). Permitted three guests, I invited, as well as Lucinda and Ciara, Sally. She had taken a generous interest in my Diogenes research since the time when we were neighbours in Bangor. I introduced her to him during a party in my flat, when, after a glass or two of wine, I feigned the risqué question "would you be interested in some squeezes?", and, to her palpable relief, instead of tightly embracing her, produced for her inspection two of the filter-paper epigraphic squeezes which I was studying at the time. She was keen on archaeology, and was to be a valued member of the Oinoanda team in 2008–2012.

In advance of the investiture, I was extremely nervous and practised the royal handshake with Ciara in our London hotel – a rehearsal which might have been more useful if we had not both had fits of hysterics. In the Palace all of us who were waiting to receive gongs were given some advice by an amusing official – his most important tip being to let go of Her Majesty's hand after the handshake and not pull her off the dais. In the event, The Queen immediately made me feel relaxed when, as she fastened the medal to my lapel, she remarked on the fiddly nature of the task. She did not actually call the medal "this flipping thing", but I sensed she might have liked to do so. I responded with "I don't know how you manage it all, Your Majesty", referring not just to the pinning of the medals, but to the whole ceremony, throughout which she, at the age of 81, was standing. What a remarkable lady she was!

In the last week of September and first week of October I was in Turkey for the first season of the new survey of Oinoanda by an international team led by Martin Bachmann. In Fethiye I met up with Jürgen Hammerstaedt in the late evening of 22 September. It was not our first meeting. That had been in Naples in 2002, and we had become better acquainted with one another and established a friendship through frequent correspondence since May 2006. The following morning I was introduced to Martin. I had not met him before, and I had a great liking and respect for him from the beginning, finding him friendly with a good sense of humour and, so far as the project was concerned, professional, purposeful, and enthusiastic. He was accompanied by two classical archaeologists, Peter Baumeister and Veli Köse, the latter being at that time the husband of Lutgarde Vandeput, the recently-appointed Director of BIAA. A bit later I was introduced to our very helpful government representative Fatih Özdel.

On the basis of my past experiences, I had advised Martin to start the process of procuring residence permits in Fethiye, but on this occasion he took different advice with the result that we all made a wasted round trip of 180 miles to Muğla, the provincial capital. But, helped by Jürgen having a laptop computer with him, the relevant applications were soon completed on our return. Martin rented accommodation in Seki for himself and everyone else except me. Knowing the usual standard of rented rooms in Seki and being now too old to share possibly-primitive sanitary facilities, I had already decided to stay in the Hotel Victoria in Fethiye – not luxurious, but adequate, and, since I would be getting up early each morning, I arranged for a refrigerator to be put in my room, so that I could be independent of the hotel staff for breakfast. I rented a car for the commute between Fethiye and İncealiler. At Oinoanda, the other members of the party naturally began by familiarising themselves with the site, while I wanted to note any changes to the state of things since my last visit in 2003, especially with regard to illegal digging. We all kept an eye out for new pieces of Diogenes' inscription and found five, although only one of these carried complete lines of text. Martin had rightly decided to carry out a survey, especially of the "Esplanade" or later agora, with the aid of the latest scientific techniques and equipment. Most of the work would be done in years to come, but a small start was made in 2007, when on 2–3 October we were joined by a team of three from the Ankara-based company SEMA Proje, who used 3D laser-scanning equipment to record part of the south side of the Esplanade.

In the coming five seasons (2008–2012) the survey continued on a much larger scale – for longer periods and with much larger teams. There was a huge expansion of the area documented by state-of-the-art technological methods, including geophysical prospection to investigate subterranean structures, terrestrial scanning, laser scanning to create 3D images, and use of GPS. Much of this work directly advanced study of Diogenes, notably in that laser-scanning was used to create 3D images of every piece of the inscription and the exact find-place of each was recorded by GPS. The creation of 3D scans can help, and indeed has already helped, to join up fragments, and, when more of Diogenes' work has been discovered, it will assist in rebuilding the inscribed wall in virtual reality.

Seventy-five new pieces of Diogenes' inscription were found in 2007–2012, and a satisfactory number of pieces not seen since they were found in the nineteenth century were rediscovered (Plate 42). All the new finds were edited by Jürgen Hammerstaedt and me and first published by us promptly each year in the journal *Epigraphica Anatolica* (2007–2012). All the articles and several other contributions by one or both of us and Greek indices were collected in our book *The Epicurean Inscription of Diogenes of Oinoanda: Ten Years of New Discoveries and Research* (Bonn, 2014). Our collaboration, both at Oinoanda and after each season, was always friendly, but unsurprisingly, given the many difficulties to do with decipherment and interpretation of often-fragmentary texts, we did not always agree, in which event we recorded our different suggestions.

A major concern of all who care about Diogenes' work has been, ever since my early investigations, the preservation of it from the elements and from damage inflicted on it, deliberately or accidentally, by visitors to Oinoanda. The number of tourists has grown, although not greatly, and the main human threat has been from treasure hunting, woodcutting, and goat-herding. A major achievement during the 2010 season was the construction on the Esplanade of a steel storehouse for the Diogenes fragments and other significant finds. The campaign to raise the estimated €45,000 to fund it began with the issue of a brochure in mid-March 2010. In the draft of it, Martin and Jürgen were named as contacts – rightly so, but they kindly accepted my suggestion that my name be added. Within not much more than twenty-four hours I was able to tell them that I had raised almost the whole sum. By far the largest donation, €35,000, came, thanks to the writer and philosopher Alain de Botton, from the Gilbert de Botton Memorial Foundation. Alain had already done excellent work to bring Diogenes to the notice of the British public. As well as mentioning him in a short talk he gave on BBC Radio 3 on 22 February 1999, he had given him prominent attention in a television programme broadcast by Channel 4 on 9 April 2000. The programme, "Epicurus on Happiness", was the third in a six-part series entitled "Philosophy: A Guide to Happiness" – a series inspired by his book *The Consolations of Philosophy* (2000). The part of the programme devoted to Diogenes was filmed and recorded at Oinoanda. The extraordinary generosity of the Foundation in memory of Alain's father meant that only €10,000 were needed from other sources, and I was able to report two or three other donations which took us to the target. In the following days there were suggestions that my first initial stood for "Midas" rather than "Martin". Further generous donations (not raised by me) from individuals and institutions followed, and the names of the principal donors are etched on the outside of the storehouse – the next best thing to their being inscribed in stone! (Plate 43).

Before the start of the 2008 season I was surprised to find advertised on the internet a newly-built luxurious house, the holiday property of an English

42) Oinoanda: Martin at work, 25 July 2008

43) Oinoanda: storehouse from SW, August 2010

lady, to let in Seki. It was on the northern fringe of the town, in an elevated position, with a view over fields and orchards to the hill of Oinoanda about five miles to the west. It had a living kitchen, sitting room, utility area, three good-sized bedrooms, a bathroom, two showers, a garden, and an outdoor swimming pool (Plate 44). Despite several failures of the electricity and water and some problems specific to the property, it was totally unlike any accommodation I had occupied in Seki before. I booked it for all five seasons (2008–2012), and Sally, Lucinda, and Ciara joined me from time to time and were very helpful on the site as well as with the cooking and housekeeping. They did not always ascend the hill of Oinoanda, and I too spent some days – typically every other day – in the villa, not just to rest my ancient limbs, but also to make drawings of the new texts.

Space allows mention of only a few of the most significant finds during the 2007–2012 survey, and I present them section by section rather than in order of discovery.

Physics

NF 182, an almost perfectly preserved block found in 2010, is a continuation

44) Seki: Snowdrop Villa, August 2008

of fragment 20 and increases to sixteen the number of consecutive columns preserved of the *Theological Physics-Sequence.* Diogenes, as part of his argument that the world is not divinely created for the benefit of human beings, lists celestial and meteorological phenomena that are harmful to them, or at least not beneficial. The list includes "flashes of lightning, claps of thunder, falls of hail, blasts and gusts of violent wind". Well, on 8 August 2010, the day after the discovery of this text and before it could be recorded, a violent storm erupted at Oinoanda and in the surrounding area with lightning, thunder, hail, heavy rain, and a high wind, causing much damage to the apple crops in Seki's orchards. Another thunderstorm on 9 August interrupted the recording of the text. The coincidence of the storms with the discovery was remarkable, although it is not suggested that it was anything more than chance. What the events of 8–9 August certainly showed was that Diogenes' list of damaging phenomena was highly relevant to weather conditions at Oinoanda.

Ethics

A very valuable addition to the treatise, made in 2012, is NF 207 (Plate 45), another superbly-preserved block carrying part of the preface and linking up with fr. 29 to make five complete columns. Diogenes asserts that happiness can be achieved only through the study of Epicurean philosophy, and that the purpose of his inscription is to bring enlightenment and salvation to readers of all ages – young, middle-aged, and old. It is never too early or late to study philosophy.

Through the spacious margin below fr. 29 and NF 207 runs a quotation of Epicurus' *Principal Doctrine* (*Kyria Doxa*) 1:

> The blessed and imperishable being neither experiences trouble itself nor causes it to another, so that it is not affected by feelings either of anger or of favour; for it is to the weak that such emotions belong.

The continuous line of previously known sayings is often of help in determining the order of the passages carved in columns above them, and the extent of gaps between them.

Less well preserved, but still substantial, new passages of the *Ethics* are NF 146 and 192, found in 2008 and 2011 respectively. The former asserts the wisdom of living a simple and wholesome life:

45) Oinoanda: Diogenes NF 207, 61.5 x 81 x 35 cm

> [Life offers us for our nutrition, although] barley-bread [is sufficient] for our nature, many foods that do not involve unpleasantness when they are taken, and a bed that does not fight against the body because of hardness, and clothes that are not indeed extremely soft, but also not so extremely rough that our nature is repelled, ...

It is to be noted that living simply does not mean practising asceticism. Diogenes goes on to describe the social behaviour suitable for Epicureans, saying that they should help others and share their possessions with them.

The content of NF 192 is polemical, being part of an argument against the Stoics' teaching that virtue (*aretē*) is the moral end. The Epicureans too advocated living virtuously, but insisted that virtue is the means to the end, not the end itself, which is pleasure (*hēdonē*). Right from the beginning, Epicurus' hedonism was often misunderstood or deliberately misrepresented, and in the new text Diogenes, like his master, denies that the pleasures recommended by the Epicureans are those of profligates or involve sensual enjoyment:

> ... it is not those, no, not those, Zeno and Cleanthes and you, Chrysippus, and all who follow the same path as you, it is not those pleasures of the masses that we advocate as being the end, but only these which we have just mentioned are an end.

The strength of Diogenes' feeling about the misrepresentation of the Epicurean doctrine of pleasure is manifested in the triple anaphora "not those (pleasures)" and in the address to the first three great Stoic philosophers.

Monolithic Maxims

NF 155, found in 2008, names another rival philosopher. It is a brief text, and I quote it in its entirety:

> Although Plato was right to acknowledge that the world had an origin, even if he was not right to introduce a divine craftsman of it, instead of employing nature as its craftsman, he was wrong to say that it is imperishable.

The Epicureans believed that our world, which is one of an infinite number of worlds in an infinite universe, is composed of two ultimate realities, atoms and void, and, like every other compound body, was created and will perish, dissolved into its constituent atoms.

The subject-matter of NF 157, located in 2008 and fully exposed in 2009, is very different:

> It is unfortunate that those who are sick with the passion of love do not realise that they derive pleasure to the highest degree from just looking, without copulation, while the sexual act itself, whether one's partner has a superior or inferior figure, is the same.

This is a welcome addition to our sources of information about the Epicurean attitude to sexual love. The fullest is Lucretius (4.1037–1287). Diogenes agrees with him in regarding sexual passion as a "sickness", but the two striking points he goes on to make are not fully paralleled in any other account.

"New" Letter

NF 209, a small fragment found in 2012, gives us the end of what seems to be a previously unknown letter addressed to two or more unnamed persons:

> As it is not possible to die twice, so it is not possible to live twice either.
>
> We should be cheerful when we die, for we shall give up not only good things but also bad ones.
>
> Farewell.

Ten-line Column Letters

NF 186, brought to light in 2010, is part of a letter from Diogenes to an unknown person, apparently an Epicurean. The main point of interest is that it mentions bringing philosophical enlightenment to unnamed women who "happen already to have done some tasting of the doctrines of Epicurus".

Unusually for a philosopher in Ancient Greece, Epicurus had admitted women to his school, and their presence in Epicurean circles in the time of Diogenes should not be a matter of great surprise. His inscription almost certainly dates from the reign of Hadrian, whose adoptive mother, Pompeia Plotina, was an Epicurean. The favour she showed to the Epicurean school in Athens will have given a boost to Epicurean fortunes throughout the

Empire and encouraged many individual women to interest themselves in Epicureanism.

While I was kneeling to study and record NF 186, I experienced mental pleasure, but also physical discomfort connected with a significant loss of function in my right leg. Naturally, as a follower of Epicurus, I used the mental pleasure to counter the physical problem and carried on as best I could, but it was a relief to be told, when I returned to Britain, that I had not had a stroke, but sustained damage to the peroneal nerve.

Old Age

One of the most popular sections of the inscription is likely to have been Diogenes' treatise *Old Age*. The advantages and disadvantages of old age were discussed by many writers in antiquity, the best known work being Cicero's *On Old Age* (*De Senectute*). But Diogenes is the only Epicurean writer known to have written a treatise on the subject. He mentions elsewhere that he is aged and in poor health, so the subject is one he was well qualified to discuss. He defends old age against charges that it is beset by physical and mental weaknesses, that it brings diminution of sensual pleasures, and that it is near to death. He is very clear that old age is not a disease: conditions often associated with it, such as dementia, myopia, and deafness are not peculiar to it, and diminution of sensual desires is actually an advantage. It is true that the elderly move about more slowly than the young, but so what? "We are certainly not entering the foot race at Olympia". This humorous statement is made in a new passage of the treatise, NF 177, found in 2009. I myself found it helpful not only in connection with the injury mentioned above, but also on other occasions. When I quoted it to a Birmingham orthopaedic consultant who had just told me that surgery would not benefit a knee injury that had been bothering me, he was so impressed that he said he would pass on Diogenes' words to some of his other patients.

During the 2011 season, an attractive and informative half-hour documentary film, *A Gigantic Jigsaw Puzzle: The Epicurean Inscription of Diogenes of Oinoanda*, directed by Nazim Güveloğlu, was shot at Oinoanda. In the following years it won prizes at several international festivals, and in March 2015 it was uploaded to YouTube, where it can still be viewed. It is obvious to viewers that my part in it was totally unrehearsed!

2012 was the last year of the survey directed by Martin Bachmann, and the last year of my work *at* Oinoanda. I stress "at", because it was not the end of my work *on* Oinoanda and Diogenes. Nor, as it turned out, was it the last year of discoveries of new pieces of the philosophical inscription. I have already mentioned Jürgen Hammerstaedt's and my republication of all the texts found in 2003–2012. Also, Martin Bachmann started to edit a book containing the results of the six-year survey of Oinoanda with contributions from all the major participants, including those of us involved with Diogenes. It was perhaps a bit of a distraction from the preparation of this volume that an international colloquium on Diogenes was held in Turkey in September 2014. I did not attend it. The proceedings were published in 2017. Nor did I join Martin and Jürgen at Oinoanda in October 2015, when they made a short visit to check some measurements and other details. As well as doing that, they were able to record an illegally-dug block assigned to the *Monolithic Maxims.* Jürgen and I published it as NF 213 in 2016.

In the afternoon of 2 August 2016 I received an email from Martin, who was in Istanbul working on the Oinoanda book. He asked me to supply photographs taken during the excavation in 1997. I immediately wrote back, saying that I did not have any in digital form, so would he like me to send him prints by airmail or have scans made for him. Since it was a straightforward question, I was a little surprised that no reply came to my inbox the next morning, but I was certainly not anxious. But when in the afternoon Jürgen telephoned me from Barcelona to say that he had some shocking news and asked me to sit down to receive it, I guessed that it concerned Martin. After arriving for work at the German Archaeological Institute in Istanbul that morning (3 August), he had suffered a fatal heart attack. He had always seemed to me fit and robust, he was only 51, and he and his wife, Jasmin, had four young children, the youngest born during the 2011 season at Oinoanda. Naturally, one's first and deepest thoughts were for his bereaved family, but, like others who worked with him at Oinoanda, I counted him a friend, and his sudden death was a shock for all of us.

It was also a serious setback for the continuation and completion of the book which he was editing. More than nine years passed before it appeared, in December 2025. It is in German, with brief summaries in English and Turkish. It contributes much to knowledge of Oinoanda, but its bulk and price are likely to restrict its readership.

To enable the editors and contributors to take more measurements and check on more details, permission was given for another short visit to Oinoanda in October 2017. One of the six participants in the expedition was Jürgen, who in a great rush skilfully recorded six new pieces of Diogenes' inscription, including two of exceptional interest and importance. One, NF 214, is part of a remarkable description of a man barely surviving a shipwreck. I had found another part of the passage in 1970. In places the language is more akin to epic poetry than to prose, and it had been widely believed that the shipwrecked man was Epicurus, who is said to have narrowly escaped death at sea and wrote about the experience in exuberant language. But the new passage reveals that the shipwrecked man was actually a contemporary of Diogenes called Niceratus (Neikeratos). Whether someone called Niceratus actually had the experience described by Diogenes one cannot tell. I have a suspicion that the description closely follows that of Epicurus, and that Diogenes has transferred the episode from him to a contemporary.

That the letters included by Diogenes in his inscription are not, or not always, letters genuinely sent by him is, in my opinion, demonstrated by NF 215, the second substantial text recorded in 2017. It is the beginning of a letter which purports to have been written not by Diogenes, but by a certain Archelaus to a certain Dion who has asked to be told what Diogenes said after the burial of his (Diogenes') son. I believe that the letter was composed by Diogenes for inclusion in his inscription as a way to vary and dramatise the presentation of his opinions. In taking this view, I am not in complete agreement with Jürgen, in collaboration with whom I edited and published the six latest fragments, including NF 214 and 215, in *Epigraphica Anatolica*, 2018.

In November 2019 I invited Ciara and her partner, Ian Birtwistle, to accompany me to Turkey and join me in climbing the hill of Oinoanda on 26 April 2020, my eightieth birthday, or soon after. I rather fancied being able to say that I had visited Oinoanda in seven decades of my life – in my twenties, thirties, forties, fifties, sixties, seventies, and eighties. I reckoned I was still capable of making the ascent, especially in the company of two expert rock-climbers, which is what Ciara and Ian were and are. But by January 2020 I was getting cold feet about the plan, which we decided to cancel. It was just as well because the outbreak of the Covid-19 pandemic would have made it impossible. Another plan of mine, a less ambitious one, to attend the Scholars' Dinner at Trinity College, Dublin, on 20 April 2020 was torpedoed by Covid-19. It would have been the 60th anniversary of my election as a Foundation Scholar and a chance to see friends from my Dublin days, one of whom, Robin Miller, died on 17 May. Another friend, whom I had hoped to visit on my way through Edinburgh, was my Oinoanda colleague Jim Coulton, who died, after a long illness, on 1 August 2020.

Since October 2017 there has been no work at Oinoanda, and the site still awaits the major programme of excavation, clearing, and restoration which it so richly deserves. If such an operation were to be carried out, it would probably at least double the extent of the known text, and although it would certainly present challenges, these would be much easier to surmount than any at Herculaneum, for Oinoanda is an uninhabited site, and, as the 1997 excavation showed, the hidden treasure lies at no great depth.

Two things give me reason for optimism. One is the publication of the Oinoanda book, which one hopes will help to inspire and facilitate further searches for Diogenes' work, with Jürgen Hammerstaedt continuing to play a leading role. The other is the greatly increased attention given to Diogenes by Turkish archaeologists and philosophers in recent years. I make special mention of two. One is Hüseyin Köktürk, who during many years of good service to the Fethiye Museum developed a special interest in Oinoanda, Diogenes, and Epicurean philosophy. His article on Diogenes in the journal *Arkeoloji ve Sanat* (2003) is, so far as I know, the first account in Turkish, and in 2022 he published an informative book in paperback, *Taşlara Kazınan Bilgelik Hazzı: Likya'da Oinoandalı Diogenes* (*The Joy of Wisdom Carved on Stones: Diogenes of Oinoanda in Lycia*), including an introduction, translation of the fragments, sections on Epicurus and Epicureanism, and notes. It is not expensive and deserves a wide readership. I thank Hüseyin not only for his enthusiasm for Diogenes and his help in the investigation of Oinoanda, but also for his friendship over several decades. The second fan of Diogenes who merits special mention is Professor H. Nur Beyaz Erkızan, of the Department of Philosophy at Muğla Sıtkı Koçman University. Recently she has done much to publicise Diogenes in Turkish academic circles, including by organising a colloquium on him in Muğla in June 2022 and another, partly devoted to him, in Bodrum in April 2023. I blush to add that the first was dedicated to me, and that I was an honorary guest at the second. I was not able to attend either, but contributed papers, read in Turkish, on "The Importance of Diogenes of Oinoanda" and "Diogenes of Oinoanda Away from Oinoanda". I wish Nur and her colleagues, as well as Hüseyin, continuing success with their admirable study and promotion of Diogenes' work.

13

Modern Studies (2009–)

I have never been solely interested in Greek and Roman antiquity or confined my reading to Classical literature, and, in my thirties and forties especially, I did much reading and re-reading of English literature and poetry. But it never occurred to me that I might produce work for publication outside my professional field. However, that changed after I inherited a collection of letters written by Henry's first cousin Rose Macaulay to his elder sister Jean Isabel Smith. Henry never saw the letters or even knew of their existence, which is just as well because he was vehemently opposed to the publication of other collections of Rose's private letters. After Jean's death in 1979, they passed to her brother Jim Smith. He and his wife, Ro, were interested in them and, after he died in 1987, she passed them to Colin, with the wish that they be preserved and, if possible, published. Colin passed them to me. In the 1990s I read and transcribed them, often during holidays and train journeys, but it was several years into my "retirement" to Foula before I had time to start the necessary research. Even then, progress was slow, because I continued to prioritise my Classical work, and I anticipated problems in getting the letters published. Was the research on Rose worthwhile? In trying to judge this, I was hampered by my closeness to her and Jean. Since both were family members, I was naturally interested, but would others be interested too? The warm reactions of many of those whom I approached as I set about my task soon convinced me that there was plenty of interest.

What attracted me to the project, apart from the family interest, was that the collection of about 100 letters was previously unpublished and unknown, and threw new light on one of the most popular and influential writers of the first half of the twentieth century and on the lively literary and social circles in which she moved. A.N. Wilson describes the letters as being "full of buried treasure". They were published in 2011 by Manchester University Press with the title *Dearest Jean*. The critical reception was favourable, and I found it refreshing and stimulating to be working in a totally new area and developed an appetite for more. One of the attractions of the project was the way it brought me into contact with many interesting people.

Among those from whom I received helpful information and friendly encouragement were my cousin Anne St Pierre in France, Celia Denney in Spain, Ana Vicente in Portugal, David Butterfield and Marjolein Wytzes (Allan) in Cambridge, Anthony Bryer and Jenny Banks Bryer in Birmingham, and HRH Princess Margaret in London, the Princess having written (19 October 1999) to confirm her enjoyment of her meeting with Rose and the delight which she and other members of the Royal Family took in *The Towers of Trebizond* (1956). All the commoners in this list I count(ed) as friends. I also established a close friendship with my cousin Victoria Chance, whose father, Sir Jeremy Chance, I had approached about Rose's friendship with his parents. Victoria, who lives in North Wales, is a cultivated person – musical, with a good singing voice, artistic, and well read. She is a loyal churchgoer, who serves as a churchwarden, and is a great asset to the wider community. At one stage she managed the local Oxfam shop. Now she works in it as an unpaid volunteer. I am not sure why she tolerates her atheistic and unsociable cousin, but guess that it may partly be that I can be a good listener and share some of her interests. Anyhow, I am very glad to have retained her friendship over two decades. In 2015 she came to visit me in Foula. I met her at Sumburgh Airport on a windy morning and told her that the only way to get across to the island that day was by sea, departing Walls at 1.30 p.m. I warned her that the boat was very small, and that the two-hour crossing would be very rough. Bravely, she said: "Let's go for it". When she saw the boat tied up at Walls Pier, she exclaimed: "Good heavens, I did not think you meant *that* small", and she soon realised why I had advised her not to have any lunch. But it was typical of her not to be put off by the prospect of sea-sickness. In any case, travelling to Foula was a doddle compared with travels she undertook in India, Nepal, and Bhutan.

In my seventies and early eighties, I wrote fourteen "modern" essays, several of which were to be reprinted in my book *In and Out of Bloomsbury* (2021). I also wrote a short book *Madeleine Symons: Social and Penal Reformer* (2017) and a biography of the artist Helen Coombe (2023). Whatever faults are found with them should not include lack of originality. Just as my work on Diogenes involved bringing to light and editing previously unknown texts, so my research on writers, artists, and social reformers born in the late nineteenth or early twentieth century is focused on extending our knowledge mainly by the presentation of previously unpublished texts, pictures, photographs, and facts, and, where the material is not new, by the independent examination of the relevant manuscripts and images.

One thing I quickly discovered is that some of the supposed authorities on the subjects I investigated were not always reliable, and it seemed important to point that out. My article "Virginia Woolf's Second Visit to Greece" (2011) was written after I had noticed that the Athenian temple in front of which she, Leonard Woolf, Roger Fry, and his sister Margery had been photographed had been misidentified as the Parthenon by Hermione Lee (*Virginia Woolf*, 1996) and Maggie Humm (*Snapshots of Bloomsbury*, 2006) among others. Humm had also done a poor job of identifying many of the photographs taken by Virginia and Leonard during their Greek holiday with the Frys in 1932. She was not pleased when in a further article, "Suicidal Mania and Flawed Psychobiography" (2014), I showed that she was mistaken in believing that Virginia herself misidentified the scene. She has recently published a second volume, *The Bloomsbury Photographs* (2024), in which she tacitly corrects her mistake about the temple (p. 134), but fails to alter the inappropriate quotation which she prints below it: "It's blazing white in Athens ... we're now changing into thin clothes and going up to the Acropolis". Virginia did not write those words on the day the photograph was taken (8 May 1932), when they did not go to the Acropolis and, as the photograph shows, were not wearing "thin clothes". Humm makes no mention of my relevant publications. The only publication of mine in her bibliography (under "Ferguson Smith") is "A Complete Strip-off", which first appeared in 2019, not, as she shows, 2021. So far as I can see, she does not use it in her book, and yet the photographs I published of Vanessa Bell, Clive Bell, and Roger Fry having a nude-posing threesome at Studland in Dorset when, unknown to Clive, Vanessa and Roger were having a passionate affair, are of obvious interest.

The misidentification of photographs was by no means the only thing I found amiss with the work of Bloomsbury scholars. There were also misreadings of Virginia Woolf's handwriting in her "Greek" *Diary* and *Letters*. Some of them are unimportant, but by no means all. None is more damaging than the one in her description of her close friend Roger Fry, who was to be the subject of her only book-length biography, as "infinitely serious" (*Diary* 4, 90). Roger could be serious, but "infinitely serious" does not suit a man whom she describes in the biography as "a saint who laughed; a saint who enjoyed life to the uttermost". What she actually called him was "infinitely porous", which perfectly suits someone who "detested fixed attitudes" and who used "to deplore the natural imperviousness of the human mind to reason". She connects porousness with creativity, as in *A Room of One's Own*:

> He [Coleridge] meant, perhaps, that the androgynous mind is resonant and porous; that it transmits emotion without impediment; that it is naturally creative, incandescent, and undivided. (Ch. 6)

Late in 2014 I consulted Richard Shone and Frances Spalding, acknowledged experts on Bloomsbury art, about two portraits by Roger Fry which I had recently acquired from separate sources in the USA. One, offered for sale as *Pencil Portrait of an Unidentified Woman*, I immediately recognised as Roger's wife, Helen Fry, *née* Coombe, and, helped by a note written by Helen while the drawing was being made, I was able to date it to the couple's wedding day (Plate 46). The other portrait, executed in pencil and gouache on paper, is of Vanessa Bell, seated, wearing a colourful headscarf, and holding an apple (Plate 47). It is to be dated to the time when she was in love with Roger, probably 1911. I sent Shone and Spalding photographs of the two portraits and found their responses astonishing. The former accepted that the first was by Roger, but not that the sitter was his wife. The latter did not even think that Roger was the artist, and thought that the sitter did not look like Helen. As for the portrait of Vanessa Bell, neither of them accepted that it is Roger's work, dismissing it as a "late pastiche" – a view that was not just improbable, but totally impossible, since on the verso the portrait is identified in Roger's handwriting as being of Vanessa, and certified as being his portrait of her by his daughter, Pamela Diamand. I offered my article, "'New' Portraits by Roger Fry (1866–1934) of Helen Fry and Vanessa Bell", first to Shone, then to Spalding, as a contribution to *The Burlington Magazine*, which she succeeded him in editing. When, after many months of time-wasting, they had both rejected it, I emailed it to Robin Simon, editor of *The British Art Journal*, who enthusiastically accepted it the same day.

My contacts with Robin about the portraits were the beginning of a friendship precious to me. He is an outstanding art historian, from whom

46) Roger Fry: Helen Coombe / Fry. Pencil on paper, 22.8 x 19.7 cm, 3 December 1896

47) Roger Fry: Vanessa Bell. Pencil and gouache on paper, 30.5 x 25.3 cm, 1911-1912

I have learned a great deal. He also interests me in matters outside the field of art, including cricket, about which he has written books, and his being Welsh. He is a son of Glyn Simon, former Bishop of Llandaff, later Archbishop of Wales, someone whom I much admired in connection with his words and actions after the Aberfan disaster of 21 October 1966, when an avalanche of coal slurry overwhelmed a school in the South Wales village, killing 116 children and 28 adults; also in connection with the campaigns against apartheid, for nuclear disarmament, and in support of the Welsh language. An early post Glyn Simon held (from 1931) was that of Church Warden at University College, Bangor. I owe a heavy debt to Robin for his encouragement and advice not only with respect to the four articles of mine he published in 2017–2021, but also regarding *In and Out of Bloomsbury* and, still more, my biography of Helen Coombe (2023). I have not met his wife, Jo Simon, the distinguished writer about food and drink, and wish I had. Nor, for that matter, have I met Robin, but I know him well from emails and telephone calls.

Two other precious friendships arose out of the research on the Roger Fry portraits. One was with Frances and Tony Bradshaw. Both had been contemporaries of mine at Trinity College, Dublin, but our paths did not cross there, and we did not meet until 30 June 2015, when I called at their London flat carrying the "new" portrait of Vanessa Bell and photographs of the drawing of Helen Fry. I wanted Tony's advice, because for many years he had run The Bloomsbury Workshop specialising in the buying and selling of artworks produced by members of the Bloomsbury Group. He did not think that Vanessa was a "late pastiche", nor did two other well-known art dealers whom I consulted the same day. One of them, Philip Mould, has written wisely about the importance of basing judgements about pictures on examination of the originals rather than on photographs. I invited both Spalding and Shone to view them, but they did not reply. The strangest thing was that, when I sold the portrait of Vanessa at Sotheby's in March 2019, and Shone was employed by the auctioneers as their expert advisor, he did not query the picture's authenticity. It was sold for over £20,000, which would have been a remarkable price for the late pastiche he earlier believed it to be!

The other friendship that arose through the two-portraits research was with the previous owner of the drawing of Helen, Dr Linda Elisabeth Beattie, now LaPinta, of Louisville, Kentucky, where she was teaching at Spalding University. She bought it from The Bloomsbury Workshop in July 1998, knowing only that it was the work of Roger Fry, and in May 2013 sold it to William Reese Company of New Haven, CT. As a teacher and researcher, she is as versatile as she is brilliant. In addition to writing numerous articles and reviews, she is the author (or editor) of *Savory Memories* (1998), *Sisters in Pain: Battered Women Fight Back* (2000), *Conversations With Kentucky Writers* (1996; vol. 2, 2000), and *Kentucky Quilts and Quiltmakers* (2023). A book on Kentucky's mineral-spring resorts is in an advanced state of preparation and eagerly awaited. She has been kind enough to take as much interest in my work as I take in hers, and her strong sense of humour always lifts my spirits.

While Linda has much expanded my knowledge of Kentucky, a piece of my own research has done the same for my knowledge of a near-neighbouring state to the southwest. I was investigating Richard ("Dickie") Williams Reynolds (1867–1947), whom I found interesting for several reasons. Educated at King Edward's School (KES), Birmingham, my native city, he returned there to teach in 1900. Before that, he worked in London, where he joined the Fabian Society and formed a close friendship with the writer Edith Nesbit, whose niece Dorothea Deakin, also a writer, he was later to marry. Someone he met and admired was Helen Coombe (later Fry). At KES his most famous pupil was J.R.R. Tolkien. In 1922, he, Dorothea, and their three young daughters moved to Capri, hoping that the climate would cure Dorothea's tuberculosis. Sadly, it did not, and, still more sadly, two of the daughters were to die very young, one in an accidental fall into the sea from a cliff-path on the island. I knew that Dickie had been born in Liverpool, his mother's home-city, but was astonished to discover the sensational facts of his paternity – that he was the unacknowledged son of Daniel Harris Reynolds of Lake Village, Arkansas, a Confederate commander in the American Civil

War. All is revealed in my article in *Arkansas Historical Quarterly* (2017), closely reproduced in *In and Out of Bloomsbury* (ch. 10).

In my next incarnation I should like to write a book arguing that the work of members of the Bloomsbury Group is, in general, overrated, and that the hagiography of Virginia Woolf, Vanessa Bell, and Duncan Grant in particular is undeserved. Sometime perhaps the rose-tinted scales will fall from the eyes of readers and viewers, and much of the current writing about them will be consigned to oblivion. I am by no means alone in my iconoclastic assessment of the Bloomsbury Group. I was heartened to read a short piece about it by Cal Revely-Calder in *The Daily Telegraph*, including:

> Vanessa's portraits seem limp. ... Virginia Woolf wrote prose devoid of rhythm or sense. People, in truth, come not for the art, but for the Bloomsbury mythology: wafty people cooking asparagus and drifting between each other's beds. They seemed to think that polyamory was interesting, which was doubtful, and that it was revolutionary, which was wrong. (Features, 12 July 2024, 3).

One inveterate Bloomsbury bed-hopper was Clive Bell, whose memoir of Annie Raven-Hill was first published by me in collaboration with Helen Walasek in *English Studies*, 2019, and reprinted in *In and Out of Bloomsbury* (ch. 3). Clive's adulterous affair with Annie, the wife of the *Punch* cartoonist Leonard Raven-Hill, was his first, beginning in 1899, when he was not quite eighteen. He gave his frank account of it to the Bloomsbury Memoir Club just over twenty years later. Whether Leonard found his wife's infidelities amusing is not known, but it seems unlikely. Helen Walasek was the ideal collaborator, being an expert researcher as well as the curator of the *Punch* archive until it was deposited in the British Library. Another of Clive's loves was his sister-in-law Virginia Woolf. In this case the relationship, which developed while on holiday in St Ives, Cornwall, in 1908, was flirtatious rather than adulterous, but it caused distress to Vanessa, coming only just over a year after she and Clive married and two months after the birth of their elder son, Julian.

In November 1940, a few weeks after the publication of Virginia's biography of Roger Fry, she received a critical letter about it. Beth Rigel Daugherty is to be congratulated on being the first to publish it, but I thought it important to republish it with corrections and commentary as part of my essay "Virginia Woolf and 'the Hermaphrodite': A Feminist Fan of *Orlando* and Critic of *Roger Fry*" (*English Studies*, 2016 = *In and Out of Bloomsbury*, ch. 6).

The letter was written by Mary Louisa Gordon, an interesting person about whom Virginia, to her discredit, writes disparagingly, more than once calling her "the hermaphrodite". Born to well-off parents in Lancashire in 1861, she chose to study medicine and entered the London School of Medicine for Women, the first of its kind in Britain, in 1886, just twelve years after it opened. She was a thoroughgoing feminist. After qualifying as a doctor, she specialised in social medicine and concerned herself with problems associated with poverty, prostitution, venereal diseases, and alcoholism. In 1908 she was appointed His Majesty's Inspector of Prisons – the first woman in Britain to hold such a post. She was responsible for nearly fifty women's prisons, borstals (young-offender institutions), and inebriate reformatories containing about 42,600 inmates. Pressing for changes, she made herself unpopular in certain quarters, and the more so when she complained about her salary being only about half of that paid to her male counterparts. There was still more of a stir when it emerged that, while in the service of the Crown, she was giving moral and financial support to the suffragettes. In 1922, the year after her retirement, she published *Penal Discipline* – a book in which she makes a devastating criticism of the prison system, as relevant to the situation today as it was a hundred years ago. In her retirement she was an ardent follower of the psychiatrist Carl Gustav Jung, and became a friend of his wife, Emma. It was to her that she dedicated her historical novel *Chase of the Wild Goose: The Story of Lady Eleanor Butler and Miss Sarah Ponsonby, Known as the Ladies of Llangollen* (1936). The book was published by Virginia and Leonard Woolf's Hogarth Press. "The wild goose" in its title and at the end of its Part II echoes the protagonist's last words in Virginia's *Orlando*, and we learn from a letter from Mary Gordon to Leonard that one of two books she had under construction was

> a work that is half finished on a very imaginative theme – the hero being a son of Virginia Woolf's Orlando and a spiritual son of Hermaphrodites. (18 February 1937, Hogarth Press Archives)

This must be the "sequel to Orlando" which Virginia earlier told Ethel Smyth "the Hermaphrodite" was writing (*Letters*, [24 October 1935]), and it is probably the main reason why she calls Mary that.

In her letter of 4 November 1940 Mary calls Virginia's biography of Roger Fry

> a story seen through the eyes of the most able of crystal gazers – written with a matchless pen

but adds: "it is quite inhuman". Her objection is, specifically, to Virginia's portrayal of Roger's wife, Helen Coombe, as "the pitiful nebulous ghost" of the woman whose company and friendship she had enjoyed when they were both young. She wishes Virginia's book

> could have said something about the courageous charming young Helen of those days, so eager to live and learn, so full of ideas, the most promising open minded of women.

Soon after her marriage to Roger in December 1896, Helen started to suffer severe episodes of a mental illness now known to have been schizophrenia. Her propensity to it was probably in her genes. Her father and four of her siblings experienced mental health problems, and two of her brothers committed suicide. But Mary Gordon was probably right in thinking that her illness was aggravated by Roger's behaviour. He admitted that he wanted a wife who would take second place to his artistic career, and Helen was not the only woman who found him difficult. So did Vanessa Bell. So too did Josette Coatmellec, who took her own life, prompting Virginia Woolf to comment: "How long can Roger love a woman without driving her mad?" (*Diary*, 14 June 1924). It is significant that in every episode of her mental illness Helen turned against him. She was a brilliant artist, superior to him, and considered by many to outclass him also in intellect and personality. Whatever the reason for her mental illness, it was a tragedy not only for her and her family, but also for British art (Plate 48).

Helen's full story is told for the first time in my book *The Artist Helen Coombe (1864–1937): The Tragedy of Roger Fry's Wife* (2023). It makes use of many sources, the most important of which is the correspondence between Helen and Roger. Thinking it best for the reader to "hear" what they have to say to one another, I include frequent quotations of their letters. The book is illustrated, mostly with Helen's artworks, many of which were previously unknown. It aims above all to restore her identity and celebrate her genius. Its

48) Helen Coombe: Martha (modelled on May Morris). Stained glass window, Church of St John the Evangelist, High Cross, 1896

reception by reviewers has been very favourable, and I like to think that Mary Gordon would have approved of it too.

When I was researching Rose Macaulay's letters to Jean Smith, I learned that Jean, who attended the Godolphin School, Salisbury, as a boarder, was a senior contemporary there of Dorothy L. Sayers, detective novelist, religious writer, and translator of Dante. She was Dorothy's head of house and preceded her as the editor of the *Godolphin School Magazine*. I have explored and described Dorothy's teenage years in three essays. One is about her major contribution, totally overlooked by her biographers, to a historical pageant in the Huntingdonshire village of Somersham, near her home in Bluntisham, in 1908, when she had just turned fifteen and had not yet started at the Godolphin School ("Dorothy L. Sayers and the Somersham Pageant of 1908", 2011 = "A Teenage Star", *In and Out of Bloomsbury*, ch. 8). The pageant was an important local event, staged under professional direction and reported in *The Morning Leader*, where the mention of Dorothy is likely to have been the earliest in a national newspaper:

> Miss Dorothy Sayers, of Bluntisham Rectory, was another most successful poetess – quite young, but amazingly fervid, and with just the right sort of fire in her. (11 August 1908)

As well as being one of the musical accompanists, she composed the verses for at least three parts of the event, perhaps four – a total of at least 56 lines. They included the words of the "Somersham Triumph Song", sung by a female professional singer.

The two other essays describe and discuss Dorothy's years at the school, where she was a star performer, including in English, foreign languages, and drama, but not always fully content, not least when she caught measles and nearly died of it. They also investigate her school friends and other contemporaries ("'Golliwog', Wolley-Dods, Wollaston, and Others", 2010, and "'She Had Quite Unusual Gifts'", *In and Out of Bloomsbury*, ch. 9.) The Godolphin's headmistress, Mary Alice Douglas, insisted on punctuality and tidiness, but rather than subject her pupils to petty rules, encouraged them to develop self-discipline. Her wise and enlightened treatment of Dorothy is illustrated by two incidents. One was her response to Dorothy's declared wish to become a professional actor. Instead of discouraging her theatrical ambitions, she remarked that she would probably be more successful as a dramatist. The other incident occurred in October 1911, during Dorothy's last term, when a company of French actors came to Salisbury to perform plays by Labiche and Molière. Directed by A. Roubaud, the company had performed also in 1909 and 1910, when Dorothy had impressed Roubaud with her fluent French. After the 1911 performance, he stood by the door and spoke to her, but she was dragged away by the school matron and the school secretary – the latter named Violet Parson, but renamed by Dorothy "The Viper". In a letter to her parents, she describes what happened afterwards:

> I came up from town in a fury. Arrived at School, I went straight to Miss Douglas and told her all about it – she was *perfectly ripping*, and said that I had done perfectly right, and Matron and Miss Parson hadn't quite understood, and it was quite right of me to come to her about it. I was awfully glad I had, for that confounded Viper had been before me – Miss D. said "Miss Parson said something to me about it, but I explained to her, and I think she understands now". I hope to Heaven she gave that woman a good dressing down. Pompous, interfering, conceited ass!!!! (29 October 1911)

Soon after leaving school, Dorothy won the triennially-awarded Gilchrist Scholarship at Somerville College, Oxford, which she took up in October 1912. It was a return home for her, because she had been born in Oxford (12 June 1893), where her father, the Revd Henry Sayers, was headmaster of Christ Church Cathedral School.

Another *alumna* of Somerville was Rose Macaulay, who entered in 1900 and studied Modern History. Despite departing with a disappointing aegrotat in 1903, she published her first novel, *Abbots Verney*, in 1906. She did so under the name "R. Macaulay". The book received a favourable critical reception. The publication least generous with praise, while still calling it "a very able and interesting piece of work", was the *Times Literary Supplement* (14 December 1906). We now know that its anonymous reviewer was Virginia Stephen (later Woolf). It would have amused and pleased Rose that the reviewer guessed she was a man.

Virginia did not publish her first novel until 1915. By that time Rose, only about six months her senior, had published, in addition to a collection of poems, seven novels, with one of which, *The Lee Shore* (1912), she won the first prize of £600 (a huge sum at that time) in Hodder & Stoughton's

Novel Competition. A few months after her success with *The Lee Shore*, she received a congratulatory letter from the Irish novelist and poet Katharine Tynan (Hinkson), her senior by over twenty years. Katharine too had entered the competition, but without success. Her letter to Rose inaugurated a friendship that was to last until Katharine's death in 1931. Our main source of information is the collection of letters which Rose wrote to her, preserved in the University of Manchester Library and first published by me in "Letters from Rose Macaulay to Katharine Tynan" (*English Studies*, 2018 = *In and Out of Bloomsbury*, ch. 7). Only Rose's letters survive. Katharine's, if Rose kept them, would have perished with the rest of the contents of Rose's flat when it was bombed in May 1941. Subjects discussed include: the Great War, in which Rose's brother Will and Katharine's two sons saw service; Katharine's war poems; Rose's friend Rupert Brooke; Rose's work in a Voluntary Aid Detachment hospital; Katharine's article about Rose in *The Queen* magazine; more of Katharine's poetry; and several of Rose's post-war novels. The only novel Rose published during the war was *Non-Combatants and Others* (1916), on which I have written:

> Among novels written about the war and during it, it is unusual for its focus on those at home, including those who have returned from the Front, for its recognition of the psychological damage caused by war, and for its whole anti-war message.
>
> (*Dearest Jean*, 11)

We do not know what Katharine thought of the book, but in 1925 she sent Rose a copy of *The Victors*, a novel by Peter Deane about an ex-serviceman, who, on becoming a non-combatant, could not get a job and could not cope with life, so put his head in a gas oven. When she received it, Rose did not know that "Peter Deane" was a pseudonym used by Katharine's daughter, Pamela Hinkson, and that the story was based on the post-war experiences of Pamela's elder brother, although he did not commit suicide.

I ended *In and Out of Bloomsbury* (ch. 11) with a near-reprint of my essay "The First Visit of Tristram Hillier (1906–1983) to Portugal", first published in *The British Art Journal*, Summer 2019. I did so, partly because Tristram was younger than the others I had discussed, partly because he can be linked to several of them – to Roger Fry, Vanessa and Clive Bell, and Duncan Grant, all of whom he met in France in 1928, and, through his love of Portugal and

Spain, to Rose Macaulay, who travelled in those countries, wrote about them, and admired his work.

Born in China and educated at Downside School in Somerset, Tristram attended the Slade School of Fine Art at University College, London. In the early 1930s he was a surrealist, a member of Paul Nash's Unit One, but, by the end of that decade, he had moved a considerable way from abstraction and surrealism to representational art, while still retaining some of his surrealist inclinations. In the same decade his personal life was eventful. He married twice. His second wife, Leda, was an Irish Protestant, which caused problems in 1946, when Tristram, a lapsed Catholic, returned to the Church. It was out of this marital crisis that his first visit to Portugal in 1947 arose, the idea being to give both of them time and space to think things over. Until early in the Second World War they had lived in Normandy. After making a hair-raising escape from the invading Germans, they and their baby daughter reached England. He enrolled in the Royal Naval Volunteer Reserve, but was invalided out in September 1942. In 1945 he and Leda returned to Normandy to see their wrecked home and retrieve his paintings. Apart from this, Portugal in 1947 was his first post-war foreign destination. He was there for four months (mid-May to late September). Just before he returned, he received the astonishing news that Leda had decided to become a Catholic. Artistically, the visit to Portugal was a resounding success. Perhaps most successful of all was the work he did in Viseu, a historic episcopal city and provincial capital in the north of the country. Enduring great heat and squalid accommodation, he spent several days making what he describes as "an ambitious and successful drawing of Cathedral Square" (Plate 49). When he got home, he used it to create a large oil painting on canvas, which is rightly considered to be one of his finest pictures. It is now in the Wolverhampton Art Gallery.

In 2018–2019 I took an interest in the preparation of an exhibition entitled "Landscapes of the Mind: The Art of Tristram Hillier" at the Museum of Somerset in Taunton. It was planned to run from 8 November 2019 to 18 April 2020, but had to close early because of the pandemic. It included the fine Viseu painting, executed in the artist's studio, but, to my regret, not the *en plein air* drawing of which he was justly proud. I found the omission particularly strange not only because comparison between painting and drawing is extraordinarily interesting and informative, but also because I offered to lend it and send it – at my own expense if funds were short. The drawing has the further interest of having been bought by Rose Macaulay in

49) Tristram Hillier: Cathedral Square, Viseu.
Pencil on paper, 34 x 42 cm, 1947

1948. After her death in 1958, it passed to Jean Smith and eventually, in 2001, to me. Rose's book *They Went to Portugal* (1946), about British visitors to Portugal, appeared shortly before Tristram went there too, and, while he was there, she was exploring Spain and Portugal in preparation for her book *Fabled Shore: From the Pyrenees to Portugal* (1949).

14

Last Thoughts and Things (2025)

The main disadvantage of my residence on Foula has been physical separation from family and close friends. Even Lucinda and Ciara have not visited often because they lead busy lives and cannot easily afford the time it takes to reach the island and be sure of getting back to work punctually. So most of our meetings have been in the areas in which they live, often combined with my research visits, on some of which Lucinda accompanied me – to London in 2016 and Somerset in 2018, in connection with Madeleine Symons and Tristram Hillier respectively. As previously mentioned, both Lucinda and Ciara assisted with the exploration of Oinoanda in 2008–2012.

These arrangements do not mean that I have loved them any less than if they could more easily visit me. They are of the greatest importance to me and my happiness, and we keep in close touch by telephone and email. I am very proud of them and their achievements, and I have a great liking for their partners – Lucinda's Chris Williams and Ciara's Ian Birtwistle. Chris is a professional gardener, whom I should love to see in action at Braidfit! Ian, of Newcastle University, is an IT expert. My first meeting with him was in 2016, when I took him and Ciara to dinner in Newcastle's Chinese quarter. Hidden in a plastic bag I had a small laptop computer, which I had just bought. Just before we parted company I said: "It is really lovely to have met you. By the way, could you possibly install Word in this device, please?" Most obligingly he delivered the laptop to my hotel the next morning. It was the first of many favours he has kindly done me. In September 2017 he designed a website www.martinfergusonsmith.com from material I had supplied. After a slow beginning, it increased steadily in popularity and at the time of writing has received over 170,000 visits. Ian continues to look after it and upload all the updates.

Ciara, born in the Princess Mary Maternity Hospital, Newcastle, on 17 September 1991, but brought up mainly in northwest Wales, soon showed herself to be academically bright and industrious and to have a particular flair for mathematics and physics. Mathematical ability does not need to have an ancestral origin, and I know little about her paternal forebears, but I have sometimes wondered if she inherited something from my great-grandfather Archibald Smith II of Jordanhill (1813–1872) who was a fine mathematician. One of his achievements was to solve the problem of ship's magnetism – a problem which had arisen when iron replaced timber in the building of ships. He came up with the calculations needed to correct the consequent deviation of the mariner's compass. Ciara, educated at Ysgol Aberconwy in Conwy, did well in all her examinations, but was handicapped in physics because the school did not have a fully-qualified teacher in the subject. That may explain why her Advanced Level grade in the subject was "A" rather than "A*" as in mathematics and media. I remember that, when Comprehensive schools were introduced, one of the arguments in their favour was that their size would enable the widest range of subjects to be expertly taught, but clearly the promise was not always fulfilled in physics any more than it was in Latin. From school Ciara went on to obtain an MPhys (Master of Physics) degree in the prestigious Department of Physics at the University of Manchester, narrowly missing out on a "first" when she graduated in 2014 (Plate 50). Since graduation, she has lived mainly in Newcastle, working tirelessly to assist the disadvantaged in various roles, all of them admirable. She was an obvious choice for dedicatee of my short biography of the social and legal reformer Madeleine Symons. She has also done splendid work as a warden of the important seabird colonies on the Farne Islands and Coquet Island off the coast of Northumbria, in this respect following in the early-twentieth century footsteps of my great-aunt Catharine ("Katy") Hodgkin. She shares her mother's and grandfather's love of gardening and her partner's passion for rock-climbing. When she and he visited me in Foula in 2018, they thoughtfully acceded to my request to refrain from climbing the island's precipitous cliffs. Her intrepid outlook is illustrated not only by her climbing of rock-faces, but also by the solo travels she undertook in her university days through China and Japan.

Lucinda, after giving Betty devoted care in the last months of her life, moved permanently from Newcastle to her mother's house in North Wales.

50) Manchester University: Ciara before graduation as MPhys. Martin and Aldus Manutius also present, 16 July 2014

Her first job there, from April 1998, was as a horticultural worker at Bryn Euryn Nursery, Colwyn Bay. The enterprise belonged to the county council. As well as growing plants, it provided placements for adults with learning difficulties. Responsibility for them made Lucinda's work extra-challenging, especially from 2002 until her departure in 2015, when she managed the daily running of the nursery in all its work, supervising its staff and co-ordinating the annual production of thousands of plants and hanging baskets for sale to the public and local town councils. It was hard work, but there were some hilarious incidents. One was when, after identifying a source of holly for Christmas wreaths, she instructed a staff-member to go to the donor's address and cut down a bush. He did indeed cut down a bush – but in the wrong garden. The same man was one of two employees who, delivering a tall Christmas tree to one of Llandudno's main hotels, attempted to take it through the revolving door and, once they had got it inside (not via the revolving door!) and were preparing to place it in the dining room, managed to sweep a mass of cutlery and glassware off a table. Laurel and Hardy would have been proud of them. In view of Lucinda's horticultural experience and expertise, it is little wonder that her own garden is stunning.

In November 2015 she embarked on a new career, still within Conwy County Borough Council, in Conwy Archives, first as Archive Assistant, then from May 2021 as Archivist. It was a post well suited to her qualifications and interests – not only her first class degree in Classics, but also the Diploma with Distinction in Archive Administration she gained from the University of Aberystwyth in 2020 after taking the course remotely. She made herself more or less fluent in Welsh. She is Honorary Secretary of the Ranulf Higden Society, concerned primarily with the study of Medieval Latin documents relating to Cheshire, Staffordshire, and Lancashire. She does much work for the Deganwy History Group and other local bodies, and she won the 2015 North Wales Short Story Competition with her hilarious entry about the thoughts and deeds of local seagulls as described by themselves. To me, both in my work and in my life generally, she is my greatest helper. For many years she has been reading and correcting my books and articles. It helps that she is an expert proof-reader. But it helps still more that she is the best critic I know. Her judgement never falters.

My sister, Carol, died in Birmingham on 15 July 2017. For some years her life had been blighted not only by her own failing health, but also by the irrational controlling behaviour of her husband, George, whose mental state had seriously deteriorated. Eventually, the situation became intolerable for her, and she moved out of the marital home to an apartment in Hagley Road Retirement Village. There at least she was spared contact with George. Her funeral on 27 July was a moving ceremony, beautifully arranged by her three children and including a notable contribution from her ten year old granddaughter. For me, the location brought some comfort. Lodge Hill Crematorium, opened in 1937 as Birmingham's first municipal crematorium, was designed by a local Arts and Crafts architect, Holland William Hobbiss (1880–1970). In retrospect, it was an additional comfort that Carol was spared the anxieties engendered by the Covid pandemic. My affectionate relationships with her children – Keith, Anna, and Christopher – and their partners and children, likewise with my friend Sally's daughters, Rebecca and Catriona, continue to be important to me, despite my rarely seeing them. With my very weak broadband connection, I cannot even meet them on my computer screen. I confess that I do not wholly regret that, for, if I were able to meet them, I would also be able to participate in online seminars and suchlike.

As I entered and moved through my seventies, I was frequently asked by well-meaning relatives and friends if it would not be a good idea to leave Foula and go to live in a house or apartment somewhere which would be less physically demanding and in easy reach of doctors' surgeries and other health facilities – and even Marks and Spencer! My brother, Colin, had moved, years earlier, into a two-bedroom apartment at Bournville Gardens, a development in Birmingham run by the same charitable trust as the one which owned the Hagley Road establishment. There he joined many other residents who could live independently if they wished, but also go to the ground floor to a small shop, a restaurant, and a gymnasium, and have access to nursing care if required. Would not something like that suit me? I thought not, and all such queries and suggestions stopped being made as soon as Covid-19 arrived. The restaurant and gymnasium at Colin's place closed immediately, and other restrictions were introduced. Even so, several residents succumbed to the pandemic, and at least one died. Naturally Colin felt very vulnerable. He caught Covid in hospital just before he died on 17 December 2021, although it was not the cause of his death.

My situation was much more comfortable, and some of those who previously thought me mad temporarily reassessed me as a sage possessed of extraordinary foresight. Although I was naturally concerned about the effects of Covid elsewhere, not least on my nearest and dearest, my own life was virtually unaffected. I could walk on the island anywhere I wanted, just as before. With my solitary life and no shops to enter, I was unlikely to contract the virus. For my writing, I had most of the material I needed at home, including for *In and Out of Bloomsbury* (2021). The main work for which I lacked what I needed was my essay "The Royal Academy of Arts Student Clubs, 1883–1902", published in *The British Art Journal,* Spring 2021. I wrote it between December 2020 and February 2021. At that time all public libraries were closed to readers, so, reasoning that buying the required books would be no more costly than my travel and accommodation expenses would have been, I went online and ordered what I needed. The most satisfying purchase was a full set of *The Year's Art* 1880–1909 and many later volumes. I put it together with acquisitions from antiquarian booksellers all around the UK and USA. It is a valuable but underused resource for research on late-nineteenth and twentieth century British art. The writing-period coincided with a prolonged spell of arctic weather, during which even sea-lochs in Shetland froze over, and, week after week, Kevin the postie valiantly negotiated the snow and ice at Braidfit carrying parcels of books, while Stuart did the same with my weekly boxes of provisions. I much enjoyed the research. Previously, very few had been aware that there had been any Royal Academy student club, let alone two clubs, the earlier of which, in its short existence, hosted important lectures by Oscar Wilde and James Abbott McNeill Whistler. The students designed delightful advertisements and invitation cards, a selection of which is included in the essay.

The pleasure I experienced at this time and throughout the period of government restrictions is like that described by Lucretius:

> It is comforting, when the winds are whipping up the waters of the vast sea, to watch from land the severe troubles of another person: not that anyone's distress is a cause of agreeable pleasure, but it is comforting to see from what troubles you yourself are exempt. It is comforting also to witness mighty clashes of warriors embattled on the plains, when you have no share in the danger. (2.1–6)

But, in the immediate continuation of this passage, he points to the even greater pleasure obtained by Epicureans when they compare their lives with those of the unenlightened:

> But nothing is more blissful than to occupy the heights effectively fortified by the teaching of the wise, tranquil sanctuaries from which you can look down upon others and see them wandering everywhere in their random search for the way of life, competing for intellectual eminence, disputing about rank, and striving night and day with prodigious effort to scale the summit of wealth and to secure power. O minds of mortals, blighted by your blindness! Amid what deep darkness and daunting dangers life's little day is passed! To think that you should fail to see that nature importunately demands only that the body may be rid of pain, and that the mind, divorced from anxiety and fear, may enjoy a feeling of contentment! (2.7–19)

During the pandemic I wrote an essay entitled "Pandemics, Plagues, and Philosophy: Moral Lessons from Antiquity for the Modern World" for the online journal *Antigone*. In it I looked back to antiquity to see what moral guidance is offered by Epicureanism and Stoicism, the two most influential systems of moral philosophy in the Hellenistic and Roman periods. I pointed out that Lucretius concludes his sixth and last book with an account of the plague which afflicted Athens in 430 BC, the second year of the Peloponnesian War, fought by the city and its allies against Sparta and its allies. For the most part it closely follows the account of the Greek historian Thucydides, but represents the Athenians, living at a time when Epicurus' teachings were not yet available, as being morally as well as medically ill-equipped to deal with the calamity. Although Lucretius does not say so explicitly, there are persuasive indications that he saw the physical condition of the plague's victims as symbolic of the moral condition of unenlightened humanity.

The idea that the unenlightened are "diseased" and require the "medicine" of Epicureanism is found both elsewhere in Lucretius and in other Epicurean sources. Epicurus himself declared:

> Vain is the word of a philosopher by which no human suffering is cured; for, just as medicine is of no use if it fails to banish the diseases of the body, so philosophy is of no use if it fails to banish the diseases of the mind.

Four maxims in which he summarised the basic principles of his moral system were known to his followers as the *tetrapharmakos* (fourfold drug therapy). According to the Epicurean spokesman in Cicero's treatise *On the Ends of Goods and Evils*, diseases of the mind are more disruptive of happiness than diseases of the body. Such diseases include unlimited and empty desires for wealth, fame, power, and sensual pleasures. In the second century AD, Diogenes, explaining his missionary purpose to the town's citizens and visitors, asserts:

> The majority of people suffer from a common disease, as in a plague, with their false notions about things, and their number is increasing, for in mutual emulation they catch the disease from one another, like sheep.

He calls the Epicurean doctrines he is propounding "the medicines (*pharmaka*) of salvation."

The perception that many, if not most, human beings are morally sick is as true today as it was in antiquity. I am not so arrogant as to claim that I am immune to sickness of this kind, but my simple way of life on Foula means that I have avoided or minimised some of the symptoms identified by Epicurus and his followers. The cultivation of the Braidfit kaleyard, until my age and poor health very recently prevented it, has been deeply satisfying. In addition to kale, I have grown enough tatties (potatoes), always of the Pentland Squire variety, not only for my own table, but also for seed, often shared with other residents. I have also grown spinach, beetroot, carrots, radishes, lettuce, French beans, broad beans, and peas. My front garden includes a herb garden, appropriately located just outside the dining room and close to the kitchen. Not all herbs withstand the climate – not basil, for example, but I have grown parsley, French tarragon, thyme, dill, chives, lovage, borage, and apple mint. The flowers in the front garden include roses, antirrhinums, pansies, viola, calendula, an enormous and ever-spreading honeysuckle, potted geraniums, and flowering shrubs.

For about five and a half years, between February 2019 and July 2024, I did not travel further afield than Lerwick, leaving Foula only for medical appointments and, whenever possible, flying out just for the day. By chance, I was one of the first folk in Shetland to receive a Covid vaccination (15 December 2020). I had been called to a different appointment, some Pfizer doses had just arrived, and being over 80, I was given the opportunity to have one. On this occasion, I had to stay in Lerwick overnight, because a fault had developed with the plane. Just one hotel was open for visitors with essential business. The next morning the plane was still out of order, necessitating a bouncy three-hour sea crossing from Scalloway to Foula. The only other passenger was Foula's resident nurse, Karen Arathoon, who was always good to me, not only medically, but also with shopping. There is no Marks & Spencer in Lerwick, no Aldi or Lidl, no Waitrose, but there are a Tesco and a Co-op. In her younger days, before marriage and motherhood, she was an army nurse, which explains how she met her soldier husband, Ivan. After years of loyal service to the Shetland Health Board, she was driven out by ill health, exacerbated by her employer's failure to keep the nurse's house in a decent habitable condition. There is now no resident nurse to deal with emergencies. Alison Rendall, the brilliant nurse based in Walls, comes in once a week, weather and her other commitments permitting, but accidents and sudden illnesses can happen at any time. Thirty years ago, it was recognised that a nurse was required around the clock throughout the year, and a doctor used to visit once every six weeks. At the time of writing no doctor has visited for over two years. There also used to be regular visits from a chiropodist until they were stopped by the Scottish government. My observation is that devolution of government to Edinburgh has been bad for health, as well as for education, transport, and policing in Scotland. It is probably superfluous to mention that police very rarely visit Foula, although I did have a visit from an officer when I was renewing my air gun licence and he wanted to see where I was storing it. I have the weapon for the control of "pests", but I have always assumed that twitchers are not *in law* recognised as that, and thought it wiser not to ask! I do not forget the true story of an American, who, at a time of frequent hijackings to Cuba, was boarding an internal flight in Florida, when he jokingly asked an air hostess if this was the plane for Havana. The airline refused to take him as a passenger.

My account of my avoidance of Covid-19 while it was raging elsewhere in the country probably sounds horribly selfish and smug. Retribution was to come in the summer of 2024. On 8 July I departed Foula on my way to Newcastle, to fulfil a three-part agenda: to see my dentist, Tony Borthwick; to have my surviving eye tested; and, most important of all, to meet up with Lucinda, Ciara, and Ian. The dental visit, my first for five years, was fine, and it was lovely to see my family and Ian. The only bad news, and it was not unexpected, came from the optometrist, who told me that he could not do anything more for my vision until I had had a cataract operation, which, given the location of my home, would involve visits to a suitable clinic. There was also the slight apprehension that, if the operation were a failure, I might be left blind. I headed back home to think things over and make enquiries. I quickly ascertained that I could not have the procedure in Shetland unless I were prepared to wait about two years, and that the Shetland health authorities would not allow me to have it elsewhere under the National Health Service. I identified a surgeon in Newcastle who would do the necessary privately. He is an Egyptian, which seemed appropriate for someone specialising in cataracts, even if he were operating on Tyneside rather than by the Nile. But on the way home I had come out with Covid, which made me feel too unwell to contemplate travelling again for several weeks. The unwellness took more than a year to go away, so was probably "long" Covid.

On 2 September, still feeling decidedly shaky, I set off for Newcastle again, for my operation on 5 September. Lucinda came up from Wales to be with me on the day and make sure I did not fall into the River Tyne or under a bus. She also accompanied me to the clinic the next morning for a check-up, when we had the thrill of an Uber taxi ride in a brand-new Tesla automatic. All was said to be fine, and I was seeing distant objects without spectacles more clearly than ever before. But I got a nasty fright on the journey home. Before catching my flight from Edinburgh to Sumburgh in the early afternoon of Sunday, 8 September, I spent a night in a hotel at Edinburgh Airport. After midnight, I awoke to find that all the restored sight had gone, and I was virtually blind. I could not read the document carrying an emergency number, and I could not read the keyboard on my mobile phone. When morning came, with the help of hotel staff, I got through to the surgeon, now on holiday abroad. I had a supply of steroid drops, and, as instructed, I had been giving the eye three each day. Now I was to give it three inside thirty minutes. To my huge relief, the vision began to return, and I was able to fly. The next night, spent in the excellent Sumburgh Hotel, exactly the same thing happened, but this time I knew what to do. A month later, I returned very briefly to Newcastle to be tested and measured for new spectacles.

I struggled through the winter of 2024–2025, battling the long Covid as well as my chronic problems, first diagnosed over twenty years ago, of bronchiectasis and cardiac arrhythmia. On 19 and 26 February 2025 Alison Rendall flew in to check me over, and on the second visit, during which she consulted the locum doctor in Walls by telephone, told me that I must go to hospital immediately. I declined to do that because Lucinda was on her way, and I had important things to show her and discuss with her before I departed, but the next morning I was flown by helicopter to the GBH in Lerwick, as described in Chapter 10. I did not know whether I would come back again, but, after various treatments and changes of medication, I returned on 7 March. I am full of gratitude to Alison and the GBH for saving my life, although the hospital, short of funds and staff, was not well equipped or well organised. My dismay at sharing a bathroom with three other men diminished slightly when I found that I was the only one able to reach it unaided. One of my ward-mates had such a remarkable cough that I was tempted to ask if he had considered offering himself as a reserve foghorn to the Northern Lighthouse Board. What I found most difficult of all was having to wait until as late as 11 p.m. or even midnight to receive my last dose of medication. It was lovely to be reunited with Lucinda at Braidfit. She had managed it superbly in my absence, despite prolonged power cuts which made it necessary for her to ask Stuart to run my emergency generator. She departed on 12 March. Since then, she has kept a close eye on me remotely, and Foula residents have been extremely kind, especially Penny Gear and her family and Fran Dyson-Sutton.

I have no wish to go back to hospital or to travel anywhere else. When I was interviewed for a radio programme about Foula, "Island on the Edge", not long after I came to the island, I remarked that it would be a wonderful place to die. I still feel that, and I hope it will happen to me. I have made it known that I wish to be buried here – preferably not (being unsociable!) in the burial ground and without any form of religious ceremony.

In my Loeb edition of Lucretius (p. xxviii), I suggest that the following lines of Shelley well describe the Roman poet:

I love all that thou lovest,
    Spirit of Delight!
The fresh Earth in new leaves dressed,
    And the starry night;
Autumn evening, and the morn
When the golden mists are born.

I love snow, and all the forms
    Of the radiant frost;
I love waves, and winds, and storms,
    Everything almost
Which is Nature's, and may be
Untainted by man's misery.

I love tranquil solitude
    And such society
As is quiet, wise, and good.

Song: Rarely, Rarely Comest Thou, 25–39

The lines also describe me, with the proviso that such society as is wise and good includes people, living and dead, whom I have never met, but know from their writings, music, and art. Prominent among them are Lucretius himself, Epicurus, and Diogenes. It is Diogenes to whom I feel closest, because of the discoveries I have made, or helped to make, and I should like these discoveries to be remembered as my most important contribution to scholarship, just as they have been acknowledged in my lifetime by fellowships of three Royal Societies (Antiquaries, Geographical, Historical), Corresponding Membership of the German Archaeological Institute, and the award of a National Honour.

In Chapter 12 I quoted Diogenes as saying:

> We should be cheerful when we die, for we shall give up not only good things, but also bad ones.

Bad things include physical and mental sickness and pain. Epicurus identified pleasure in its purest form as *aponia* (freedom from pain) in the body and, most importantly, *ataraxia* (freedom from disturbance) in the mind. *Ataraxia* is a metaphor from calm water and weather, the idea and ideal being to make your mind as tranquil as the water of a harbour undisturbed by currents, tides, and winds. Although Epicureans recognised and valued the positive bodily and mental pleasures human beings can enjoy if they live their lives wisely, death is nothing to fear: so long as we exist, it is not with us; and when it comes, we do not exist. Hell exists only in the sense that fools make one of their lives on earth. Death is no more to be feared than a deep sleep, and the eternity of time that elapsed before we were born mirrors the eternity of time – *mors ... immortalis* as Lucretius (3.869) puts it – that will follow our death. Not everyone fancies the idea of being annihilated, but, since death brings both *aponia* and *ataraxia*, it is, logically, something to welcome. The only thing I dread is outliving my physical and/or mental capacities and losing my ability to live independently, both for my own sake and for the sake of those who might feel obliged to shoulder the burden of looking after me when my life is no longer worth living. To avoid that, living on Foula may be advantageous, in that its remoteness reduces the chances of being resuscitated.

15

Key to Selected First Names

Alan: Alan Stirling Hall, director of work at Oinoanda 1974–1983
Barbara: Barbara Catharine Smith, *née* Tangye, mother
Betty: Elizabeth Mary Smith, *née* Dempsey, girlfriend, then wife until divorce
Carol: (Alison) Caroline Ferguson Smith, sister
Ciara: Ciara Barrett Smith, granddaughter
Colin: Colin Ferguson Smith, brother
Henry: Henry Ferguson Smith, father
Hilde: Hilde Thomas
Jean: Jean Isabel Smith, aunt
José: José Kany-Turpin
Judith: Judith Higgens, later Stancomb
Jürgen: Jürgen Hammerstaedt, Oinoanda collaborator
Lucinda: (Catharine) Lucinda Ferguson Smith, daughter
Manuela: Manuela Maria Tecuşan, second wife until annulment
Martin: Martin Ferguson Smith
or Martin Bachmann, director of work at Oinoanda 2007–2016
Miranda: Miranda Kynoch Clark, later Overend, first cousin
Moira: Moira Dempsey, *née* Crone, Betty's mother
Petru: Petru Creţia, Manuela's uncle
Ro: Rosemary Stella Middlemore Smith, *née* Hughes, aunt
Sally: Sally Lovecy

16

Publications of Martin Ferguson Smith

Books

1. *Lucretius. On the Nature of Things*, Sphere Books, London, 1969.

2. *Thirteen New Fragments of Diogenes of Oenoanda*, Österreichische Akademie der Wissenschaften, Vienna, 1974. Illustrated. ISBN 3-7001-0085-X.

3. *Lucretius. De Rerum Natura*, Heinemann and Harvard University Press (Loeb Classical Library), London and Cambridge, Mass., 1975. Edited, with the revised translation of W.H.D. Rouse. Further editions in 1982, 1992. ISBN 0-674-99200-8.

4. *Classics in Albania*, The Albanian Society, Ilford, 1984. Illustrated.

5. *Diogenes of Oinoanda. The Epicurean Inscription*, Bibliopolis, Naples, 1993. Illustrated. ISBN 88-7088-270-5.

6. *The Philosophical Inscription of Diogenes of Oinoanda*, Österreichische Akademie der Wissenschaften, Vienna, 1996. Illustrated. ISBN 3-7001-2596-8.

7. *Lucretius. On the Nature of Things*, Hackett, Indianapolis and Cambridge, Mass., 2001. ISBN 0-87220-588-6 (hardback), 0-87220-587-8 (paperback).

8. *Supplement to Diogenes of Oinoanda. The Epicurean Inscription*, Bibliopolis, Naples, 2003. Illustrated. ISBN 88-7088-441-4.

Awarded the International Theodor Mommsen Prize for Herculaneum Papyrology, 2004.

9. *Dearest Jean. Rose Macaulay's Letters to a Cousin*, Manchester University Press, Manchester, 2011. ISBN 978-0-7190-8521 (hardback). Revised edition, 2017. Illustrated. ISBN 978-1-5261-2300 (paperback).

10. *The Epicurean Inscription of Diogenes of Oinoanda. Ten Years of New Discoveries and Research*, Habelt Verlag, Bonn, 2014. Illustrated. ISBN 978-3-7749-3927-1. Co-author with Jürgen Hammerstaedt.

11. *Madeleine Symons, Social and Penal Reformer*, SilverWood, Bristol, 2017. Illustrated. ISBN 978-1-7813719-7 (paperback), 978-1-78132-748-7 (ebook).

12. *In and Out of Bloomsbury: Biographical Essays on Twentieth-Century Writers and Artists*, Manchester Press, Manchester, 2021. Illustrated. ISBN: 978-1-5261-5744-7; paperback, 2023, ISBN 978-1-5261-7193-1.

Longlisted for the William M. B. Berger Prize for British Art History, 2022.

13. *The Artist Helen Coombe (1864–1937): The Tragedy of Roger Fry's Wife*, Paul Holberton Publishing for Hogarth Arts, London, 2023. Illustrated. ISBN: 978-1-913645-53-3.

Longlisted for a Historians of British Art Book Award, 2025.

14. *Martin the Epicurean*, SilverWood Books, Bristol, 2026. Illustrated. ISBN: 978-1-80042-324-4 (paperback and e-book).

15. *Urbi et Orbi: The Epicurean Inscription and Prescription of Diogenes of Oinoanda*, tab edizioni, Rome, 2026, Doxai Series: testi e studi di filosofia antica (paperback and Open Access). English Translation with Introduction and Notes.

Articles

16. "Lucretius, De Rerum Natura, V.1440–7", *Hermathena* 98 (1964) 45–52.

17. "Textual Notes on Sophocles' *Antigone*", *Classical Review* 15 (1965) 5–6.

18. "Some Lucretian Thought Processes", *Hermathena* 102 (1966) 73–83.

19. "Three Textual Notes on Lucretius", *Classical Review* 16 (1966) 264–266.

20. "Fragments of Diogenes of Oenoanda Discovered and Rediscovered", *American Journal of Archaeology*, 74 (1970) 51–62.

21. "Observations on the Text of Diogenes of Oenoanda", *Hermathena* 110 (1970) 52–78.

22. "Philosophy and Philanthropy in the Mountains of Lycia. The Inscription of Diogenes of Oenoanda", *Proceedings of the Classical Association* 67 (1970) 28–29.

23. "Lucretius V. 1442", *Greece and Rome* 18 (1971) 102–103.

24. "New Fragments of Diogenes of Oenoanda", *American Journal of Archaeology* 75 (1971) 357–389.

25. New Readings in the Text of Diogenes of Oenoanda", *Classical Quarterly* 22 (1972) 159–162.

26. "Two New Fragments of Diogenes of Oenoanda", *Journal of Hellenic Studies* 92 (1972) 147–155.

27. "Termessus Minor. An Inscription", *Anatolian Studies* 23 (1973) 62.

28. "Seven New Fragments of Diogenes of Oenoanda", *Hermathena* 118 (1974) 110–129.

29. "More New Fragments of Diogenes of Oenoanda", in J. Bollack & A. Laks (eds), *Études sur l'épicurisme antique* (Lille, 1976) 279–318.

30. "Diogenes of Oenoanda and l'École française d'Athènes", *Bulletin de Correspondance Hellénique* 101 (1977) 353–381.

31. "An Association Copy of Charles Fellows' 1838 Journal", *Türk Tarih Kurumu Belleten* (= *Turkish Historical Society Bulletin*) 41 (1977) 383–387.

32. "Oenoanda. The Epicurean Inscription", *Proceedings of the Tenth International Congress of Classical Archaeology* (Ankara, 1978) 841–847.

33. "Diogenes of Oenoanda, New Fragment 24", *American Journal of Philology* 99 (1978) 329–331.

34. "Fifty-five New Fragments of Diogenes of Oenoanda", *Anatolian Studies* 28 (1978) 39–92.

35. "Eight New Fragments of Diogenes of Oenoanda", *Anatolian Studies* 29 (1979) 69–89.

36. "New Epicurean Texts from Oenoanda in Lycia", *Proceedings of the Classical Association* 76 (1979) 39–40.

37. "Oenoanda and its Philosophical Inscription", *Actes du Colloque sur la Lycie antique*, Bibliothèque de l'Institut français d'études anatoliennes d'Istanbul (Paris, 1980) 73–87.

38. "Archaeology in Albania", *Albanian Life* 20 (1982) 24–30.

39. "Diogenes of Oenoanda, New Fragments 115–121", *Prometheus* 8 (1982) 193–212.

40. "A Bibliography of Work on Diogenes of Oenoanda, 1892–1981", *Syzêtêsis: Studi sull'epicureismo greco e romano offerti a Marcello Gigante* (Napoli, 1983) 683–695.

41. "Epicureanism in a Stoa. The Philosophical Inscription of Diogenes of Oenoanda", in P. Oliva & A. Frolíková (eds), *Proceedings of the 16th International Eirene Conference* (Prague, 1983) I 241–244.

42. "Diogenes of Oenoanda, New Fragments 122–124", *Anatolian Studies* 34 (1984) 43–57.

43. "Archaeology in Albania, 1973–83", *Archaeological Reports for 1983–84* (1984) 102–119. A report by Z. Andrea, edited and adapted (see prefatory note on p. 102) by MFS.

44. "Notes on Lucretius", *Studi in onore di Adelmo Barigazzi* (Rome, 1986) II 219–225.

45. "Lucretius and Diogenes of Oenoanda", *Prometheus* 12 (1986) 193–207.

46. Regular reports on current research in Classics and Ancient History for the "Findings" column in *The Times* during the three years (1986–87–88) of the column's existence.

47. "Havercamp's Sigla", *Liverpool Classical Monthly* 12 (1987) 127.

48. "A Note on Colonel W.M. Leake", *Anatolian Studies* 38 (1988) 185.

49. "Roundish rather than Round. *Epistroggylos* in Diogenes of Oenoanda and Aristotle", *Prometheus* 14 (1988) 199–201.

50. "Trees, Fire and Sex in Lucretius", *Liverpool Classical Monthly* 17 (1992) 40–41.

51. "Notes on Sophocles' Oedipus Coloneus", *Prometheus* 18 (1992) 227–230.

52. "Notes on Lucretius", *Classical Quarterly* 43 (1993) 336–339.

53. "The Philosophical Inscription at Oinoanda in Lycia. The Austrian Contribution", in J. Borchhardt & G. Dobesch (eds), *Akten des zweiten Internationalen Lykien-Symposions* (Wien 6–12 Mai 1990), Österreichische Akademie der Wissenschaften (Vienna, 1993) II 221–228.

54. "In the Footsteps of Heberdey and Kalinka. Recent and Current Work on Diogenes of Oinoanda", in G. Dobesch and G. Rehrenböck (eds), *Die epigraphische und altertumskundliche Erforschung Kleinasiens: Hundert Jahre Kleinasiatische Kommission der österreichischen Akademie der Wissenschaften, ÖAW* (Vienna, 1993) 339–348.

55. "Did Diogenes of Oinoanda Know Lucretius? A Reply to Professor Canfora", *Rivista di Filologia* 121 (1993) 478–492.

56. "Lucretius 3.962", *Mnemosyne* 46 (1993) 377.

57. "The Millionaire Philosopher's Precious Stones", *Ad familiares* 6 (1994) 14–15.

58. "Firs meter graesk filosofi" (= "Eighty Metres of Greek Philosophy"), *Sfinx* 17, 3 (1994) 105–108. In Danish.

59. "New Readings in the Demostheneia Inscription from Oinoanda", *Anatolian Studies* 44 (1994) 59–64.

60. "New Votive Reliefs from Oinoanda", *Anatolian Studies* 44 (1994) 65–76. Co-author with N.P. Milner.

61. "Support from Oinoanda for a Variant Reading in Dionysius of Halicarnassus", *Hermes* 122 (1994) 503–504.

62. "Ducks' Eggs in Statius, *Silvae* 4.9.30?", *Classical Quarterly* 44 (1994) 551–554.

63. "A 'Herculaneum' in the Mountains of Turkey. Oinoanda as a Source of Epicurean Texts", in G. Giannantoni & M. Gigante (eds), *Epicureismo greco e romano: Atti del Congresso Internazionale, Napoli, 19–26 maggio 1993* (Napoli, 1996) 951–968.

64. "An Epicurean Priest from Apamea in Syria", *Zeitschrift für Papyrologie und Epigraphik* 112 (1996) 120–130.

65. "Lucretius 5.201", *Rivista di Filologia* 124 (1996) 285–289.

66. "The Chisel and the Muse. Diogenes of Oinoanda and Lucretius", in K.A. Algra, M.H. Koenen & P.H. Schrijvers (eds), *Lucretius and his Intellectual Background* (Amsterdam, 1997) 67–78.

67. "Oinoanda" (excavation report), *Anatolian Archaeology: Research Reports of the British Institute of Archaeology at Ankara* 3 (1997) 11–12.

68. "Problems in PHerc. 1018 col. II", *Cronache Ercolanesi* 28 (1998) 105–110.

69. "Epicurus' *Kyria Doxa* 26 and a New Fragment of Diogenes of Oinoanda", *Hyperboreus* 4 (1998) 193–195.

70. "Excavations at Oinoanda 1997. The New Epicurean Texts", *Anatolian Studies* 48 (1998) 125–170.

71. "A New Reading in Diogenes of Oinoanda fr. 69", *Classical Quarterly* 49 (1999) 639–640.

72. "Digging up Diogenes. New Epicurean Texts from Oinoanda in Lycia", in M. Erler (ed), *Epikureismus in der späten Republik und der Kaiserzeit* (Stuttgart, 2000) 64–75.

73. "Lucretius 3.955", *Prometheus* 26 (2000) 35–40.

74. "The Introduction to Diogenes of Oinoanda's *Physics*", *Classical Quarterly* 50 (2000) 238–246.

75. "The Dates of Cyril Bailey's Oxford Classical Texts of Lucretius", *Classical Quarterly* 50 (2000) 307–308. Co-author with L. Holford-Strevens.

76. "Nêssos at Oinoanda in Lycia. Misspelling or Genuine Variant?", *Zeitschrift für Papyrologie und Epigraphik* 130 (2000) 127–130.

77. "Elementary, my Dear Lycians. A Pronouncement on Physics from Diogenes of Oinoanda", *Anatolian Studies* 50 (2000) 133–137.

78. "Quotations of Epicurus Common to Diogenes of Oinoanda and Diogenes Laertius", *Hyperboreus* 6 (2000) 188–197.

79. "Fresh Thoughts on Diogenes of Oinoanda fr. 68", *Zeitschrift für Papyrologie und Epigraphik,* 133 (2000) 51–55.

80. "A Mass of Dross and one Particle of Gold. Observations on a New Text of Lucretius", *Prometheus* 26 (2000) 233–240.

81. "Lucretius 6.799–803", *Museum Helveticum* 58 (2001) 65–69.

82. "New Thoughts on New Fragments of Diogenes of Oinoanda", *Hyperboreus* 6 (2000), 430–436.

83. "Lucretius 2.547", *Classical Quarterly* 51(2001) 617–620.

84. "Herculaneum and Oinoanda, Philodemus and Diogenes. Comparison of Two Epicurean Discoveries and Two Epicurean Teachers", *Cronache Ercolanesi* 33 (2003) 267–278.

85. "Lucretius 5.1105–7", *Classical Quarterly* 54 (2004) 298–299.

86. "Epicurus' Whirlpool Bath. Diogenes of Oinoanda fr. 72 Smith", in S. Cerasuolo (ed.), *Mathesis e Mneme. Studi in memoria di Marcello Gigante* I (Napoli, 2004) 247–257.

87. "The Title of Diogenes of Oinoanda's *Physics*", in H. Heftner and K. Tomaschitz (eds), *Ad Fontes! Festschrift für Gerhard Dobesch zum fünfundsechzigsten Geburtstag* (Wien, 2004) 431–434.

88. "In Praise of the Simple Life. A New Fragment of Diogenes of Oinoanda", *Anatolian Studies* 54 (2004) 35–46.

89. Remarks after receiving the Theodor Mommsen Prize for Herculaneum Papyrology, in Pozzuoli, 12 January 2005, *Cronache Ercolanesi* 35 (2005) 249. In Italian.

90. Remarks after the "presentazione", by Professors Alberto Grilli and Nicola Pace, of *Supplement to Diogenes of Oinoanda, The Epicurean Inscription*, in Naples, 13 January 2005, *Cronache Ercolanesi* 35 (2005) 249–250. In Italian.

91. Introduction to Th. Antoniadis and Roula Chameti (trans.), *Loukrētios. Gia tēn Physē tōn Pragmatōn: De Rerum Natura* (Thessaloniki, 2005) 11–51. Translation into Modern Greek of the introduction to the Loeb edition to Lucretius (see above, no. 3).

92. "Lucretius, *On the Nature of Things* 2.1–61", *A Loeb Classical Library Reader* (Cambridge, MA; London, 2006) 144–149. With W.H.D. Rouse.

93. "Diogenes of Oinoanda. News and Notes, 2005", *Cronache Ercolanesi* 36 (2006) 233–245.

94. "Professor Courtney's Suggestions on Lucretius", *Prometheus* 32 (2006) 228–230.

95. "The Inscription of Diogenes of Oinoanda. New Investigations and Discoveries (NF 137–141)", *Epigraphica Anatolica* 40 (2007) 1–11. With Jürgen Hammerstaedt.

96. "Diogenes of Oinoanda. News and Notes II (2007), *Cronache Ercolanesi* 38 (2008) 309–317.

97. "Diogenes of Oinoanda. The Discoveries of 2008 (NF 142–167)", *Epigraphica Anatolica* 41 (2008) 1–37. With Jürgen Hammerstaedt.

98. “Diogenes of Oinoanda. News and Notes III (2008), *Cronache Ercolanesi* 39 (2009) 301–312.

99. “‘Golliwog’, Wolley-Dod, Wollaston, and Others. Some Contemporaries of Dorothy L. Sayers at the Godolphin School, Salisbury”, *Proceedings* of the Dorothy L. Sayers Society 34th Annual Convention 14th–17th August, 2009 (Hurstpierpoint, 2010) 81–100.

100. “Diogenes of Oinoanda. The Discoveries of 2009 (NF 167–181)”, *Epigraphica Anatolica* 42 (2009) 1–37. With Jürgen Hammerstaedt.

101. “Diogenes of Oinoanda. News and Notes IV (2009)”, *Cronache Ercolanesi* 40 (2010) 223–238.

102. “Not a Ghost: The 1496 Brescia Edition of Lucretius”, *Aevum* 84 (2010) 683–693. With David Butterfield.

103. “Virginia Woolf’s Second Visit to Greece”, *English Studies* 92 (2011) 55–83.

104. “Diogenes of Oinoanda. The Discoveries of 2010 (NF 182–190)”, *Epigraphica Anatolica* 43 (2010) 1–29. With J. Hammerstaedt.

105. “Diogenes of Oinoanda. News and Notes V (2010)”, *Cronache Ercolanesi* 41 (2011) 235–250.

106. “Dorothy L. Sayers and the Somersham Pageant of 1908”, *VII: An Anglo-American Literary Review* 28 (2011) 79–96.

107. “Diogenes of Oinoanda. The Discoveries of 2011 (NF 191–205, and Additions to NF 127 and 130)”, *Epigraphica Anatolica* 44 (2011) 79–114. With J. Hammerstaedt.

108. “Diogenes of Oinoanda. News and Notes VI (2011)”, *Cronache Ercolanesi* 42 (2012) 303–318.

109. “A Good Rector Playing a Bad Bishop: Henry Sayers in the Somersham Pageant”, *The Dorothy L. Sayers Society Bulletin* 226 (March 2013) 15–17, online issue.

110. “Diogenes of Oinoanda: New Discoveries of 2012 (NF 206–212) and New Light on “Old” Fragments”, *Epigraphica Anatolica* 45 (2012) 1–38. With J. Hammerstaedt.

111. “Diogenes of Oinoanda: News and Notes VII (2012)”, *Cronache Ercolanesi* 43 (2013) 161–175.

112. "'Suicidal Mania' and Flawed Psychobiography: Two Discussions of Virginia Woolf", *English Studies* 95 (2014) 538–556.

113. Diogenes of Oinoanda: News and Notes VIII (2013)", *Cronache Ercolanesi* 44 (2014) 179–191.

114. "Diogenes of Oinoanda: News and Notes IX (2014)", *Cronache Ercolanesi* 45 (2015) 189–197. With J. Hammerstaedt.

115. "Virginia Woolf and 'The Hermaphrodite': A Feminist Fan of *Orlando* and Critic of *Roger Fry*", *English Studies* 97 (2016) 277–297.

116. "New Research at Oinoanda and a New Fragment of the Epicurean Diogenes (NF 213)", *Epigraphica Anatolica* 49 (2016) 109–125. With J. Hammerstaedt.

117. "Diogenes of Oinoanda: News and Notes X (2015)", *Cronache Ercolanesi* 46 (2016) 161–167. With J. Hammerstaedt.

118. "Foreword: The Importance of Diogenes of Oinoanda", in J. Hammerstaedt, P-M. Morel, and R. Güremen (eds), *Diogenes of Oinoanda: Epicureanism and Philosophical Debates*, Leuven University Press (2017) xi-xvii. ISBN 978-94-6270-101-4.

119. "'New' Portraits by Roger Fry (1866--1934) of Helen Fry and Vanessa Bell", *British Art Journal* 17, no. 3 (Spring 2017) 34–39.

120. "The British Connection: The Secret Son of Brig.-Gen. Daniel Harris Reynolds", *Arkansas Historical Quarterly* 76, no. 2 (Summer 2017) 144–176.

121. "Diogenes of Oinoanda: News and Notes XI (2016), *Cronache Ercolanesi* 47 (2017) 305–315. With J. Hammerstaedt.

122. "Letters from Rose Macaulay to Katharine Tynan", *English Studies* 99 (2018) 517–537.

123. "Diogenes of Oinoanda: News and Notes XII (2017)", *Cronache Ercolanesi* 48 (2018) 203–210. With J. Hammerstaedt.

124. "The First Visit of Tristram Hillier (1905–1983) to Portugal", *British Art Journal* 20, 1 (Spring 2019) 90–97.

125. "Diogenes of Oinoanda: News and Notes XIII (2018)", *Cronache Ercolanesi* 49 (2019) 301–313.

126. "Diogenes of Oinoanda: The New and Unexpected Discoveries of 2017

(NF 214–219), With a Re-edition of Fr. 70–72", *Epigraphica Anatolica* 51 (2018) 43–79. With J. Hammerstaedt.

127. "Clive Bell's Memoir of Annie Raven-Hill", *English Studies* 100 (2019) 823–824. With Helen Walasek.

128. "A Complete Strip-off: A Bloomsbury Threesome in the Nude at Studland", *British Art Journal* 20, 2 (Autumn 2019) 72–77.

129. "Tribute to Diskin Clay and His Work on Diogenes of Oinoanda", in F. Burian, J. Strauss Clay, & G. Davis (eds), *Euphrosyne: Studies in Ancient Philosophy, History, and Literature in Memory of Diskin Clay* (Berlin, 2020) 109–111.

130. "A New Look at Diogenes of Oinoanda, Fr. 157 Smith", *Hyperboreus* 25, 2 (2019) 351–362.

131. "Confronting Covid-19 with Help from Greek Philosophy", www.martinfergusonsmith.com – republication, in April 2020, of MFS, "Ancient Plagues Displayed Similar Symptoms", *The Shetland Times*, 10 April 2020, 16.

132. Online republication of last item, with minor alterations, in the Durham University Classics Society's blog, *Ostraka*, 24 April 2020, and Classics For All's magazine *Ad Familiares*, 15 June 2020.

133. "Covid-19 and Greek Philosophy", *The Philosophers' Magazine* 90 (3rd quarter 2020) 53–56. Invited contribution to a special issue, *Thinking Through the Pandemic.*

134. "Fifty Years of New Epicurean Discoveries at Oinoanda", *Cronache Ercolanesi* 50 (2020) 241–258.

135. "The Royal Academy of Arts Students' Clubs, 1883–1902", *British Art Journal* 22, 1 (Spring 2021) 78–88. Illustrated.

136. "Pandemics, Plagues, and Philosophy: Moral Lessons from Antiquity for the Modern World, *Antigone* [online classical journal], January 2022. Illustrated.

137. "Diogenes of Oinoanda: News and Notes XIV (2019–2021)", *Cronache Ercolanesi* 52 (2022) 383–399. One illustration.

138. "Diogenes of Oinoanda Fr. 65 + Fr. 78: A Join Enabled by Digital Models", *Epigraphica Anatolica* 55 (2022) [2024], 121–129. Illustrated. With Jürgen Hammerstaedt.

139. "The Stephen and Macaulay Families: Two New Letters", *Virginia Woolf Bulletin* No. 75, January 2024, 28–39.

140–141. Papers read in Muğla (June 2022) and Bodrum (April 2023). Published versions in Turkish in *Arkhe-logos*.

142. "Die epikureische Inschrift des Diogenes von Oinoanda", in M. Bachmann, J. Hammerstaedt, E. Laufer (eds), *Oinoanda: Ergebnisse der Surveys 2007-2015: Bauforschung, Archäologie, Epigraphik*, Deutsches Archäologisches Institut, Istanbuler Forschungen 57, Wiesbaden, 2025, 371-393. With Jürgen Hammerstaedt. In German.

Reviews

143. C.W. Chilton, *Diogenis Oenoandensis fragmenta*, in *Hermathena* 108 (1969) 60–62.

144. C.A. Gordon, *A Bibliography of Lucretius*, in *Hermathena* 109 (1969) 70–72.

145. C.W. Chilton, *Diogenes of Oenoanda. The Fragments*, in *Journal of Hellenic Studies* 92 (1973) 234–236.

146. E.J. Kenney, *Lucretius, De Rerum Natura, Book III*, in *Classical Review* 24 (1974) 204–207.

147. F. Wooby, *Lucretius, About Reality*, in *Hermathena* 117 (1974) 91–93.

148. A. Barigazzi, *Lucrezio. Vita e morte nell'universo. Antologia dal "De Rerum Natura"*, in *Classical Review* 26 (1976) 270.

149. G. Maurach (ed.), *Römische Philosophie*, in *Classical Review* 28 (1978) 172.

150. K. Müller, *T. Lucreti Cari De Rerum Natura*, in *Classical Review* 28 (1978) 29–31.

151. P. Gordon, *Epicurus in Lycia. The Second-Century World of Diogenes of Oinoanda*, in *Ancient Philosophy* 18 (1998) 216–220.

Forthcoming Articles

"The Artist and Suffragette Marie Jane Naylor (1856-1940)". Illustrated.

"The Artist Helen Coombe (1864-1937): Addenda". Illustrated.

Index

www.ingramcontent.com/pod-product-compliance
Lightning Source LLC
LaVergne TN
LVHW091026080826
845145LV00002B/371

* 9 7 8 1 8 0 0 4 2 3 2 4 4 *